The Islamist Challenge and Africa

The Islamist Challenge and Africa

Samory Rashid

LEXINGTON BOOKS
Lanham • Boulder • New York • London

Published by Lexington Books
An imprint of The Rowman & Littlefield Publishing Group, Inc.
4501 Forbes Boulevard, Suite 200, Lanham, Maryland 20706
www.rowman.com

6 Tinworth Street, London SE11 5AL, United Kingdom

British Library Cataloguing in Publication Information Available

Library of Congress Cataloging-in-Publication Data

Names: Rashid, Samory, 1948- author.
Title: The Islamist challenge and Africa / Samory Rashid.
Description: Lanham, Maryland : Lexington Books, 2019. | Includes bibliographical
   references and index.
Identifiers: LCCN 2018043235 (print) | LCCN 2018046051 (ebook) |
   ISBN 9781498564434 (electronic) | ISBN 9781498564427 (cloth : alk. paper)
Subjects: LCSH: Islamic fundamentalism—Africa. | Islamic fundamentalism—Political
   aspects—Africa. | Terrorism—Africa. | Terrorism—Religious aspects—Islam. |
   Islam and politics—Africa. | Political violence—Africa.
Classification: LCC BP166.14.F85 (ebook) | LCC BP166.14.F85 R37 2019 (print) |
   DDC 320.557096—dc23
LC record available at https://lccn.loc.gov/2018043235

Printed in the United States of America

To Elizabeth W. Walker and Family

Contents

Preface

This is a study of one of the most dangerous regions in the world. Africa south of the Sahara (hereafter referred to as Africa) has been described as "the world's deadliest region" by William Thom (2010) and "second most dangerous region" by John Davis (2010). By the start of the twenty-first century more people had died from political conflict in Africa than any other place on earth.[1] Between 1999 and 2008, for instance, Africa experienced thirteen major armed conflicts, the highest total for any region of the world."[2] In addition to the general issue of political violence "terrorist safe havens have exploded across Africa," according to one observer, to such an extent that safe havens have served as sanctuaries for insurgents operating in weak and failed states. Once established, these safe havens have allowed insurgents to organize and train recruits to launch cross-border strikes.[3] Yet, in our efforts to understand and cope with this, another observer reminds us of the difficulty involved in defining, interpreting, and measuring political violence.[4]

Could it be, as Mahmoud Mamdani (2005) suggests, that political violence is the "midwife of [human] history," precisely because our modern sensibilities encourage us to rationalize violence as "necessary to human progress?"[5] Although political violence in Africa and elsewhere may be staggering, Mamdani concludes that "it never fails to astound us." From the Spanish Inquisition to the annihilation of Americas' native people, violence has been justified as "necessary."[6] Violence in the War on Terror (WOT) seems no exception given our common use of expressions like "taking out" an enemy as a euphemism for killing, "going after" someone (or something) as a euphemism for aggression, or Enhanced Interrogation Techniques as a euphemism for torture. Could it be as Mamdani suggests that WOT is a continuation of the unfinished politics of the Cold War and that contemporary confrontations with Islamist insurgencies represent the latest form of anti-western "proxy wars" of the 1970s and 1980s? Whatever the answer, Mamdani's observations encourage us to confront the causes and cures of political violence in the routinely marginalized region we call Africa.

It is important to acknowledge from the start that there is hardly a zone of conflict in contemporary Africa that cannot be traced to colonialism.[7] Perhaps because of these colonial roots, Africa south of the Sahara continues to suffer from state versus society and intra-societal violence. Between 1993 and 2014 the continent suffered nearly 50 percent of the world's genocides and politicides,[8] and at just 28 percent of the UN's member-states and 14 percent of the world's population, Africa has witnessed more than its fair share of armed conflicts.[9] Religion in general and Islam in particular have been blamed for conflicts in Sudan, Nigeria, Ethiopia, Chad, Kenya, and Tanzania.[10] For instance, the *Economist* magazine in 2015 identified Islamism as "the biggest threat to African peace and prosperity."[11] And yet because religion can be used to justify either peace or violence, it is doubtful that such a view is a valid explanation of these events.[12]

Nevertheless, Africa may also lead the world in the number of internally and externally displaced persons and international peacekeepers deployed. But once again, oversimplified images of Africa as a land of starvation and misery obscure the deeper, more profound reality that war-related starvation, displacement, and despair claim more lives than bombs and bullets combined. For instance, war zones in and around the city of Goma in the eastern DRC during the late 1990s earned a reputation for being among the most dangerous places on earth for women. Rape in the DRC is estimated to have occurred at a rate of one every twenty minutes. This study devotes particular attention to violence associated with Islamists militancy among Africans where women and girls sometimes as young as ten have been kidnapped, raped, and forced to marry Islamist fighters often after witnessing the killing of their loved ones. But whose ethics ultimately matters in these instances: the secular "authority" of the state (or warlord) or the moral authority of religion? Are secular values the only values that matter, or do religious values still matter? Can a distinction be made between excess and moderation in matters of religion or does all religious authority inevitably lead to excess and therefore conflict with the state?

A well-known saying among Egyptian Muslims seems worth noting for its possible relevance: "there is nothing more pious than a political leader who consults a sheikh nor more despicable than a sheikh who consults a political leader." This study offers (1) evidence of Africa's important and significant role in the worldwide Islamist challenge, (2) an analysis of the ideology of Islamist militancy among Africans and (3) ways to minimize if not eliminate the spread of its terrorist violence. One critic describes the worldwide Islamist challenge as one that presents a choice not just between war and peace but between war and endless war! But whether this is true or not, a change in the status of Africa in US policy circles is long overdue.

This study attempts to appeal to a broad audience of undergraduate and graduate students in African/Africana/Black Studies, Political Science, Public Policy, and International Relations as well as policy makers, researchers, activists, and library collections. While the hope of every scholar, consciously or unconsciously, is to generate new knowledge or new analyses of existing knowledge, this study contributes more to the latter than to the former. In this regard, aspects of this study include items of interest to the general public and policy makers, as well as items of special interest to scholars including the *sunnah*, *hadith*, and *Wahhabi* movement. This study has made prominent use of eyewitness accounts, British Broadcasting Corporation (BBC) interviews, case-study techniques identified by Robert K. Yin, and field study methods popularized by anthropologist Clifford Geertz. Observations derived from interviews and cases drawn from the literature will be mediated by my own experiences in Africa, Europe, and the Middle East. This study also offers new ways of viewing militant Islamism in an ever-expanding 1.8 billion-strong Muslim community (*ummah*), which according to the Pew Research Center will become the world's single largest religious community by the year 2050.

Within the vast domain of the Islamist challenge currently confronting the world community, Africa, Africans, and African Muslims will remain the central focus of this study. This study welcomes "progress" made by policy makers to emancipate Africa from its marginalized status in world affairs, a status that President Trump describes in more colorful terms, but a status of neglect, nonetheless. Scholarly manifestations of this change are apparent from studies including Davis's *Terrorism in Africa* (2010) and Jack Mangola's *New Security Threats and Crises in Africa* (2010). However, if de-marginalization represents a genuine change in our thinking, then more studies devoted to this phenomenon are desperately needed. Studies of terrorist violence linked to Islamist militancy in Africa can be categorized in one of three ways. An older category of studies taking the form of anti-colonial resistance emphasizing the historical aspects of African insurgencies constitutes the first category. Studies bringing together collections of readings devoted to Islamist militancy in different parts of Africa as seen in Davis (2010) represent a second category. A third category perhaps illustrated by Williams (2017) emphasizes an international relations approach. Although this study intends to contribute to the third of these three categories, elements of both historical and to a lesser extent comparative analysis are also included herein. For instance, the subject of "foreign fighters" in the WOT may have puzzled recent readers of the *New York Times* with its Africa-related characterization of Trinidad and Tobago as the world's largest per capita source of "foreign fighters." However, an important source of this concern no doubt may have been the Times' and other influential news outlets' focus since September 11, 2001 on world regions other than the Americas. Information included in chapter 7 of this study offers valuable insights, designed to offset deficits in our knowledge of African Muslim influence which continue to survive in regions including the Caribbean. Although this study offers no hypotheses or formal models for testing, it offers novel ways of understanding existing knowledge of value to scholars and policy makers alike.

Chapter 1 offers a descriptive assessment of recent episodes of terrorist violence among Africans. Chapter 2 offers an analysis of non-terrorist Muslim struggle (*jihad*), including an assessment of its overall features among Africans. Chapter 3 offers an analysis of the politics of Muslim struggle (*jihad*) among Africans and ways to diminish if not eliminate it among Africans. Chapter 4 examines eight prominent cases of non-terrorist Muslim struggle (*jihad*) and Africans. Chapter 5 examines eight prominent cases of terrorist violence among Africans. Chapter 6 examines Muslim flight (*hijra*) from the Old to the New World and its implications. Chapter 7 explores the resulting presence of Islam and Muslims in the Americas. Chapter 8 offers the study's conclusions and recommendations for policy makers.

While primary attention is devoted to militant Islamist insurgencies among Africans, other Islamists movements involving Africans, including the very first *jihad*, *hijra*, and *ummah* led by the Prophet Muhammad in seventh-century Arabia, are also examined. Both the original Muslim fighters (*mujahedeen*) and companions (*al-sahaba*) of the Prophet reveal a significant African presence. While this history is well-known to many older Muslims and students of world and Middle East history, it is often less well known to younger Muslims or students less versed in history. Special attention is devoted to the key role of Africans in the development and spread of Islam and its contemporary implications. Central to this study are the essential Islamic institutions of Muslim struggle (*jihad*), flight (*hijra*), and community (*ummah*).

NOTES

1. Paul D. Williams, *War & Conflict in Africa*, second edition (Cambridge, UK: Polity Press, 2017), 5.

2. Ibid.

3. John Davis, *Terrorism in Africa: The Evolving Front in the War on Terror* (Lanham, MD: Lexington Books, 2010), 241.

4. Williams, *War & Conflict in Africa*, 15.

5. Mahmoud Mamdani, *Good Muslim, Bad Muslim* (New York: Doubleday, 2005), 3–4.

6. Ibid., 7–8.

7. Williams, *War & Conflict in Africa*, 8.

8. Ibid., 19.

9. Ibid., 20 and 21.

10. Ibid., 160.

11. Ibid.

12. Ibid.

Acknowledgments

First, I wish to thank the anonymous readers who struggled to bring this project to fruition and my editors Courtney Morales and Emily Roderick for their guidance, patience, and perseverance. Many other professionals helped make this project possible, including Michael A. Gomez of New York University, John Padgett and Charles Lipson of the University of Chicago, David Laitin of Stanford University, Duncan Snidal of Oxford University, John and Jean Comaroff of Harvard University, Muhammad Ali Abdul Salaam of Atlanta, Arif Jamal of the University of Pittsburgh, Sulayman Nyang and Marilyn Lashley of Howard University, the late Akbar Muhammad of Binghamton University, Douglas Allen, Yvone Labe and Bill Munsey of the University of Maine, Dean Lenz, Steven Raymer, Robert Terrell, and John and Audrey McCluskey of Indiana University, Edmond Keller and Leonard Binder of UCLA, Andrew McFarland and W. Clarke Douglass of the University of Illinois at Chicago, Robert and Josephine Dibie of Indiana University Kokomo, Mark Levine, business executive and Frank Morris formerly of Northwestern University, Salta Liebert of Virginia Commonwealth University, Sultana Afroz formerly of the University of the West Indies, Milton Morris of the University of the West Indies, Frank Southard and Andrea Southard formerly of the University of Maine Farmington, Sunil Sahu of DePaw University, John Duke Anthony of Washington, DC, Sayyid Muhammad Syeed of ISNA, and Abigail Hauslohner of the *Washington Post*. A note of thanks goes to the following professional journals for publishing earlier versions of portions of this book. These journals include the *Journal of Muslim Minority Affairs*, *Hamdard Islamicus*, the *Journal of Islamic Law*, the *Journal of Islamic Law and Culture*, *Arab World Geographer*, *American Journal of Islamic Social Sciences*, and *Islamic Studies*. I also wish to thank my colleagues at Indiana State University, including Stan Buchanan, Christopher

Olsen, Andrea Arrington, Barbara Skinner, Anne Foster, James Gustafson, Namita Goswami, Kathleen Heath, Paul Burkett, Ralph Leck, Ann Rider, Mark Hamm, Adeyemi Doss, David Polizi, Glenn Perry, David Nichols, Bassam Yousif, Tom Derrick, Kieth Byerman, Charles and Scotia Brown, Laura Wilburn, Valentine Muyumba, Yasmine Haiti, Ethan Doig, and Idris Sababu. Finally, I wish to thank a number of long-time friends and family for their tireless support, including Elizabeth W. Walker and family, Idris and Sadieka Qadeem, Cedric and Ernestine Cheatom, George Russell Pope, Bill and Barbara Moody, Albert and Barbara Harold, Wayne and Maria Nehrt, Judy Smith, Marsha P. Cannon, Ameer Ali, Abdul Malik, Richard and Collette Smith, Cass and Ofori Sabur, Abdul Latif Mutakkabir, Bennie Gordon Jr., Edward Mead, Lemont Sanders, Harvy Blanks, Hannah Jon Taylor, Hasaan Rashid, Aleeya Reynolds, Noah Rashid, Leyla Rashid, Shandris Rashid, Trina Akins, Angie Akins, Phyllis Henderson, Marie, Steven and Rhonda McDaniel, Steven and Michael Houseworth, Tony Zamora, Galen Abdurrazzaq, Preston Jackson, Ms. Gossie Harold Hudson, Clara Small and Judge Brown. A special note of thanks goes to my wife, Dr. Nancy J. Obermeyer, the love of my life, for her enduring love, support, and patience. Of course, I alone am responsible for the errors and shortcomings of this book.

Introduction

Policy makers are often ill served by their misperceptions of world events and nowhere is this more evident than in the "War on Terror (WOT)," a term first coined by President George W. Bush in the aftermath of 9/11.[1] Who can forget Mr. Bush's now famous appearance aboard the US Abraham Lincoln in May 2003 before a banner reading "Mission Accomplished" or assertions like "we fight them *there* so we do not have to fight them *here,*" or "you're either with us or you're with the terrorists"? Who can forget President Obama's utterances, some thirty-two times according to one source, that al-Qaeda was "weakened," "decimated," "on the run," "on its heels," "on the path of defeat,"[2] in a war that was "coming to an end," fought by an "Islamic State" described as "contained," and ridiculed as al-Qaeda's "jayvee team"?[3] Some predicted the United States would be welcomed as liberators in Iraq, in a war that would be over in weeks and paid for with Iraqi oil! Candidate Trump's proposed Muslim ban was widely ridiculed as "ignorant" and unlikely in 2016 though it remained an issue until it was upheld by the US Supreme Court in a 5–4 ruling on June 26, 2018.[4] President Trump savored his own "mission accomplished" moment after bombing Syria on April 14, 2018. Yet assessments of Mr. Trump were not the only misperceptions. For instance, the *New York Times* prematurely assessed the "Islamic State" as "one of the greatest global security challenges since the end of the Cold War."[5] But this view has been challenged by empirical data released in December 2015 showing Boko Haram rather than ISIS or "al-Qaeda central" as "the world's most deadly terrorist group." Boko Haram has been linked to 6,664 deaths while ISIS has been linked to 6,073 deaths in 2014.[6] The same terrorism index cited ISIS *and* Boko Haram as responsible for roughly half of all deaths from terrorism in 2014.[7] Since then ISIS has experienced major setbacks as African terrorists continue to kill, maim, and displace victims by the thousands. While the chief culprits include Boko Haram of Nigeria, al-Qaeda in the Islamic Maghreb (AQIM), al-Shabab of Somalia, Ansar Dine of Mali, the Seleka of the Central African Republic (CAR), and the Allied Democratic Forces (ADF) of Uganda,[8] Boko Haram has been linked to the deaths of over 20,000 with some estimates ranging as high as 31,000.[9] Testifying before Congress in 2018, General Thomas D. Waldhauser, head of the US Africa Command, described the group as "the most deplorable organization on the planet." Africa may be "the most conflict prone region in the world," yet it "remains one of the least understood."[10] Writing in 2010, one retired US intelligence official described it as "the only area of the world we could write off as a backwater not worthy of full intelligence coverage,"[11] a "prevailing attitude" he fought against "for years with little success."[12] Mr. Trump's alleged 2018 description of Africa as "sh_thole" countries reinforces this view. This study explores Islamist violence among Africans to improve our overall awareness and understanding of militant Islamism. Throughout this study the authoritative institutions of *jihad, hijra,* and *ummah* are explored along with Jervis's classic *Perceptions and Misperceptions in International Relations* (1976) to (1) debunk myths and stereotypes about Africans, (2) improve our understanding of militant Islamism, and (3) minimize if not eliminate Islamist-driven violence among Africans and their progeny throughout the world.[13]

The late scholar, historian, and self-described neoconservative Bernard Lewis was widely regarded as the Dean of Islamic and Middle East studies in the United States. He was an advisor to President George W. Bush and Vice-President Dick Cheney, and a student of the orientalist, H. R. Gibb.[14] But Lewis also has been described as "the founding father of contemporary "Culture Talk" which among other things represented the politicization of culture.[15] Culture Talk assumes that every culture has a tangible essence that defines it and then explains politics as a consequence of that essence.[16] Based on this logic, Africa is seen as being incapable of modernity, while "hardcore" Islam is seen as being both incapable of and resistant to modernity.[17] After September 11, 2001, it qualified and explained the practice of "terrorism" as "Islamic" allowing all Muslims from this perspective to be viewed as "just plain bad."[18] Muslims were "no longer just an earthly enemy, the Crusades demonized the Muslim as evil incarnate and personification of the religion of the Antichrist," as perhaps best illustrated by St. Bernard's assertion "that to kill an infidel was not homicide but 'malicide,' annihilation of evil and that a pagan's death was a Christian's glory because, in it, Christ was glorified."[19]

The orientalism with which Lewis is associated was widely criticized during the 1960s and famously so by Edward Said, in *Orientalism* (1978).[20] Yet, despite this checkered past, Mamdani has marveled at just how much "Orientalist histories have managed to rebound."[21] For instance, Lewis's article "The Roots of Muslim Rage," published in the Atlantic in 1990 was the first to contain the phrase, "Clash of Civilization." It later became the title of Samuel Huntington's 1993 article and book of the same name.[22] But obituaries following Lewis's death in 2018 also recounted the misperceptions he promoted including one that appeared in the *Wall Street Journal* in 2002 wherein he predicted Iraqis would "rejoice" over an American invasion.[23] On the NBC News show Meet the Press, he predicted incorrectly that "a strong, firm US response to terror and threats to the United States would go a long way, frankly to calming things down in that part of the world."[24]

Given the level and significance of these misperceptions rational choice theory (RCT), the most prominent theory in the discipline of Political Science seems the appropriate theoretical perspective for use in this study. RCT, the most prominent theory in Political Science, was one of the perspectives used in Graham Allison's classic work *the Essence of Decision* (1971) examining decision making in the Cuban Missile Crisis, widely regarded as one of the most influential studies in Political Science in the post–World War II era. Jervis's classic *Perceptions and Misperceptions in International Relations* (1976) examining RCT decision making during the Vietnam War is also used. Given the successful use of RCT as a theoretical device in analyses of decision making in the Cuban missile crisis and Vietnam RTC seems the appropriate device for analyzing misperceptions in the WOT.

This study also relies on a mixture of quantitative and qualitative data plus case studies presented in chapters 4 and 5. Robert K. Lin's (2018) *Case Study Research and Applications: Design and Methods* and Clifford Geertz's (1968) *Islam Observed: Religious Development in Morocco and Indonesia* will be used to organize and select the cases along with intermittent eyewitness accounts and interviews referenced throughout the study. Of special value are the insight of anthropologist Clifford Geertz (1968) and the participatory observation method he introduced as an alternative to the orientalism of Lewis and his teacher H. R. Gibb whom Edward Said passionately criticized in Orientalism (1978). More about the case studies used herein is provided in chapters 4 and 5.

THE TASK AHEAD

This study explores the Islamist challenge to expose popular misperceptions of Africans and Islamism and shed new light on contemporary militant Islamism. This chapter includes sections devoted to (1) "The Task Ahead"; (2) "Theoretical Considerations"; (3) "Myths and Stereotypes"; (4) "Origins and Characteristics of Islamism"; (5) "Africa in the Wider World of Islam"; (6) "Islamism and Political Change"; (7) "Africans and US Foreign Policy Makers"; and

(8) "Africa in the WOT." Beyond this chapter, this study provides a preface, introduction, and eight chapters, with each (except chapter 1) beginning with a reiteration of the main idea from the previous chapter followed by a statement of the main idea to be explored. The Preface frames the larger challenge of political violence in Africa while eventually shifting attention to violence involving Africans sparked by the ideology of militant Islamism.

The Introduction to this study offers an overview of the book's focus, components, central argument, and theoretical perspective. Contrary to the myth of Africa as "the dark continent" of marginal importance and significance, it argues for the need to recognize Africa as a major political arena in the US-led WOT. Chapter 1, on terrorism, examines recent episodes of terrorism and Africa including many that remain largely ignored. Evidence is offered to challenge the view still held by some, (though not all) that Africa and Africans are of marginal importance and significance. Chapter 2 examines Muslim struggle (*jihad*) to understand more clearly how basic Islamic beliefs and practices as delineated in the authoritative sources of Islam, differ substantially from "terrorism" or "jihadism" discussed in chapter 1. Chapter 2 also attempts to clarify the often-ignored distinction between terrorist violence and Muslim struggle (*jihad*) and the need to correct this and other important though widely overlooked distinctions as a first step toward better understanding and undertaking a sustainable response to the worldwide Islamist challenge.

Chapter 3 explores the politics of Africans and Muslim struggle (*jihad*) as distinct from the terrorist violence of "jihadists," to document Africans' long-standing involvement with mainstream Islam and question the misperception that non-Arab Islamists are mere "copy-cat," "home-grown," "want-to-be," "jihadists" with little or no legitimate links to the religion of Islam or its history, politics, or traditions. Chapter 3 clarifies the widely misunderstood meaning of Muslim struggle (*jihad*) by exploring its descriptions in the authoritative sources and history dating to the Prophet Muhammad (570–632 AD). Chapter 4 examines eight prominent cases of Muslim struggle (*jihad*) involving Africans to refute the misperception that Africans have little or no experience with the Islamic institution of Muslim struggle (*jihad*). Chapter 5 examines eight prominent cases of terrorist violence involving Africans or persons of African descent that document Africans' significant role in the ongoing WOT.

Chapter 6, Flight (*hijra*) to the Americas, explores the Islamic institution of flight (*hijra*) which first brought *Moors* (*moriscos*) and Jews (*morenos*) attempting to escape the long reach of the Inquisition in Iberia to the Americas. Later, more massively, enslaved Africans, some of whom were Muslim, were also brought to the Americas. Their arrival and presence in the New World planted the earliest seeds of Islam, Islamism, and quite possibly Judaism in the New World. A small but growing number of writers view this early arrival of Muslims in the New World as the nucleus of the contemporary Muslim community (*ummah*) in the Americas.[25]

Chapter 7 develops this theme more fully first by distinguishing Islam, Islamism, and the Islamist challenge, and second by inviting scholars of Islam to reimagine if not redefine what it means to be "African" in the context of contemporary Islamist militancy. Several obvious reasons necessitate this reimagining or redefinition, including the globalization of Muslim struggle (*jihad*), the dispersal of Africans throughout the African diaspora and the rise of Islamist militancy among Africans.[26] These factors necessitate new conceptualizations of an evolving black/African identity exposing the inadequacy of Eurocentric notions of identity based on the modern secular state that fail to reflect notions of identity commonplace among Islamist militants. For instance, Boko Haram, like Islamists elsewhere, promotes the authority of God (*Allah*) and the religion of Islam over the authority of the state and international system. To understand this phenomenon more fully, this study examines the Islamist challenge as a political alternative to the existing order and offers recommendations for minimizing if not eliminating the terrorist violence among Africans that have emerged in its wake.

Before discussing rational choice and the bounded rationality paradigm used in this study, a brief description of the Global Terrorism Database (GTD) and other databases used in this study are provided. GTD is an open sourced database compiled by the University of Maryland and largest database of its kind. GTD data document Africa's rising incidence of violence including violent incidents observed in Somalia, Burundi, Ethiopia, Democratic Republic of the Congo (DRC), Sudan, the CAR, Nigeria, Kenya, and Cameroon. It displays a growing rate of violence in Africa since 2002.[27] A second prominent database, the Social Conflict in Africa Database (SCAD) compiled by the University of Denver offers another source of empirical data documenting some 7,900 social conflict events across Africa from 1990 to 2011. The Denver database records incidents of riots, strikes, protests, coups, and communal violence.[28]

A third empirical database upon which this study relies is the RAND Corporation, which identified 1,487 terrorist incidents in Africa in 2016, alone. According to this database, states associated with Islamist violence in Africa formed the majority of terrorist incidents around the world, led by Somalia whose violent explosions in the form of "suicide bombings" may be the signature weapon of choice among militants.[29] While these data appear significant, they are not offered as part of a full formal analysis. Rather, their inclusion is meant to help substantiate the empirical claim that terrorist violence among Africans is significant, growing and deadly. This if true supports the need for remedies that minimize if not eliminate violence of the sort witnessed in Rwanda.

This study assumes that the goal of eliminating terrorist violence is more or less shared by Africanists and policy makers, alike. The Maryland GTD reveals a 220 percent increase in the rate of terrorist violence among Africans since 2013 and a pattern of largely increasing terrorist violence since 2004.[30] Although significant political and military responses to Islamist violence have emerged in the interim, no evidence to date scholarly or otherwise suggest that terrorist violence in Africa is declining or nearing an end. Hence, there continues to be a need for new and improved ways of understanding this challenge as a first step toward hastening its demise. This study draws on the collective wisdom of over forty peer-reviewed scholarly sources appearing in journals, books, and reference materials. Reports in the *New York Times* and *Wall Street Journal*, indispensable to policy analysis, are also tapped to capture the evolving views and responses of policy makers and prominent think-tank experts.

Reports from these and other accounts produced by journalists like Smith (2016) and Bauer (2016) augment (rather than replace) scholarly peer-reviewed studies and empirical databases. These reports are valuable for the rich details they offer on violence involving Africans not always apparent from empirical databases or media reports that frequently marginalize subjects related to Africa. Descriptive accounts gleaned primarily from journalists are primarily used in the Introduction, chapter 1, and in case studies presented in chapters 4 and 5 and these are among the shortest chapters in this study; empirical data and more analytic treatments appear in chapters 2, 3, 6, 7, 8, and these are among the longest chapters in this study.

A terrorism study conducted by the US State Department found that among five perpetrator groups displaying the highest number of terrorist attacks, Boko Haram recorded the highest number of deaths at 6, 663 in 2014 and the second highest number of deaths at 5,450 for the year 2015.[31] Assistant Secretary of State Linda Thomas-Greenfield told the Senate Foreign Relations committee that the number of people killed by African groups is "as large, if not larger, than the number of people killed by ISIL."[32] In addition to this, Africa may be home to eight of the largest UN peacekeeping operations in the world,[33] a fact that may have led Virginia Senator and 2016 Democratic vice presidential candidate, Tom Kaine, to question why the United States is not more actively involved in Africa. According to Kaine, "we've got to look in the mirror and ask if race is a reason" for this predicament in light of (1) the United States' internment of Japanese-Americans while refusing to intern German-Americans during World War II and (2) the decision to intervene in the Balkans in the 1990s to stop potential genocide there, while doing nothing to stop actual genocide in Rwanda.[34] The harsh treatment of refugees fleeing violence in Central America in 2018 may be a third example of this practice.

References will be made to passages from (1) the Qur'an most often cited by Islamists, (2) the tradition of Islam (*sunnah*), and (3) the sayings of Prophet Muhammed (*hadiths*) in keeping with this study's attempt to make primary use of the voices/ideology of the subjects themselves. Collectively referred to as the authoritative sources of Islam in this study, play a crucial role in delineating the core tenets of militant Islamist ideology to offer a rare glimpse into the heart and soul of Islamism providing a degree of Islamic authenticity not often found in studies written after September 11, 2001. The essential Islamic institutions of Muslim struggle (*jihad*), flight (*hijra*), and community (*ummah*) are examined herein to distinguish this study from purely normative approaches to the Islamist challenge in an effort to derive a more dispassionate, nonjudgmental, objective analysis aimed at diminishing and ultimately eliminating Islamist terrorist violence.

Violence among Africans may be underreported and even worsened by government impotence and heavy-handed policies as seen in the case of Nigeria.[35] Moreover, it is difficult to conduct a major study on the Islamist challenge and Africa, overall and in historical perspective, when relatively few such studies exist. Another obstacle is the formidable linguistic challenge presented by African place names like Timbuktu, a once-thriving world center of Islamic learning in Mali, though now a synonym for a place in the middle of nowhere of little or no significance. This is especially problematical for a study that seeks to demonstrate just the opposite image of Africa. Nevertheless, it is a mistake to assume that Timbuktu is without major significance as a historical site and contemporary flash point in the US-led WOT.[36] Despite these obstacles, we must never be tired of asking, why? Why have we failed to eliminate terrorist violence among Africans and what can be done to change this?

Nothing in the scholarly, media, or government literature suggests the end of terrorist violence among Africans is near. Indeed, terrorist violence among Africans is increasing and not decreasing. No other evidence demonstrates the inadequacy of existing approaches and strategies and the need for new ones more than this. Violence linked to Islamist militants is on the increase in Europe where violence linked to terrorists often with family ties to North or West Africa have occurred at the rate of one episode per month in early 2017. The mindset of denial, that is, "if it didn't happen to us, it didn't happen," is a luxury the United States (and Europe) can no longer afford. Indeed, with the decline of ISIS in the Middle East, Islamist controlled sites in Africa, Afghanistan, and elsewhere are bound to acquire greater significance. In the words of one long-term observer and former US security expert, "lawlessness in Africa constitutes a threat to the United States because it allows Africa to become a breeding ground for terrorists, political instability, and global health issues."[37]

The US Department of Homeland Security is very much aware of the Islamist militant challenge in Africa. The report "Terrorism in Africa: the Imminent Threat to the United States," published by the Subcommittee on Counterterrorism and Intelligence of the Committee on Homeland Security of the US House of Representatives during open hearings in 2015 examined a June 2006 issue of the publication, Echo of Jihad (*Sada al-Jihad*) featuring an article by Abu Azzam al-Ansari titled, "Al-Qaeda is Moving to Africa," in which the author claimed "Africa is a fertile soil for the advance of jihad and the jihadi cause." The congressional subcommittee examining this article asserted in retrospect that "it was clearly a mistake for many to have dismissed Abu Azzam's analysis as devoid of operational effect," because shortly before the publication of Azzam's article, the Somali Islamist movement, the Islamic Courts Union whose leaders included a number of al-Qaeda linked figures seized control of the intermittent Somali capital in Mogadishu in late December 2006. This action led the subcommittee to conclude that "there is no doubt that the US is behind the curve in taking threats from terror groups in Africa seriously," because "we have seen on too many occasions that al-Qaeda-affiliated groups in Africa will attack American and Western interests when they see an opening."[38]

Combatting this challenge may be the political equivalent of halting the spread of Africa's HIV/AIDS and Ebola diseases under the Bush and Obama presidencies, respectively. Indeed, one observer describes how preoccupation with the Ebola epidemic and other urgent issues facing African societies may have distracted the attention of US policy makers away from the danger of terrorist violence among Africans.[39] Yet, if the presence of disease anywhere threatens the spread of disease everywhere, the presence of terrorism anywhere threatens the spread of terrorism everywhere. Like Ebola or HIV/AIDS, this is *not* an African problem but a world problem threatening Africa and everything in its path as evidenced by Boko Haram and ISIS propaganda videos displaying African appearing militants vowing attacks on the United States, Paris, and beyond.

This study challenges the US-led WOT primarily aimed at ISIS and al-Qaeda "central" to the neglect of lesser-known possibly deadlier Islamist insurgencies like Boko Haram, affiliated with ISIS since 2015 and al-Shabaab, affiliated with al-Qaeda since 2012.[40] Only when Boko Haram gained recognition as an "international crisis" did it became officially recognized as a "terrorist organization."[41] And while this designation brought valuable US assistance to the government of Nigeria, thousands of lives had already been lost before significant outside help arrived. The fact that ISIS and al-Qaeda "central" have remained the primary focus of US anti-terrorist policy to the neglect of a Boko Haram insurgency that began in 2009 is indefensible. As cited in the opening paragraph of this study, "for the past forty years

Africa south of the Sahara has been the most conflict prone region in the world."[42] Yet, despite its growing importance in the WOT, Africa remains "one of the least understood regions of the world."[43]

Despite its marginalization, Africa's ties to Muslim struggle (*jihad*) can be traced to the earliest beginnings of Islam itself and to the rise of the Prophet Muhammad in Mecca whose original companions (*sahaba*) included many blacks. Indeed, blacks are mentioned in the Qur'anic chapter (*sura*), the Elephant (*al-fil*), which describes how divine intervention caused the elephants of would-be African conquerors that once controlled the region, to flea in panic saving the Meccans from near certain defeat. Muslims believe that were it not for God's (Allah's) intervention, Mecca, the center of the Arab world, may have become a colony of Africa in 570 AD, the year of the Prophet's birth. Awareness of this event as described in chapter (*sura*) 105 of the Qu'ran makes it difficult to marginalize Africans in the Muslim world.[44] But lack of historical awareness is not the only obstacle to understanding the Islamist challenge as the language we use often falls short of accurately identifying even the most basic of concepts we use, raising questions over the appropriateness of our word choices as seen in distinctions that include Islamic versus Islamist, "holy war" versus Muslim struggle (*jihad*), and "radical Islamic terrorist" versus Islamist militant. Carelessness in our choice of words undermines the goal of diminishing, if not eliminating terrorist violence, as words matter in the Muslim world. This study warns against ignoring these and other distinctions.

THEORETICAL CONSIDERATIONS

There is a need to explain and avoid the practice of marginalizing Africa in the future, while remaining mindful of Vincent Ostrom's assertion that "theory without practice is fantasy; but practice without theory is blind." RCT and the related though distinct bounded rationality paradigm are theoretical constructs used in this study to explain the past behavior of US policy makers of marginalizing Africa prior to its latest "rediscovery." RCT assumes that human beings are equipped with perfect knowledge and possess infinite problem solving capacity. It further assumes that all humans maximize their utilities (goals) while minimizing their losses. By contrast, the bounded rationality paradigm assumes that human beings are limited problem solvers who possess finite problem solving capacity who seek nonoptimal instead of optimal decision outcomes.[45] Nobel Prize winning social scientist Herbert Simon, who first coined the phrase "bounded rationality" argued that instead of optimizing or maximizing their utilities (goals), human beings simply satisfice in their actual-observed behavior.[46] "Fully rational man," the mythical

hero who knows the solutions to all mathematical problems who can immediately perform all computations, regardless of how difficult, was metaphori-
cally laid to rest by Simon's notion of satisficing.[47] Satisficing suggests that
humans by necessity seek outcomes described as nonoptimizing or "good
enough" instead of optimal. For Simon, humans are intendedly rational rather
than actually rational creatures who typically pursue incremental rather than
comprehensive goals.[48]

The challenge for US decision makers to either embrace or avoid Africa
has always been one that is surrounded by risk, ambiguity, and uncertainty[49]
beset by flawed and incomplete information. When these circumstances
persist, decision makers may feel forced to rely more on misperceptions,
stereotypes, and myths rather than on reliable information, leading Jervis in
his (1976) classic study of misperception to ask:

> Do important explanatory variables in international relations involve decision
> making? In terms of perceptions this can be separated into two subsidiary ques-
> tions: are important differences in policy preferences traceable to differences
> in decision makers' perceptions of their environment? And are there important
> differences between reality and shared or common perceptions?[50]

Consistent with findings by Jervis, this study answers "yes" to these
questions, as explanatory variables in international relations of course may
involve decision making and misperceptions that reflect (1) mistakes or (2)
systematically shared differences between reality and perceptions, described
by cognitive theorists as perceptual or implicit biases. Analysis of these
maladies can be helpful in explaining past avoidance behavior by US policy
makers toward Africa. But they may also offer insights into how best to reject
knee-jerk avoidance behavior in the future especially when they unfold at the
expense of broader US interests. If misperceptions spring from ignorance,
myth, and stereotypes then eliminating ignorance, myth, and stereotype
seems a fitting starting place for the removal of misperceptions about the
Islamist challenge and Africa.

This study explores what Stefano describes as the central concern of
models of bounded rationality, namely, "how people make judgements on
the basis of incomplete and imperfect information," and their frequently dire
consequences. Jervis is correct when he admits that "there is no easy way to
determine the accuracy of perceptions,"[51] because "it is hard to know what a
person's perceptions are and even harder to know whether they are correct."[52]
Yet, if US decision makers are able to resist avoiding Africa based on very
limited information—then potential errors in judgment associated with "writing off" Africa might be avoided. Africa in the minds of most nonexperts is
a place of little importance, value, or significance, located on the margins of

civilization and world affairs. This view is not the exclusive view of the bigot, but may well be the mindset of the otherwise open-minded and well-educated observer. If the United States is to meet the Islamist challenge in the future, a change in this mindset is urgently needed (for most).

Citing the work of Jervis (1976), Kaufman's descriptions of decision-making behavior among US policy makers offers additional support for the idea that implicit bias permeates decision making especially when it involves international phenomena.

> The role of the decision maker is to filter the information received in order to arrive at a decision that also builds in bias. Information screens are subconscious filters through which people put the information coming in from the world around them. Often they simply ignore any information that does not fit their expectations. Thus most decision makers will look for information or even "evidence" that supports what they already believe. . . . In terms of policy making what this means is that information can and will be screened as it passes from person to person. . . . By the time it gets to the end of the chain, it is a totally different statement.[53]

Misperceptions of Africa in US corporate circles became a matter of widespread debate among Africanists in 1990 when the *Economist* magazine printed a controversial magazine cover titled, "Africa: the hopeless continent" followed by an equally controversial and troubling *Economist* magazine cover titled "Africa Rising" in 2000. This sharp reversal in the depiction of Africa made it difficult for President Obama to challenge stereotyped images of Africa held by some US officials who depict it as a "backwater." This depiction is refuted by Africa and other regions' role in facilitating China's emergence as arguably the engine of world trade.[54] Is it possible to go from being "hopeless" (whatever that means) to "rising" in a mere decade? Was the *Economist* magazine's assessment a misperception or a random mistake? Perhaps the magazine decided to avoid further embarrassment by simply embracing empirical reality.[55] But taking a decade to do so, did little to repair negative perceptions among Africans toward the *Economist* and like-minded US officials as President Obama learned firsthand during two official African visits in 2013 and 2015.[56]

Efforts to present a more positive image of Africa during President Trump's much heralded address before the UN were dashed by his failure to refer to Africa as a continent instead of a country and mispronunciation of the African state name of Namibia in September 2017. After, President Trump's reference to Africa, Haiti, and El Salvador as "sh_thole" countries and a five-nation African tour by US Secretary of State Rex Tillerson seeking to make amends for Mr. Trump's earlier remark was later called off after the secretary became ill, leaving Africa to become marginalized once again. Tillerson, who was reportedly not a big twitter user, received word of his firing via twitter while travelling home from Africa on March 13, 2018. He reportedly had called his boss, President Trump, a "f_ing moron!"

The decision to marginalize Africa (perhaps similar to the decision to fire Tillerson) may be an example of a decision Jervis believes can be explained "without over psychologizing." Yet, of greater concern to the aims of this study is the question, do decision makers perceive the world accurately and when misperceptions do occur can they be explained away as random accidents? Jervis answers "no" to this question, for in his view, rather than random mistakes, "perceptions of the world and of other actors diverge from reality in patterns that we can detect and for reasons that we can understand."[57] The idea of cognitive maps first introduced by Edward Tolman in 1948 and their impact on our decisions lend credence to Jervis's observation that patterns exist in our perceptions and misperceptions of the world and of actors who inhabit it.

Africa for better or worse is not normally a part of the cognitive or mental map that readily comes to mind when thinking of US interests; but then neither were Vietnam nor Afghanistan. Perennially beset by conflict, poverty, and despair, Africa at best is treated as a non-priority, by most. Because the label one assigns to an object shapes the way it is perceived—it is easy to see how the "backwater" label associated with Africa and described by a former official led Africa to be marginalized if not ignored in certain intelligence circles.[58] Jervis argues that decision makers inclined to perceive a thing in a certain way are likely to evaluate it in that same way. Thus, characterizing a region like Africa for example, in a way that diverges from one's preconceived expectations, can lead to what psychologists describe as incongruent images that are easily discarded for their cognitive dissonance with one's pre-existing cognitive or mental map of "reality."

Beyond theory and misperceptions, David Robinson, author of *Muslim Societies in African History*, describes how Europeans and North Americans have had difficulty understanding Islam and Muslims and even greater difficulty understanding Muslims, socially and individually. Their greatest difficulty in Robinson's view has been their struggle to understand Islam and Muslims in Africa and African history.[59] While colonial governments accepted the Muslim identities of those over whom they ruled, Robinson, who spent thirty years researching and writing on Islam in West Africa at Yale reminds us that the memory of condescension experienced by colonial subjects outlasted colonial rule to fuel the anger strikingly expressed against the West on September 11, 2001.[60]

Attacks in 2015–2016 on Paris, Brussels, Nice, and Normandy, and on the United Kingdom and Barcelona in 2017 may be reminders of Robinson's observation of anti-colonial outrage as nearly all the terrorists linked to these attacks were young men from immigrant Muslim families from formerly colonized North and West Africa. It seems difficult to ignore how recent incidents of terrorist violence in London, Paris, and Berlin against western occupations in Iraq and Syria inspired by the ideology of prison Islamism and minority subculture explored by Hamm (2013) share a political kinship with the anti-colonial struggles of their great grandparents in places like Algeria, Guinea, and Ghana with ideological roots linking them to Fanon, Sekou Toure, and Nkrumah. Yet, from Algeria's FLN to South Africa's ANC anti-colonial revolutionary parties have had greater success at struggling than they have at governing.

With 1.8 billion adherents compared to 2.3 billion Christian, Islam is the world's second largest and fastest growing religion. The Pew Memorial Trust forecasts that Islam will pass Christianity to become the world's largest religion by the year 2050. African Muslims account for nearly 25 percent of the world's Muslims. About half of all Africans identify themselves as Muslim.[61] Africa's current population of just over 1 billion people is projected to double to 2.5 billion by 2050. The heavily Islamic states of Nigeria and Kenya are among Africa's largest and fastest growing states, respectively. Nigeria's rapidly growing population of 190 million people exceeds Russia's declining population of 140 million and is expected to reach 400 million to surpass the population of the United States by the year 2050 according to UN projections.[62] Nigeria's commercial hub in Lagos includes over 21 million people. Four fifths of the world's Muslims live outside the Arab Middle East. Of the five most populous Muslim states, Indonesia, India, Pakistan, Iran, and Nigeria, none are of these countries are located in the Arab Middle East. In fact, Nigeria has more people than Egypt, the largest Sunni Arab state and Iran the largest Shia Muslim state, combined! Nearly half of Nigeria's population is Muslim. Muslims in Africa occupy an area nearly twice the size of the United States, which is enveloped by porous borders providing free access to the adjoining Sahara, the world's largest desert and major hub for international arms, drugs, and other trafficking.[63] Africa also contains the world's fastest growing youth population. Quite sadly, African and Arab-world youth unemployment is the major contributor to a refugee crisis, wreaking havoc on the EU political landscape.

MYTHS AND STEREOTYPES

Before Americans can truly move beyond their stereotypes of Africa and Africans as President Obama first called for in 2013, they must first be reminded of what these stereotypes and myths actually are. This task is both essential and unavoidable. Drawing on primary source historical material, this study identifies stereotypes and myths that include (1) the myth of the docile and acquiescent African "slave," (2) the myth of "black inferiority," (3) the myth of the Negro past, (4) the myth of the "dark continent," and (5) the myth of the White Man's Burden. Primary source material that negatively depicts black Africans include Ibn Khaldun's *al-Muqaddimah* written in ca. 1377, Kipling's classic poem "The White Man's Burden," first published in 1899, and Kipling's classic ode to the "Fuzzy-Wuzzy" (Muslims) of Africa's Eastern Sudan. Each falsely portrays blacks as infantile, savage, and not fully human. A recent obituary for the late scholar Jack Sheheen, for example, describes how he fought Arab stereotypes like those found in the original lyrics of a song in the Disney film *Aladin* (1992) depicted as follows:

> Oh, I come from a land, from a faraway place, where the caravan camels roam, where they cut off your ear if they don't like your face, its barbaric, but hey, its home.

Despite Barack Hussein Obama's avowed Christian belief and demonstrated American citizenship, he too was unable to escape one or more of these stereotypes. The myth of the White Man's Burden by novelist and poet Rudyard Kipling became a euphemism for imperialism in 1899. The following is a brief excerpt of this poem.

> Take up the White Man's Burden send forth the best ye breed—Go send your sons to exile To serve your captives' need To wait in heavy harness your new— caught sullen peoples, half devil and half child.[64]

The myth of the Negro past which holds that Africans had no past worth examining inspired anthropologist Melville Herskovits to devote his entire career to disproving it. Along the way, he founded the first and oldest African studies program in the United States and authored the classic, though mistitled book, *The Myth of the Negro Past* (1941). Another prominent myth, the myth of the "dark continent" similarly holds that Africa has no significant history or culture.

From this perspective, Africa is a land of isolated and legendary backwardness. The "dark continent" myth joins similar myths of black inferiority that attribute nothing of merit to Africans. Students of anthropology are familiar with this bias especially given the systematic practice of attributing achievements like the building of the great pyramids to people regarded as not fully African.[65] Examples of this myth are apparent from the treatment of Barack Obama by Republicans popularly known as "birthers" who believed Mr. Obama was not a US citizen but rather was a Muslim from Kenya, an

Arab and therefore not an American. Donald Trump was a leading figure in the birther movement. Yet, Ibn Khaldun's *An Introduction to History (The Muqaddimah)* ca. 1377 translated from Arabic by Franz Rosenthal and J. J. Dawood reveals how nineteenth- and twentieth-centuries European writers were not the only sources of stereotyped images of Africans. *Al-Muquaddimah*, published in the fourteenth-century Arab world is a celebrated classical work written by a pioneering social scientist. Yet, it contains the following images of blacks:

> Negroes are in general characterized by levity, excitability and great emotionalism. They are found eager to dance whenever they hear a melody. They are everywhere described as stupid. . . . Therefore, the Negro nations are, as a rule, submissive to slavery, because (Negroes) have little that is (essentially) human and possess attributes that are quite similar to those of dumb animals, as we have stated.[66]

Nevertheless, underscoring the role that Europe played in the manufacturing of bigoted stereotypes, one study concludes that "if the prejudice of 'us versus them' ever had a homeland, it was Ottoman-threatened central Europe."[67] Anti-black and anti-Muslim bigotry displays deep roots in the western world. "The stereotype of the Turk as the bloodthirsty and barbarian Muslim conqueror in central Europe and elsewhere morphed into the less daunting image of the Turk as a trivial, ignorant and hapless fool." Western laughs at the expense of Islam are not the least bit out of step with news that "Europeans . . . had always enjoyed bits of private mischief at the expense of Islam."[68] While contemporary western leaders too, extensive to name, have made disparaging remarks about Islam and Muslim, "the Koran did not have Voltaire's respect either." Immersed in a climate of bigotry the Qur'an was regarded as an empty babble for a French *philosophe*,[69] and as a result of this climate "ignorance and fear led most Europeans to think of Muslims and their faith in terms of negative and distorted stereotypes."[70] The WOT has created its own climate of bigotry like the racist remarked hurled by a prominent Hollywood star at a former advisor to President Obama. Yet, it is difficult to avoid viewing contemporary racism as a vestige of an earlier European bigotry that once depicted Muslims as idolaters who rejected the Trinity, accepted polygamy, homosexuality, and pedophilia and who espoused notions of paradise (or if you like, heaven) widely viewed as inexcusably erotic.[71]

However, like other "inferior" people, "Turks and Muslims were 'bad' but not all the time," as the so-called "the Terrible Turk retained his presence in all forms of entertainment in the Habsburg empire,"[72] Yet, Muslim Turks and other dark-skinned people remained the butt of European jokes and revile as seen in the following excerpt:

> The Turk as a comic ignoramus was not the only unflattering and unrealistic stereotype drawn from his culture to amuse the much-relaxed Viennese theatregoer in the eighteenth century. The term "Moor" (Germ. *Mohr*), generally associated with black skin tones, evil and sexual excess was conceptually interchangeable with Turk and Muslim in early modern Europe.[73]

Yet, beyond Habsburg Europe's theatergoers, preachers "pulled no punches" as far as language was concerned, especially when major Ottoman offenses loomed. For instance, in Vienna midway through the fifteenth century, "a Franciscan Minorite, Johannes Capistrano, called Muslims 'dogs,' with Muhammad himself the 'giant dog' among them." Indeed, one account describes how even Pope Calixus III advised homilists to alert congregations to the dangers of the man he called "Muhammad the Son of the Devil."[74]

Modern African stereotypes join these earlier stereotypes to promote ubiquitous images of buffoon-like African Muslim leaders like Uganda's Idi Amin. Amin's image joins non-Muslim African leaders like Zaire's Mobutu Sese Seko and Zimbabwe's Robert Mugabe depicted as savage and stupid. Meanwhile, dignified African Muslim leaders like Nigeria's Sir Abu Bakar Tafawa Balewa and non-Muslim leaders like Tanzania's Julius Nyerere to say nothing of South Africa's Nelson Mandela are all but ignored. One US military intelligence official described Ugandan dictator Idi Amin (d. 2014) as "a six-foot-five inch brute of a man" and "an embarrassment to Africa."[75] Yet, in spite of these images and a reputation for being hated by most of his own people, Amin could not escape the adoring gaze of Hollywood. These images join Africa's gun-toting child soldiers widely posted online depicting Africans as uncivilized and savage.

ORIGINS AND CHARACTERISTICS OF ISLAMISM

Despite the fact that it is often depicted as a war between Islam and the West, more Muslims are killed by militants than any other group. This truism illustrates the point that the Islamist challenge among other things is a battle for the hearts and minds of the Muslim world. Most militant Islamists believe the WOT is a war on Islam itself. During the last quarter of the twentieth century, Africa and the Islamic world experienced a postmodern revival (*tajdid*) aimed at confronting the question: why is the Muslim community (*ummah*), described in the Qur'an as being exalted among the nations of the world, left so far behind? If Islam is God's gift to humanity and God's perfected religion, then why are Muslims from Syria to Afghanistan in such dire straits? Why do Muslims continue to suffer as seen in the 2010/2011 Arab Spring movement which began in Tunisia yet culminated in a refugee crisis forcing thousands of Muslims and others desperately to flee to the West? Why are Muslims a far cry from the status they once enjoyed during Islam's golden age when Europe once languished in what historian label the dark ages? And why are Muslims so often among what the Qur'an describes as the downtrodden (*al-mustad'fin*) or what Fanon once famously labelled *The Wretched of the Earth*?

The proponents of Islamic revival (*tajdid*) seeking answers to these questions believe that an Islamic revival (*tajdid*) occurs at least once every century.[76] The phenomenon of Islamism complements *tajdid* and shares many of its same attributes including resurgence, renewal, revival, purification, and rejuvenation. Although differences exist over the precise start date for its most recent appearance, a consensus holds that the current wave of Islamism, that is, the application of Islamic values, principles, and law (*shari'ah*) to the challenges of modern life, began sometime during the 1970s. Most experts agree that the movement was in full swing by the time of the 1979 Iranian revolution, which deposed the despotic US-installed Shah of Iran. While all Muslims did not experience the Shah's oppression, the experience struck a chord with many Muslims around the world. For example, despite the dominance of Sunni Islam in northern Nigeria a Shia-oriented sect led by Yakubu Yahya in Katsina, Nigeria, triggered clashes with Nigerian authorities in March/April 1991 opposed to the politics of stagnation.[77]

A 1997 study of the origins and characteristics of Islamist movements depicted them correctly as remaining remarkably unchanged over time, notwithstanding their evolving tactics.[78] Except for the Islamist-led government in Khartoum, Sudan, which came to power in a 1989 coup under the influence Hassan al-Turabi, the Seleka of the CAR with the rise of Michael Mjotodia, and Islamists in east and southern Africa, respectively, most Islamists parties have been outlawed throughout Africa. This quite clearly results from Islamism's role as a force of opposition, resistance, and a challenge to the political status quo.[79] For example, the Sunni Islamist and scholar Abubakar Gumi of northern Nigeria led the Yan Izala reform movement in 1978 soundly criticized Sufi Muslims for their subjectivism and forcefully condemning them as fraudulent by noting that Sufis did not exist during the time of the Prophet. Gumi vehemently condemned Sufis for their use of charms, amulets, and drums.[80]

Sufi collaboration with secular and colonial authorities in the post-colonial period made them easy targets for Islamists.[81] Moreover, the anti-Sufi doctrine of Wahhabism or more accurately Salafism, popular among Islamist militants, is a major source of Sufi-Sunni tensions. Salafist influence in West Africa most likely derive from the influence of Africans returning from the pilgrimage (*hajj*) to Mecca, contacts with Saudi Arabians and access to Salafist literature, tapes, videos, practitioners, and/or ideas. The internet has accelerated and expanded this trend at a phenomenal rate. Salafist influence has been more predominant in West than in East and southern Africa—though its presence as seen in the al-Qaeda linked bombing of the US embassies in Kenya and Tanzania killing 224 in August 1998 are major exceptions to this rule. Islamist organizations tend to be based in urban areas and attract followers from younger rather than older Muslims. The rise of Islamism is often associated with new mosque construction and the establishment of Muslim educational, health care, recreational, and religious centers (*madrasas*) funded by Saudis.[82] When access to politics is curtailed, the mosque has become an alternative political rallying point.[83] Islamism therefore can also be seen as a movement of discontent whose adherents most often reject secularism and unchecked westernization.[84]

While most Americans link Osama bin Laden to the 9/11 attacks on the World Trade Center from his base in Afghanistan, Osama bin Laden's very first "base" of operations was actually in the African country of Sudan where he plotted the very first World Trade Center bombing that killed 6 and injured over 1,000 in 1993. Before his death in 2016, Sudan's Hassan al-Turabi (1932–2016) arguably Africa's leading Islamist militant, "power behind the throne," and "de facto leader" of Sudan during the 1990s, facilitated training camps in Sudan for Islamist militants from Chad, Ethiopia, Somalia, Bosnia, and Afghanistan.[85] Once described as "Africa's most active contemporary Islamic ideologue," Turabi is quoted as saying in 1997 that "America incarnates the devil for all Muslims in the world."[86] He came to power in a military coup in 1989 and served from 1990 ot 1996 as host, "friend," and "mentor" to Osama bin Laden. According to one source, Osama bin Laden was married to Hassan al-Turabi's niece.[87] As a measure of his prominence, Osama bin Laden is described as looking up to his host, Dr. al-Turabi," during his 1990–1996 stay in Sudan before moving on to Afghanistan.[88] He "had expansive plans for a new jihad which would establish a true Islamic government across Muslim countries in Africa and further afield."[89] According to the BBC, the war he led in southern Sudan (now South Sudan) caused the deaths of 2 million people and the displacement of 4 million more. The UN imposed sanctions on Sudan for allegedly attempting to assassinate Egypt's Hosni Mubarak in 1995. Turabi has been recognized "for his scholarly brilliance, with degrees from the University of Khartoum, the University of London and a PhD from the Sorbonne in Paris. He was fluent in Arabic, English, French and German."[90] These facts fail to describe a leader or African state of marginal significance for Africa and Africans for they lie at the heart of the WOT. Sudan became one of six states included in President Trump's Muslim ban of 2016/2017. But decades before this, Turabi was placed under house arrest in Sudan after falling out with his sponsor President Omar al-Bashir in 1999 and may have suffered a fate similar to that of the turn-of-the-century pioneer of the pan-Islamism, Jamal a-din al-Afghani, who died mysteriously while in the custody of the Ottoman Sultan in Turkey.

Turabi was already in poor health after suffering a savage beating on May 26, 1992, in an Ottawa, Canada, airport administered by a 300-pound Sufi opponent and martial arts expert, Hashim Bedreddin Mohammed. Turabi was knocked unconscious and left for dead following the beating and remained in a comma and was hospitalized for four weeks. After the assault he was forced to walk with a cane. Ironically, Turabi was the son of a religious judge and Sufi sheikh.[91] As an early mentor to Osama bin Laden, Turabi's influence rests firmly among the leading voices of contemporary Islamic revival and postmodern Islamism, which includes Sayyid Abu'l-A'la Mawdudi (1903–1979), Hasan al-Bana (1906–1949), Sayyid Qutb (1906–1966), Ayyatollah Khomeini (1902–1989), and Ali Shariati (1933–1977).[92] The arrest of over 60,000 opponents of President Recep Tayyip Erdogen of Turkey following a failed military coup in 2016 bears some resemblance to the treatment of Islamists like Jamal a-din al-Afghani and Hassan al-Turabi. Yet secularists are not the only actors fearful of Islamists. President Trump for example has threatened Islamists opponents, real or imagined, with reprisals ranging from arrest to waterboarding. His original Muslim travel ban affected some six Muslim states. While President Trump may have impressed the rich and powerful in Riyadh following his 2017 visit, most agree that little has been done to endear the "Arab Street."

Hunwick's discussion of Sub Saharan Africa in the wider Islamic world asserts

> The colonial period . . . was a time during which West Africa was perhaps more cut off from the rest of the Muslim world than ever before. Colonial authorities, British and French, were ever watchful for signs of what they perceived as the dangerous phenomenon of pan-Islamism and were able to keep an eye on the movements of Muslim leaders from both ends of the lines of communication—sub-Saharan African and Mediterranean Africa including Egypt. Colonial authorities tried either to co-opt or control Muslim leadership. . . . Saudi Arabia was a poor country hemmed in for the most part . . . and in no position to have a very profound impact on African Muslims except through the pilgrimage.[93]

But significantly more avenues for the promotion of pan-Islamism and Islamist agendas existed during colonialism than Hunwick and others like him have been able to discern. Even under the most compelling of circumstances including the enslavement of Muslims in the Americas, the persecution of Muslims during the Spanish Inquisition and the arrest, detention, and imprisonment of Muslims in contemporary United States and Europe,

Muslims have always found ways to survive. Malcolm X and Sayyid Qutb, the "godfather of militant Islamism," though imprisoned and ultimately killed, may illustrate this point, nonetheless.

Existing perspectives understandably exaggerate the success of various western projects, including slavery, colonialism and the modern African state as history is always written by the victors. Western projects appear legendary in their near endless goal of "Westernizing" or "civilizing" Africans. But the European practice of promoting indirect rule as seen in Nigeria, the CAR and remnants of the old Kanem-Bornu Empire enabled West and Central African Muslims to engage with other Muslims, long before the arrival of full political independence in 1960.[94] The West African states of Ghana, Guinea, Liberia, and Sierra Leone independent before 1960 contained Muslim groups who most certainly interacted with other Muslims.

The fact that emerging leaders in West Africa were closely watched by Europeans for signs of pan-Islamism and targeted for cooptation, says nothing about how successful these officials were at actually containing Islam! The blossoming of Islamist revival (*tajdid*) movements worldwide by the 1970s in former colonial regions raises serious doubts as to the complete effectiveness of European projects aimed at controlling the emergence of Islamism before 1960. It seems possible to argue that efforts to control Muslim societies whether by former colonial powers or by the post-colonial modern African state were simply no match for African societal forces not the least of which included Islamism. Rothschild and others have long argued this point persuasively in their weak state, strong society paradigm of the post-independence modern African state.[95]

Yet, also ignored by Hunwick are the numerous opportunities enjoyed by African elites in the 1950s to meet students in the United States and Europe long before becoming West African officials and heads of state. For instance, Kwame Nkrumah (not a Muslim) who became president of Ghana in 1957 married Fathia Rizak (d. 2007), an Arab Christian from Egypt and is known to have met with other prominent African and African American intellectuals including George Padmore while studying at the historically black Lincoln University in Pennsylvania. Nkrumah introduced the anti-colonial doctrine of Pan Africanism that helped propel his native Ghana to political independence, lifting the aspirations of Africans everywhere, including many who were no doubt African Muslims.

While malleable and compliant elites of northern Nigeria may have conformed to Hunwick's observation, other less malleable Islamists as possible forerunners to Boko Haram militants did not. Would greater colonial surveillance or cooptation have stopped them from emerging? Probably not: the Egyptian Islamist Sayyid Qutb may have met as early as the 1950s with black Muslim leader, Malcolm X, of the quasi-Islamic Nation of Islam movement in the United States during Qutb's studies in the United States. The two may have met in 1951 around the time of Malcolm's release from prison and Qutb's return to Egypt. Malcolm may have returned the favor with visits to Egypt in 1964 and 1965 including meetings with Qutb's Muslim Brotherhood.[96]

At least three generations (if not more) of Hausa and Fulani Muslims primarily from Nigeria and across West African survive to this day in the Saudi Arabian cities of Jedda, Medina, and Mecca.[97] For instance, Mustafa Ahmed al-Hawsawi, described by Corbin as "Bin Laden's money man, who masterminded the funding of the September attacks" is a black Saudi who based on his last (i.e., tribal) name is a member of the Hawsawi tribe which migrated to Saudi Arabia from Nigeria well over a century ago.[98] Former African pilgrims and their progeny who chose to remain in Saudi Arabia form the core of these contemporary Afro-Saudi communities.[99] It seems fair to assume that some of these Africans must have remained in touch with relatives back home in Africa paving the way for subsequent African pilgrims journeying to Mecca, allowing them to benefit from valuable contacts in the Saudi kingdom.

As an African American professor of Political Science and international relations at a medium size public university since 1990, a small but regular contingent of mostly male college students primarily from Saudi Arabia conscious of their Islamic and sometimes African Islamic identity ask me: When did you become Muslim? Have you made your pilgrimage (*hajj*) and are your wife and family Muslim? When I answer (in Arabic) that I am a Muslim from Chicago, some eventually say, yes, but where are you *really* from? Non-Muslim students rarely ask me these questions. One of the insights I have gained from these encounters is that the idea of a color-blind society whether in the Middle East or the United States is a myth and that most of my students from the Middle East know more about Africa than blacks born in the United States.

Others from Africa following the same well-travelled routes as Mustafa Ahmed al-Hawsawi's family may have followed found their way to the ranks of Saudi Arabia's Islamist militants. These same well-travelled routes may explain the visible presence of Africans in the ranks of al-Qaeda and ISIS, as Saudi Arabia remains the leading source of "foreign fighters" in the ranks of al-Qaeda and ISIS. These communities and the social networks they produced refute the argument advanced by Hunwick that West Africa was "cut off" from the rest of the Muslim world from roughly 1860 to 1960 except for those who performed the pilgrimage or participated in foreign language study. This argument ignores the full impact of the annual pilgrimage (*hajj*) on the subsequent emergence of *tajdid* and Islamism in Africa. Far from being a mere by-product of the pilgrimage (*hajj*) and language study, Islamic revival (*tajdid*), Islamism, and Africans can be traced to years of Islamic acculturation, education, and socioeconomic exchanges, initiated perhaps by the pilgrimage to Mecca (*hajj*) and Arabic language study especially in Medina, but by no means limited to them.

African sheikhs with links to Saudi Arabia serve as prayer and mosque leaders (*imams*) throughout Saudi Arabia and the Gulf and are sometimes highly sought-after for their piety (*al-taqwa*) and religious skills.[100] For instance, a black Saudi sheikh, Imam Adil Kalbani, led prayers at the Grand mosque in Mecca in 2008 the same year that President Barak Obama was elected US president leading some to dub him the "Saudi Obama." While travelling in 2013 to the UAE, I prayed behind a highly respected sheikh in Sharjah who came to the UAE from Ethiopia. I also met an African American Muslim woman from Michigan who studied Arabic in the United States and taught English in the UAE. Those who are unaware of this long history and the rich social ties it has forged erroneously view Africa as a "marginal," "backwater," "cut off" from the Islamic world.

At the time of his 1997 book chapter Hunwick may have been unaware of these and other avenues for the dissemination of Islamist ideas among West Africans. Nevertheless, the suggestion that the Muslims of colonial West Africa were "cut off " from the rest of the Muslim world more than ever during 1860–1960 strains credulity. Such a view overlooks how the system of British indirect rule fostered a legacy of tribal favoritism, corruption, and undeterred Islamism that survives to this day in Nigeria. Key members of the British administration, including Sir Frederick Lugard, for whom many regarded as the most enlightened colonial civil servant of his age, "tended to have something of an exaggerated regard for native aristocracies of the Islamic north of Nigeria." A London Times editorial written in 1904 by Flora Shaw, who also happened to be the wife of Lord Lugard, asserted: "The Fulani were a striking people, dark in complexion, but of the distinguished features, small hands, and fine, rather aristocratic carriage of Arabs on the Mediterranean coast."[101] "*Indirect Rule*, which was a concept conceived and implement [*sic*] by Lord Frederick Lugard himself, implied the devolution of all the day-to-day administrative responsibilities of government to the pre-existing traditional authority, with imperial superintendentship visible only at the center, and existing at all times within an advisory capacity."[102]

Reflective of European stereotypes of Africans, and his own bias toward the Muslims of the northern Nigeria, Lugard crudely asserted that "The great Ibo [Igbo] race to the East of the Niger, numbering some 3 millions [*sic*] and their cognate tribes had not developed beyond the state of primitive savagery."[103] Lugard's anti-Igbo bigotry and Hunwick's suggestion that

Africa Muslims might possibly be controlled to the point of determining their inner-most thoughts and beliefs in addition to monitoring literature written by the eighteenth-century sheikh Abd al-Wahhab (in Arabic no less!) seems astonishingly naïve. The religious movement known as Wahhabism (or *Wahhabiya*) was founded on the teachings of Muhammad Ibn 'Abd al-Wahhab (1703–1791) whose writings covered the subjects of religion (*din*), exegesis, Islamic jurisprudence (*fiq*), and the life of the Prophet Muhammad. A set of core issues distinguish Wahhabism from other Islamic movements including the unity of God (*Allah*) (*tawhid*), intercession (*tawassul*), the visitation of graves and erection of tombs (*ziyarat al-qubur*), change of unbelief (*takfir*), innovation (*bid'a*), and original juristic opinions, and imitation of tradition (*itihad* and *taqlid*).

Tawhid, the unity of God (*Allah*), represents the central theme of Wahhabism which is manifested in three distinct ways. First, *Tawhid* holds that God (*Allah*) alone is the creator, provider, and disposer of the universe. Second, the unity of names and attributes (*tawhid al-asma' wa-alsifat*) elaborates the attributes of God (*Allah*) including the Beneficent (al-*Rahman*), the Merciful (al-*Rahim*), the Knowing (*al-Alim*), and so on. Third, tawhid, stipulates that worship must be devoted to God (*Allah*) and God (*Allah*) alone (*tawhid al-Ilahiyah*). Wahhabis strongly disagree with their opponents regarding the question of intercession (*tawassul*) or seeking protection from anything or anyone other than God (*Allah*) which is considered tantamount to polytheism. Wahhabis became the dominant religio-political force of the Arabian Peninsula around 1746 when Al Sa'ud combined their political force with Wahhabi religious teachings.[104]

Retracing the evolution of Africa's most violent terrorist group whose ideological roots spring from Wahhabism, William notes:

> Today's Boko Haram emerged from a secret created around Mohammed Yusuf, a charismatic preacher inspired by Salafi/Wahhabi religion ideals and who initially followed the Izala movement in Nigeria. By 2003, however, Yusuf was prevented from preaching in Izala mosques.[105]

Advocates of what Mamdani calls Culture Talk who turn religion into a political category attribute the theological roots of Islamist terrorism to Wahhabism.[106] Culture when interpreted in this way describes certain people by ascribing to them a set of unchanging attributes functioning as a latter-day counterpart of race talk.[107] It also "becomes a code word for describing certain people by ascribing to them a set of unchanging attributes. Such is the case, in most "Culture Talk" descriptions of Wahhabism/salafism.[108] Yet, the challenge of violence and militant Islamists among Africans would be incomplete without mentioning concerns raised by the predicament of the post-independence African state, which Mamdani confronts by asking:

> Could it be that the African problem was not colonial but an incomplete penetration of traditional society by a weak colonial state or deference to it by prudent but shortsighted colonizers? Could it be that Europe's mission to Africa was left half finished?[109]

Other observations raise further doubts as to the validity of Hunwick's assertions.

> There is little disagreement that the states constructed by African elites are weak, poorly focused, and their writ rarely runs through the "political kingdom." The Central African Republic is doubtless an extreme case in which "the state stops at PK 12" (i.e., twelve kilometers from the capital).[110]

Colonial Nigeria maintained the longstanding practice of recruiting Hausa Muslims from the North to serve as British army auxiliaries who formed the majority of Nigeria's seemingly loyal officer corps during the colonial period. As perhaps the primary African beneficiary of indirect British colonial rule in Nigeria, Hausa prime minister Sir Abubakar Tafawa Balewa, whose British title of "sir" alone suggests he enjoyed a status higher than that of most other Africans, further undermines the religiously controlled image of the West African Muslims offered by Hunwick.[111] Yet, if Nigeria's Muslims were as politically controlled as Hunwick suggest, it was certainly not apparent to their rivals among Nigeria's predominantly Catholic Igbo. An Igbo-led military coup seeking revenge for perceived injustices committed by northerners killed many northern officers and high government officials including Prime Minister Sir Abubakar Tafawa Balewa, a Muslim, "who died under murky circumstances" in 1966.[112]

Abubakar Gumi (d. September 11, 1992) and the Yan Izala (Sunni) reform movement offer an excellent example of an Islamist movement in Africa. The movement shocked the Muslim establishment of northern Nigeria sparking heated and violent confrontations between Yan Izala supporters and the vast and well-established Qadiriyya and Tijaniyya Sufi Muslim brotherhoods and others.[113] Gumi, a former Grand Qadi (paramount Islamic judge) and author of the book *al-Aqida es-Sahiha* in 1972 single-handedly inspired Nigeria's Sufi Muslims to unite in response to Yan Izala.[114] The message of the movement was simple. All evil innovations (*bid'a*) such as the Sufi Muslim practice of intercession (*tawwasul*) at the tombs of the dead, pilgrimages to the tombs of saints, and the singing of hymns of praise to the Prophet

Muhammad were forbidden (*haram*).[115] Gumi declared in an interview with Loimeier in 1987 that "his own efforts at *tajdid* would have been useless had it not been for the achievements of the legendary Sheiykh Usman dan Fodio" (d. 1817).[116] While Islamic revival (*tajdid*) movements such as Yan Izala since 1978 sought to "purify" Sunni Muslim practice in Nigeria, they also aggravated intra-Muslim Shia-Sunni-Sufi conflicts and longer-term Muslim-non-Muslim tensions culminating in the Biafran civil war of 1966–1970.[117]

For example, although the Igbo commander Major-General Johnson Aguiyi-Ironsi remained loyal to the government causing the Igbo-led military coup of 1966 to fail, subsequent events fell short of establishing peace and stability within Nigeria.[118] With the support of the Cabinet, Ironsi assumed power though he inflamed tribal animosities after driving around Lagos, the then capital of Nigeria, in the presidential Rolls Royce, while his wife elected to be addressed as "Lady Ironsi."[119] The final straw came when General Ironsi refused to punish the so-called January (Igbo) boys responsible for carrying out what up to then had been Nigeria's bloodiest coup, infuriating Muslim northerners who scoffed at the Igbo-dominated senior officer corps comprised primarily of Igbo officers.[120] Seventy percent of all lower-level enlisted men were northerners.[121] Months later northerners struck back killing Ironsi and hundreds of other federal officers and non-officers most of whom were Igbo. "Most of the victims were savagely beaten and tortured before being shot."[122] One Igbo officer was tied to an iron cross and whipped nearly to death before being cut down and left to die.[123] Three days later, a triumphant insurgent named Lieutenant Colonel Yakubu "Jack" Gowan, an Anglican, professional soldier and Sand Hurst graduate, stepped forth to head the new federal military government.[124]

Previously targeted for death in a 1964 military coup, Gowan escaped his assassins' arrival at his hotel by simply not being there.[125] According to one source, he was away from his hotel while walking his Igbo companion home;[126] despite his father's objection to his marrying her, his love and sheer "luck" according to one source may have saved his life.[127] Gowan was overthrown in a military coup while attending an Organization of African Unity (OAU) summit in Kampala. He later went into exile in Britain where he earned a PhD in Political Science. He was later implicated in a coup resulting in the death of Murtala Muhammed for which he was eventually exonerated. He returned to Nigeria and has remained a military professional.

AFRICANS AND US FOREIGN POLICY MAKERS

Recounting his long career in military intelligence Thom describes how "one of the hidden advantages of working on Africa was that very few people knew anything about it," but it was also "tough on the Africa analysts' morale and made retention of bright up and coming analysts difficult," because of "the ignorance of senior managers who knew little about the forty eight Sub Saharan African countries."[128] As a branch chief in the 1980s, he describes dispatching a subordinate with a PhD to provide a briefing to the upper brass. "When he [the subordinate] arrived at the VIP's office in the Pentagon, the first question he had to answer was "where the hell is Liberia?"[129] Thom candidly admits that "peeling back ignorance about Africa [in US military Defense Intelligence agencies] is still a mighty and continuous chore."[130] Thom's assessment of Afro-pessimists is further revealing.

> The list of Afro-pessimists includes the military, defense and intelligence communities, political conservatives, investors, the ex-colonial powers, and the so called "K Street racists"—the Washington insiders in and out of government who employ impeccable logic to dismiss Africa as a strategic nonentity but whose position really reflects racial attitudes.[131]

While Thom acknowledged that Afro-pessimism is no crime, the lingering biases and stereotypes that he witnessed among Washington, DC, based officials left the distinct impression that Africa had never been important and that its status was unlikely to change any time soon.

Given the continued US dependence on overseas petroleum, Afro-pessimists ignore Africa at their own peril.[132] The adage, a pessimist sees difficulty in every opportunity, while an optimist sees opportunity in every difficulty, may offer important insights of special value to those seeking to understand African Muslims. Yet, corruption and ineffective government remain major challenges facing African states that undermine development and play into the hands of criminal elites whether in the bush or in the parliament.[133] For example, the United States once labelled guerrilla fighters "communist" for simply being armed with communist-origin weapons and receiving training from communist countries.[134] This logic ignored the fact that African insurgents fighting to overthrow oppressive minority governments took arms from wherever and whomever they could. Did these African insurgents become Marxist by necessity?[135] Might a similar logic explain contemporary Islamist labelled "terrorists" in the WOT? A recent study of violence in northeastern Nigeria describes how "the persistent brutality displayed by Nigerian security forces towards ordinary civilians living in areas where Boko Haram was active turned many ordinary Muslims against the government. This did not always translate into direct support for Boko Haram but did amount to an unwillingness to assist the government."[136] Could it be that police brutality as seen in the case of Nigeria drive some otherwise ordinary citizens into the arms of the terrorists?

AFRICA IN THE WOT

What happened in Somalia between 1988 and 1992 was unprecedented as UNOSOM (United Nations Operation in Somalia) troops seized the airport and seaport in Somalia.[137] But US and UN operations in Somalia went sadly aerie. In the words of one US official, Somalis were "good fighters" who were "lightly armed but cleaver and fearless."[138] The Somali warlord, General Mohammed Farrah Aidid lured a Pakistani detachment of UN troops into an ambush that killed twenty-four soldiers to culminate in the infamous Black Hawk Down debacle which produced further casualties including the killing of an American soldier whose corpse was dragged through the streets of Mogadishu by anti-American Somali demonstrators.[139] US Special Forces were dispatched to provide support but to no avail. The US Black Hawk helicopter downed in 1993 left an indelible wound on US military psyche.[140] Never before had the United States suffered such a humiliating setback. The debacle may have led the United States to balk in the face of the 1994 Rwandan genocide. But reports of US Special Forces in Somalia and elsewhere in Africa have reversed this hesitancy.

Confrontations with African Muslims in Sudan over an alleged chemical weapons factory destroyed by a direct US missile strike (the first of its kind on an African country) occurred during early 1998. The bombing of the US embassies in Kenya and Tanzania killed 224 people in August 1998 and the Darfur "genocide" crisis of 2006/2007 have further challenged US foreign policy makers.[141] These episodes undermine the assertion that Africa is a "backwater" in world affairs. The emergence of AQIM, al-Shabab, and Boko Haram lend support to this view. President George W. Bush's decision in 2007 to create an Africa Command on African soil for the first time was hailed by some as a remarkable achievement. Yet, the historical record displays the need for greater US attention to Africa as displayed in the following excerpt:

> Washington's obsession with the Cold War placed America on the wrong side of Africa's history. We just could not see the forest for the trees. We used the flimsiest "evidence" to condemn liberation movements as "communist . . . Most of the liberation movements were communist at least on paper, but Africa analysts for the most part knew that Marxism was hardly even skin-deep.[142]

The above words are not those of a communist or Islamist militant. They are the words of a retired US Intelligence official who acknowledges that "policymakers and intelligence professionals have recently taken Africa more seriously."[143] According to various sources, 25 percent of US petroleum imports will come from the African region by 2025.[144]

Former UN Secretary General Kofi Annan in a BBC Television News interview on May 10, 2014, publicly criticized the Nigerian government on its slow reaction to the Chibok schoolgirl kidnappings and its failure to reach out for help. The Nigerian state may have spurned offers of help from the United States because it believed it would allow the United States to pry into its private internal affairs. But reactions from the international community were equally slow. After waiting three weeks for the state to rescue the kidnapped girls, parents and relatives formed #BringBackOurGirls as a protest movement that went viral on social media to attract the support of then-First Lady, Michelle Obama. The Nigerian state eventually requested help from Britain and the United States after the loss of many lives. Meanwhile, China and France have provided satellite technology assistance.

Boko Haram reportedly killed 1,500 people in the first four months of 2014 alone, and thousands more before that according to Amnesty International. Abubakar Shekau, the group's leader mocked Nigerian President Goodluck Jonathan in April 2014, by declaring "[Goodluck] Jonathan, you are too small for us, let's address your masters, like Obama."[145] With a demeanor bordering on the bazaar Shekau has been compared to the equally bazaar Joseph Kony, former head of the Lord's Resistance Army (LRA) of Uganda. Shekau filmed himself ridiculing a $7 million offer by the US State Department for his arrest. Some allege that the Nigerian state, which was warned four hours in advance of an imminent attack on Chibok, in an area already under a state of emergency for nearly a year, underscores the Nigerian state's incompetence and lack of credibility.

This study adopts a different approach to Islamist violence among Africans that avoids characterizing African Islamist as mere offshoots of al-Qaeda or ISIS. While these groups share a common ideology, training, and goals, they have differed especially before 2014 in their tactics, strategies, and targets, as perhaps best illustrated by Osama bin Laden's refusal to accept Shabab as a member of the al-Qaeda organization. Yet, there is much that remains unknown about Islamist militants among Africans as seen in the little-known ADF group. Operating in the Congo, though based in Uganda ADF has killed more than 500 people in military actions including actions against UN peacekeepers in 2017. Despite its reticence to do so in the past, the United States is no longer deterred from working with the Nigerian state. The Pentagon has sent dozens of Special Operations Advisors to Nigeria to shore up the fight against terrorist violence. Despite losing territory in 2015, Boko Haram remains a challenge. While many still fear US weapons may fall into the wrong hands, based on rumors of Boko Haram spies in the Nigerian state, President Obama approved the sale of American-made Cobra attack helicopters to Nigeria before leaving office in 2016. Media accounts of Secretary of State, Rex Tillerson's ill-fated 2018 visit to Africa may be evidence of a shift in US policy—from an emphasis on African development to an emphasis on African security. President Muhammadu Buhari succeeded in forging closer military ties with the United States following successful meetings with President Donald Trump in 2018. Chapter 1 on terrorism in Africa explores these developments and the possible reasons behind them.

This Introduction has offered an overview of the contents, subject matter, methods, and theories contained in this study as discussed in sections devoted to (1) "The Task Ahead"; (2) "Theoretical Considerations"; (3) "Myths and Stereotypes"; (4) "Origins and Characteristics of Islamism"; (5) "Africa in the Wider World of Islam"; (6) "Islamism and Political Change"; (7) "Africans and US Foreign Policy"; and (8) "Africa in the WOT." The following chapter explores terrorism in Africa, why Africa is one of the world's deadliest terrorist regions, and what must be done to eliminate it.

NOTES

1. President Barack Obama rejected this term as unduly provocative but it survives to this day, nonetheless.

2. CNS.News.com http://cnsnews.com/news/article/obama-touts-al-qaeda-s-demise-32-times-benghazi-attack-0.

3. "Obama Faces a Crossroads," *Wall Street Journal*, November 16, 2015.

4. An important limitation in Jervis's study is his omission of cultural differences and the influence of ego psychology. These omissions by Jervis are explained in the following excerpt: "I have ignored two well-known approaches to the study of perceptions—cultural differences and ego psychology. I have instead found it fruitful to look for patterns of misperceptions that occur within a shared culture and that are not strongly influenced by personality characteristics." See Robert Jervis, *Perceptions and Misperceptions in International Relations* (Princeton, NJ: Princeton University Press, 1976), 8.

5. "Islamic State Spreads its Tentacles," *Wall Street Journal*, December 21, 2015.

6. "Boko Haram Tops ISIS in Ranking Terror Groups," *New York Times*, November 19, 2015.

7. Ibid. Also see "Nigerians Brave Threat of Attacks," *Wall Street Journal*, November 21–22, 2015.

8. For a detailed introduction to South Africa's Zanzibari Muslims see "Muslims in Post-Apartheid South Africa," *About Islam*, November 28, 2017. http://abo utislam.net/muslim-issues/opinion-analysis/muslims-in-post-apartheid-south-africa/.

9. "Nigerian Military Jet on the Hunt for Boko Haram Bombs Refugee Camp by Mistake," *Wall Street Journal*, January 18, 2017. Another report estimates the number of deaths linked to Boko Haram at 31,000 since 2009, with two million displaced. See "Boko Haram Militants Seize More Nigerian Schoolgirls," *Wall Street Journal*, February 22, 2018.

10. William G. Thom, *African Wars: A Defense Intelligence Perspective* (Calgary: University of Calgary, 2010), dust cover.

11. Ibid., 27.

12. Ibid.

13. See John L. Esposito (ed.), *The Oxford Encyclopedia of the Modern Islamic World* (New York: Oxford University Press, 1995), vol. 2, 111–112, vol. 2, 369–373 and vol. 4, 267–270.

14. "Bernard Lewis, Scholar of Islam Who Advised Bush After 9/11, Dies at 101," *New York Times*, May 22, 2018.

15. Mahmood Mamdani, *Good Muslim, Bad Muslim: America the Cold War and the Roots of Terror* (New York: Doubleday, 2005), 17–18.

16. Ibid.

17. Ibid., 19.

18. Ibid.

19. Ibid., 25–26.

20. "Bernard Lewis, Scholar of Islam Who Advised Bush After 9/11, Dies at 101," *New York Times*, May 22, 2018.

21. Ibid.

22. Mamdani, *Good Muslim, Bad Muslim*, 17–18.

23. "Bernard Lewis, Scholar of Islam Who Advised Bush After 9/11, Dies at 101," *New York Times*, May 22, 2018.

24. Ibid.

25. Sultana Afroz, "From Moors to Marronage: The Islamic Heritage of the Maroons in Jamaica," *Journal of Muslim Minority Affairs*, vol. 19, no. 2, 1999; and Sultana Afroz, "The Jihad of 1831–1832: The Misunderstood Baptist Rebellion in Jamaica," *The Journal of Muslim Minority Affairs*, vol. 21, no. 2, 2001.

26. For an interesting study of this phenomenon see Bryan Cheyette, *Diasporas of the Mind: Jewish and Postcolonial Writing and the Nightmare of History* (New Haven, CT: Yale University Press, 2013).

27. From the Global Terrorism Database, compiled by the University of Maryland, 2017. For a more detailed description of this information source, see https://www.start.umd.edu/gtd/.

28. For a detailed description of this information source, see http://www.du.edu/korbel/sie/research/hendrix_scad_database.html.

29. For a detailed description of this information source, see http://datalab.alcafricanos.com/node/73.

30. This figure is confirmed by the HIS Jane's Terrorism and Insurgency Center which describes how "terror attacks by radical groups in Africa have increased by 200 per cent and fatalities by more than 750 percent during 2009–2015." See Ruchita Beri, "Rise of Terrorism in Africa," April 13, 2017. http://www.idsa.in/idsacomment s/rise-of-terrorism-in-africa_rberi_130417.

31. See US State Department, "Diplomacy in Action, National Consortium for the Study of Terrorism and Responses to Terrorism: Annex of Statistical Information," 2015. www.state.gov/documents/organization/257738.pdf. Also see John O. Voll, "Boko Haram: Religion and Violence in the Century," *Religions*, vol. 6, no. 4, 2015, 1182–1202.

32. Nicole Gaouette, "US Official: Terror Kills as Many or More in Africa than Mideast," *CNN*, May 10, 2016. http://www.cnn.com/2016/05/10/politics/africa-terror-isis-boko-haram/index.html.

33. Ibid.

34. Ibid.

35. Daniel E. Agbiboa, "(Sp)oiling Domestic Terrorism? Boko Haram and State Responses," *Peace Review*, vol. 25, no. 3, 2013, 431–438.

36. For an article illustrating the importance of Mali and Timbuktu in the WOT, see David Gutelius, "Islam in Northern Mali and the War on Terror," *Journal of Contemporary African Studies*, vol. 25, no. 1, 2007, 59–76.

37. Thom, *African Wars*, 33.

38. Subcommittee on Counterterrorism and Intelligence of the Committee on Homeland Security House of Representatives *Terrorism in Africa: The Imminent Threat to the United States* (Washington, DC: US Government Publishing Office, 2015), 10.

39. John Davis (ed.), *Terrorism in Africa: The Evolving Front in the War on Terror* (Lanham, MD: Lexington Books, 2010), 240.

40. Boko Haram has renamed itself "Islamic State West African Province." Considerable speculation surrounds this change. For example, "American military officials have said the two groups [Boko Haram and ISIS] have started collaborating more closely. . . . Some analysts have speculated that Mr. Shekau" former leader of Boko Haram, "may be dead." "Others think he has been marginalized, or is perhaps leading a core group of fighters while others have split-off. Abu Musab al-Barrnawi is now the wali or leader and Shekou is not," said Jacob Zenn, an African affairs fellow at the Jamesstown Foundation, a Washington-based research organization. "But Shekau likely would not accept a demotion, so I imagine in order to get him demoted they had to eliminate him." "In June 2016 Gen. Thomas D. Waldhauser, the head of the Pentagon's Africa Command, told the Senate at his confirmation hearing that the Islamic State had disavowed Mr. Shekau because of his tactics which are extreme even by the Islamic State's standards." He told the committee that half of Boko Haram's members had broken off "because they were not happy with the amount of buy-in if you will, from Boko Haram into the ISIL brand." "During the hearing, the general indicated that the Islamic State was trying to reconcile the two groups but that Mr. Shekau had not really fallen into line with what ISIL would like him to do. Some security analysts think Mr. al-Barnawi is the leader of the group of Boko Haram fighters who have split from Mr. Shekau over disputes about attacking mosques." See "Boko Haram May have a New Leader, ISIS Magazine Suggests," *New York Times*, August 4, 2016. Also see "Islamic State Names Boko Haram Leader," *Wall Street Journal*, August 4, 2016.

41. F. C. Onuoha, "The Audacity of the BoKo Haram: Background, Analysis and Emerging Trend," *Security Journal*, vol. 25, no. 2, 2012, 134–151.

42. Thom, *Africa Wars*, dust cover.

43. Ibid.

44. See *The Holy Qur'an Text, Translation and Commentary* by Abdullah Yusuf Ali (Qatar: Publications of The Presidency of Islamic Courts and Affairs, State of Qatar, copyrighted 1946 by Khalil al-Rawaf), The Elephant (*al-fil*), 1792. References

throughout this study to the Qur'an shall refer to the Yusuf Ali translation and commentary. Like Christians, Muslims believe the Qur'an is the word of God (*Allah*). However, instead of the original Qur'an written in Arabic, this study makes references to Yusuf Ali's Translation of the Qur'an written in English which for Muslims remains an important distinction. The former is considered perfect while the latter may vary in accuracy given the level of skilled involved in translating the Arabic Qur'an to English and differences derived from linguistic interpretation. After the death of the Prophet Muhammad in 632 AD, before it became canonized and before every Muslim was required to commit all or a portion of it to memory in Arabic different version of the book (al-kitab) existed. For a discussion of this and how this issue was resolved, see Ibn Warraq (ed.), *Which Koran? Variants, Manuscripts, Linguistics* (Amherst, MA: Prometheus Books, 2011). For a useful aide to navigating the Qur'an see Abdulazziz A. Al-Saleem (ed.), *Index of Qur'anic Topics*, Compiled by Ashfaque Ullah Syed (Washington, DC: IFTA Office, 1998). Finally, for an authoritative discussion of the life and times of Prophet Muhammad, see Safiur-Rahman Al-Mubarakpuri, *The Sealed Nectar Ar-Raheequl-Makhtum* (New York: Darussalam Islamic Books, 2008).

45. For important discussions of the bounded rationality paradigm, see Gerd Gigerenzer and Reinhard Selten (eds.), *Bounded Rationality: The Adaptive Toolbox* (Cambridge: MIT Press, 2001), Bryan D. Jones, "Bounded Rationality and Public Policy: Herbert A. Simon and Decisional Foundation of Collective Choice," *Policy Sciences*, no. 35, 2002, 269–284 and the classic, Richard Cyert and James March, *Behavioral Theory of the Firm* (New York: Blackwell Business, 1992). Jones describes how the notion of bounded rationality first introduced and expanded by Herbert Simon was expanded further by James March. For instance, Cyert and March's, *Behavioral Theory of the Firm* first published in 1963 offers several important concepts essential to the main argument presented in this study. Indeed, uncertainty avoidance may explain in large part US State Department and multinational corporations' (MNC) avoidance of Africa. Finally, for an overview of research on bounded rationality see Fiori Stefano, "Forms of Bounded Rationality: The Reception and Redefinition of Herbert Simon's Perspective," *Review of Political Economy*, vol. 23, no. 4, 2011, 587–612.

46. Since the appearance of Simon's landmark study, *Administrative Behavior*, in 1958, and his Nobel prize in economics in 1978, Simon has influenced generations of scholars in the field of behavioral economics and beyond. The Nobel Prize winner in Economics for 2017 from the University of Chicago continues Simon's tradition of bounded rationality.

47. See Reinhard Selten, "What is Bounded Rationality?" in Gerd Gigerenzer & Reinhard Selten (eds.), *Bounded Rationality: The Adaptive Toolbox* (Cambridge, MA: MIT Press, 2001), 14.

48. Simon's assumption that human beings are intendedly rational was first introduced in his landmark study, *Administrative Behavior*, fourth edition (New York: Free Press, 1997). Simon's original assumption regarding the intended rationality of humans is relaxed by most contemporary researchers. Jon Elster's examination of "thin" as opposed to "thick" rationality is a case in point. See Jon Elster, *Reason and Rationality* (Princeton, NJ: Princeton University Press, 2009).

49. See Cyert and March, *Behavioral Theory of the Firm*, 290.

50. Jervis, *Perceptions and Misperceptions*, 14.

51. Ibid., introduction.

52. Ibid.

53. Joyce P. Kaufmann, *Introduction to International Relations: Theory and Practice* (New York: Rowman & Littlefield, 2013), 149–150.

54. For a discussion of China's role in the "Africa Rising" phenomenon, see Howard W. French, *China's Second Continent: How a Million Migrants Are Building a New Empire in Africa* (New York: Vintage Books, 2015).

55. See "Hopeless Africa," *The Economist* Magazine (cover), 1990 and "Rising Africa," *The Economist* magazine (cover), May 11, 2000.

56. Further evidence that the magazine cover, Africa: the Hopeless Continent, may have been an uncharacteristic departure from *The Economist*'s otherwise stellar reputation seems apparent from the following, "The Danger in the Desert, Jihad in Africa," *The Economist*, vol. 406, no. 8820, 2013, 21, and "Faithful, but not Fanatics: Islam in Africa," *The Economist*, vol. 367, no. 8330, 2003, 50.

57. Jervis, *Perceptions and Misperceptions*, introduction, 3.

58. Ibid., 162.

59. David Robinson, *Muslim Societies in African History* (New York: Cambridge University Press, 2007) introduction, xv.

60. Ibid. "Introduction," xvii. Also see "Muslims Projected to Outnumber Christians by 2100," *New York Times*, April 3, 2015.

61. Ibid., "Introduction," xviii.

62. "Nigeria's Burgeoning Middle Class Hangs Out at the Mall," *New York Times*, January 6, 2016.

63. Africa' porous borders are a special problem in the WOT acknowledged in public remarks by President Obama. These borders are alluded to recent reports on Boko Haram and its elusive leader, Abubakar Shekau, in the following manner: "Islamic State said it appointed a new leader for Boko Haram, in a sign that the Nigerian Islamist insurgency is retooling under the command of the Terrorist group, . . . [t]he group didn't say what happened to Abubakar Shekau the former face of Boko Haram, who hasn't been seen in videos since 2015 . . . for months, Nigerian officials have warned that Boko Haram members' are slipping into the Sahara, joining Islamic State in Libya or for meetings in Sudan. Intelligence reports and officials in neighboring countries have supported that view." See "Islamic State Names Boko Haram Leader," *Wall Street Journal*, August 4, 2016.

64. Rudyard Kipling, "The White Man's Burden," *McClure's Magazine*, February 1899.

65. For a detailed discussion of the Hamitic Hypothesis see Edith R. Sanders, "The Hamitic Hypothesis: Its Origin and Functions In Time Perspective," *Journal of African History*, vol. 10, no. 4, 1969, 521–532.

66. Ibn Khaldun, *The Muqaddimah: An Introduction to History*, Translated from the Arabic by Franz Rosenthal, and J. J. Dawood, eds. (Princeton, NJ: Princeton University Press, 1989), "Introduction," vii, ix, 63, and 117.

67. Paula Sutter Fichtner, *Terror and Toleration: The Hasburg Empire Confronts Islam, 1526–1850* (London: Reaktion Books, 2008), 18.

68. Ibid., 98.

69. Ibid., 99.

70. Ibid., 25.

71. Ibid.

72. Ibid., 82, 96.

73. Ibid., 102.

74. Ibid., 24.

75. Thom, *African Wars*, 130.

76. For a broader discussion of Islamic revival and its major spokespersons, see Ali Rahnema (ed.), *Pioneers of Islamic Revival* (New York: Zed Books, 1994).

77. Toyin Falola, "Violence and Conflict in the 1990s," in Tom Young (ed.), *Readings in African Politics* (Bloomington: Indiana University Press, 2003), 68.

78. See David Westerlund, "Reaction and Action: Accounting for the Rise of Islamism," in David Westerlund and Eva Evers Rosander (eds.), *African Islam and Islam in Africa: Encounters between Sufis and Islamists* (Athens: Ohio University Press, 1997), 308.

79. Ibid., 309.

80. Ibid., 309–310.

81. Ibid., 310–311.

82. See David Westerlund, "Reaction and Action: Accounting for the Rise of Islamism," in Westerlund et al. (eds.), *African Islam and Islam in Africa…*, 313.

83. Ibid., 314.

84. Ibid., 313.

85. Hassan al-Turabi Obituary, *The Guardian,* UK, March 11, 2016. https://www.theguardian.com/world/2016/mar/11/hassan-al-turabi-obituary. Also see Peter Woodward, "Hasan al-Turabi," in John L. Esposito (ed.), *The Oxford Encyclopedia of the Modern Islamic World* (New York: Oxford University Press, 1995), 240–241.

86. Ibid.

87. Ibid.

88. Jane Corbin, *Al-Qaeda: The Terror Network that Threatens the World* (New York: Thunder Mouth Press/Nation Books, 2002), 30 and photo section.

89. Ibid., 36.

90. Hassan al-Turabi Obituary, *The Guardian*, UK, March 5, 2016. https://www.theguardian.com/world/2016/mar/06/hassan-al-turabi-sudan-opposition-leader-who-hosted-osama-bin-laden-dies.

91. Hassan al-Turabi Obituary, *The Guardian*, UK, March 11, 2016. https://www.theguardian.com/world/2016/mar/11/hassan-al-turabi-obituary.

92. See Ali Rehnema (ed.), *Pioneers of Islamic Revival* (New York: Zed Books Ltd., 1994).

93. John Hunwick, "Sub Saharan Africa and the Wider World of Islam," in Eva Evers Rosander and David David Westerlund (eds.), *African Islam and Islam in Africa* (Athens: Ohio University Press, 1997), 33.

94. Jim Crow segregation had a similar effect of providing space for the survival of Islamic belief and practice for well over a century among blacks in the United

States. This space existed well beyond the surveillance and reach of white authorities similar to the description offered by Hunwick of the surveillance of African Muslim leaders by colonial officials during roughly 1860–1960.

95. See Philip G. Roeder and Donald Rothschild (eds.), *Sustainable Peace: Power and Democracy after Civil Wars* (Ithaca: Cornel University Press, 2005).

96. See Charles Tripp, "Sayyid Qutb: The Political Vision," in Ali Rahnema (ed.), *Pioneers of Islamic Revival* (New York: Zed Publication, 1994), 154–184.

97. The former Ugandan Muslim dictator, Idi Amin, died in the city of Jedda, Saudi Arabia in 2014.

98. See Jane Corbin, *Al-Qaeda: The Terror Network that Threatens the World* (New York: Thunder's Mouth Press/Nation Books, 2002), see photo 13.

99. Similar communities exist in contemporary Iraq as we shall see later on in this study.

100. I have witnessed this first-hand in the UAE and find it difficult to image that it is merely a recent phenomenon.

101. Charles River Editors, *Boko Haram: The History of Africa's Most Notorious Terrorist Group* (Lexington, Kentucky: Charles River Editors, 2017), 3.

102. Ibid.

103. Ibid., 3–4.

104. See Ayman al-Yassini, "Wahhabiyah," in John L. Esposito (ed.), *The Oxford Encyclopedia of the Modern Islamic World* (New York: Oxford University Press, 1995), 307–308.

105. Paul D. Williams, *War & Conflict in Africa*, Second edition (Cambridge, UK: Polity Press, 2017), 161.

106. Mamdani, *Good Muslim, Bad Muslim*, 24–26.

107. Ibid.

108. Ibid.

109. Mahmood Mamdani, "Linking the Urban & the Rural," in Tom Young (ed.), *Readings in African Politics* (Bloomington: Indiana University Press, 2003), 45.

110. Tom Young, "Introduction," in Tom Young (ed.), *Readings in African Politics* (Bloomington: Indiana University Press, 2003), 5.

111. This narrative in no way intends to ignore the colonial practice of divide and rule as a system of control and domination, which the British were as skilled at using as any of the European colonial power.

112. See Robert E. Edgerton, *Africa's Armies: From Honor to Infamy A History from 1791 to the present* (Boulder, CO: Westview Press, 2002), 104.

113. Roman Loimeier, "Islamic Reform and Political Change: The Example of Abubakar Gumi and the Yan Izala Movement in Northern Nigeria," in David Westerlund and Eva Evers Rosander (eds.), *African Islam and Islam in Africa* (Athens: Ohio University Press, 1997), 286 and 291.

114. Ibid., 296

115. Ibid.

116. Ibid., 286–287.

117. Ibid., 296–298. Also see Robert B. Edgerton, *Africa's Armies: From Honor to Infamy*, 103–107.

118. Edgerton, *Africa's Armies: From Honor to Infamy,* 104.
119. Ibid.
120. Ibid.
121. Ibid., 104–105.
122. Ibid., 105.
123. Ibid.
124. Ibid.
125. Ibid.
126. Ibid.
127. Ibid.
128. Thom, *African Wars*, 28–29.
129. Ibid., 32–33.
130. Ibid., 34.
131. Ibid., 40–41.
132. Ibid., 226.
133. Ibid., 43.
134. Ibid., 48.
135. Ibid.
136. Williams, *War & Conflict in Africa*, second edition, 170–171.
137. Thom, *African Wars*, 145.
138. Ibid., 148.
139. Ibid., 145.
140. Ibid., 145–147.
141. Ibid., 153–154.
142. Ibid., 225.
143. Ibid., 223.
144. Ibid., 224 and 228.
145. "Stumbling Government Search Torments Parents," *Wall Street Journal*, May 9, 2014.

Chapter 1

Terrorism and Africa

Louis Brenner reminds us that Islam has become a major factor in world politics and many Africans are injecting themselves into the political arena as *Muslims*.[1] While the majority of them practice mainstream Islam, a growing number of African Muslims embrace militant Islamism and contribute to its path of death and destruction.[2] This chapter offers a broad and descriptive overview of recent terrorist violence among Africans with sections that explore (1) "A 'Good Muslim, Bad Muslim' Device"; (2) "The Mysterious Crash of Air Algérie Flight 5017"; (3) "Africa's Slow-Motion Disasters"; (4) "With Friends Like These . . ."; (5) "Shabab and Its Contenders"; (6) "Africa's Anti-Terrorism Politics"; (7) "Africa's other Terrorist Groups"; (8) "#BringBackOurGirls"; (9) "The Special Case of Carlos the Jackal"; and (10) "Distinctive Features of Terrorism in Africa." Emphasis in this chapter is placed on descriptions of recent terrorist violence among Africans to set the stage for more rigorous analyses in subsequent chapters.[3]

This chapter examines recent episodes of terrorist violence linked to Islamist militants and Africans. Although the terrorist episodes covered in this chapter primarily involve the experiences of Islamist militants in East, West, and Central Africa, they nonetheless shed new light on the ideology of militant Islamism in parts of the Islamic world not normally associated with Islamist militant terrorism (e.g., The Central African Republic, Mali, and Burkina Faso). This chapter also seeks to expand the discourse on terrorism to include actions such as the kidnapping of mostly westerners to finance Islamist militant activities among Africans that are not widely discussions in debates on Islamist militancy.

A "GOOD MUSLIM, BAD MUSLIM" DEVICE

Mamdani's *Good Muslim Bad Muslim* offers an analytical device for under-standing the emergence of a new mindset following policy shifts introduced by presidents Ronald Reagan and George W. Bush. This new mindset replaced world communism as the chief adversary of the United States and facilitated the emergence of "Muslim terrorism" as the new chief adversary of the United States going forward.[4] "Culture talk," the term Mamdani used to describe Huntington and Lewis's notion of a "clash of civilizations" pro-moted the demonization of Muslims, especially after September 11, 2001, wherein those who cooperated with the United States were considered good; while all other Muslims were considered bad. This view is apparent from the phrase associated with President George W. Bush, "you're either with us or you're with the terrorists," which implies Muslims are inherently bad except when cooperating with the United States. Also implied is the view that "good Muslims" are modern, secular, and westernized; while "bad Muslims" are anti-modern, doctrinal, and virulent. Secular Muslims are good, but Muslims who take their religion seriously like Wahhabis, are bad.[5] Muslims prove their credentials by joining in the war against "bad Muslims."[6]

Mamdani's discussion of the Muslim obligation to wage *jihad* acknowl-edges that the debate around radical political Islam (or militant Islamism) increasingly focuses on the meaning of *jihad*. Accordingly, *al-jihad al-akbar* denotes the greater jihad while *al-jihad al-asghar* denotes the lesser *jihad*.[7] The greater jihad is the struggle against one's passions; the lesser *jihad* is the obligation to resist oppression. While *jihad* for mainstream Muslims is a doctrine of spiritual struggle or effort, of which military action is but one of its many forms, for the Islamist militant "jihad" is an instrument of terror.[8] Muslims also distinguish the near enemy including one's passions from the far enemy, which typically includes more distant opponents.

THE MYSTERIOUS CRASH OF
AIR ALGÉRIE FLIGHT 5017

The crash of Air Algérie Flight 5017, which killed all 116 passengers and crew of six shortly after takeoff on July 24, 2014, over Gossi, Mali, seems a fitting point of departure.[9] The flight departed from Ouagadougou, Burkina Faso, for France with scheduled connecting flights and a brief layover in Algiers, the capital of Algeria. Officials lost contact with the plane fifty minutes after takeoff. The official cause of the crash was bad weather. Both flight recorder boxes were found. The flight's passengers came from nine different countries, including fifty-four from France and twenty-three from

Burkina Faso planning to make connecting flights in Algiers for Paris. Officials reported no signs of foul play, but ruled nothing out, at least initially.[10] The crash investigation got off to a rocky start after the plane went missing for nearly an entire day![11] Despite improvements in its safety record, Africa remains one of the most dangerous and accident-prone regions in the world for air travel. Burkina Faso and Algeria were mediators in talks design to end the conflict involving Islamist militants, local governments in the Sahel and western powers led by France. A Spanish plane leasing company, Swift air, faced charges including manslaughter and negligence for failure to ensure the safety of passengers.

The US Federal Aviation Administration (FAA) warned airlines of the dangers of flying over conflict zones in 2014 citing risks from rocket-propelled grenades fired at low flying aircraft. French troops allegedly regained "control" over the area eighteen months before the crash from militants linked to four different al-Qaeda groups that controlled two-thirds of the country in 2012.[12] Since then, the region also known as the Sahel remained awash in Libyan arms left over from the 2011 "Arab Spring" and beset by terrorist attacks like one that ambushed and killed four US Green Beret fighters in Niger on October 4, 2017. A series of mysterious plane crashes over "conflict zones" as witnessed in the Ukraine led the United States and other state officials to discourage air travel over conflict zones.[13] One week before the crash of Air Algérie Flight 5017, Malaysia Airlines Flight 17, departing from Amsterdam was shot down by a missile over a conflict zone in eastern Ukraine, killing 298. The crash was blamed on pro-Russian separatists for which the United States and EU imposed sanctions on Russia for its role. Malaysia Airlines Flight 17, departing from Amsterdam and shot down over Ukraine received major news coverage while the crash of Air Algerie Flight 5017 over Gossi, Mali, received practically no news coverage in the United States. The crash of TransAsia Airways Flight 222, departing from Taiwan within days of Air Algérie Flight 5017, killing 28, raised questions over whether 2014 was the deadliest year on record for air travel with 700 passengers killed in just 138 days.[14]

All flights to and from Tel Aviv were suspended due to rocket fire from Gaza in July of 2014. Rumors of stacks of manuals left behind by fleeing al-Qaeda Islamists in northern Mali (*Azawad*) explaining how to use shoulder fired antiaircraft missiles to down low flying aircraft, heightened fears. Claims by French officials that "the plane probably hit the ground intact" were contradicted by eyewitness accounts on the ground including one by General Gilbert Diendéré, chief of the Burkino Faso general staff describing the remains of the plane as totally burned out and scattered. Videos of the crash scene taken by Burkino Faso soldiers and broadcast on French television showed fragmented and charred remains of the plane "scattered over a broad area of muddy terrain." Another eyewitness who described the plane flying at a low altitude before crashing contradict French government accounts that described the plane as sharply plunging 10,000 meters in the three minutes prior to crashing. Muhammed El Moctar, a Malian living in Burkino Faso, said he spoke through cellphone with a cousin, a shepherd, who "saw the plane descending to a low altitude then hearing a loud rumbling followed by lots of smoke."[15]

Do eyewitness and videotaped accounts produced by local officials of charred, fragmented remains scattered over a broad area of muddy terrain seem consistent with evidence of a plane crash caused by bad weather? Can a plane crash be explained away entirely by a sand storm when the plane may have been a target of militants who forced it to fly at low altitudes in a conflict zone? Might a plane flying French nationals over a conflict zone been the target of militants French authorities purportedly cleared out months earlier in Africa's version of Afghanistan? Were terrorist attacks throughout 2014 and 2015 on French and UN interests in Mali a harbinger of things to come in 2015 and 2016 in Mali, Paris, Côte d'Ivoire, Burkina Faso, Nice, and Normandy? Additional Air tragedies possibly related to these events include the crash of Russian Flight A321, departing from the Egyptian resort city of Sharm-al-Sheikh on October 21, 2015, killing 224. ISIS claimed responsibility for the crash as retaliation for Russia's role in Syria. The crash of Egypt Flight MS804 on May 19, 2016, which departed from Paris for Cairo, killing sixty-six people over the Mediterranean raised further questions. Were these tragedies associated with Islamists in North and West Africa merely a coincidence? We may never know for sure. But the time lines tied to these events suggest they may have been linked.

A string of terrorist attacks since the July 24, 2014, crash of Flight Algérie 5017 over Gossi, Mali, have emerged including the October 4, 2017, ambush along the Mali-Niger border killing five Nigeriens and four US Green Beret Special Forces troops near Tongo Tongo in Niger. Nigerien officials are quoted as saying at least forty attacks by militant Islamists were witnessed in the region from 2016 to 2017. An estimated 800 US troops were deployed to Niger by President Obama to operate a $50 million US drone facility scheduled for completion in 2018. Michael R. Shurkin, a senior political scientist at RAND and former CIA analyst, is quoted as saying, "since Trump took office, US policy in the region has been more or less adrift."[16] Others however describe the Niger ambush as the first US overseas casualties of the Trump administration and perhaps more cynically as "Trump's Benghazi." Other reports issued in 2018 have suggested that thousands of US troops have been operating in Africa under little or no public scrutiny. When Republican Senator John McCain was asked in a brief televised interview if he thought Mr. Trump was being forthcoming regarding the American troop ambush in

Niger, his answer was "of course not." Although we may never know the full extent of US military involvement in Africa, a 6,000-page classified report on the Niger ambush issued on April 25, 2018, suggests that terrorist violence in Africa is far from being marginal.

In fact, events in Mali in 2012 became so dire that experts began referring to it as "Malistan," shorthand for Mali's (or Africa's) version of Afghanistan, where militants from far and wide were flocking to train and engage in terrorist plots.[17] As the situation deteriorated in Spring of 2012, the region of the Sahel which envelops Mali was described as "an African powder keg on Europe's doorstep."[18] The Sahel is home to "some of the most ruthless terrorists in Africa."[19] "France's six month attempt to lead the Africans from behind into a military action against al-Qa'ida collapsed in a few short days in early January 2013 when several hundred jihadists breached the Niger Bend in an armed convoy and sped toward Bamako."[20] The French looked on from Paris with fear, as Bamako's population of over a million was described as defenseless, not because it was without protection but because it lacked effective and capable military protection.[21]

Mali's US-trained defenders reportedly "fled the scene, leaving the French and their two helicopters the only barrier that stood between al Qa'ida and Bamako."[22] "By the time [US Defense Secretary] Panetta and Minister Le Drian spoke [by phone] the first French soldier had already been killed in action" and "the French war on al-Qa'ida in Africa" or what would later be called operation Wildcat (*Serval*) was under way.[23] The attack on Bamako was not just a threat to Mali's capital city, but a security challenge to western capitals, as well.[24] According to one account, this threat if left unchecked could metastasize and threaten the United States and France in particular.[25] France, the former colonial power in the Sahel was unable to maintain order around the northern city of Kidal, where Tuareg and Islamist militants battled for supremacy in 2012. French intervention to resolve Mali's North-South divide plus efforts to quell new outbreaks of unrest in May 2014 were unsuccessful and continued throughout 2014 and 2015.[26]

A common theme in the history and politics of Mali is the North-South geographic divide pitting black Malians of the South like the Bambara who were primarily Sufi Muslims against Tuareg, Arabs, and others of the North who were primarily Sunni Muslims. "For centuries the Tuareg eeked out an existence in the extraordinarily harsh environment of the Sahara."[27] One account depicted them as "great serried squadrons of tall, blue-veiled men, mounted on fast white camels, crashing forward like a vast roller . . . one of the most stunning spectacles to be seen on any battlefield."[28] But Tuaregs were also known for their viciousness including raids that carried off livestock, slaves and other loot from southerners.[29] For this reason, southerners in and around Bamako resented Tuaregs and others in the

North of Mali. Understanding the North-South divide in Mali is essential to understanding the conflict.

Though both communities are Muslim, the North unlike the South is awash with money, arms, and Wahhabi-Salafi ideology, wed to a strict interpretation of Islamic law (*shar'iah*) and harsh living conditions. Wahhabi-Salafi ascendancy during 2012–2014 came to dominate Tuareg leaders who looked more to nationalism than Islamism for identity. The West African Movement for Unity and Jihad, known by the French acronym Majao, was led by a Mauritanian, but composed largely of largely radicalized black Malians especially from Gao.[30] Also on the rise were the Islamist groups Ansar al-Din drawn from the Tuareq stronghold of Kidal and the Tuareg independence movement spearheaded by the *Movement Nationale pour la Liberation de l Azawad* (MNLA).[31] But Tuaregs of the North were eventually weakened greatly by the emergence of Wahhabi-Salafists and al-Qaeda in the Islamic Maghreb (AQIM). Around this time (2012–2014) the Arab movement of Azawad (MAA) emerged. What followed was a harsh form of Islamic law (*shari'ah*) widely associated with Islamist militants.

Sadly, two years after the French intervention in 2012, little progress had been made on reconciliation.[32] The North-South divide endured. The situation got worse in 2014 when a faction within the Malian army of over 1,000 troops attempting to settle old scores by marching on the town of Kidal in northern Mali to attack Islamists there but was forced to retreat to the safety of UN and French troops. At least forty Mali government fighters were killed in the episode.[33] Further attacks by Mulathamin, Ansar al Din, and AQIM continued in 2014 and 2015 with new Islamist groups like the Macina Liberation Front joining the fray.[34] A total of thirty-five UN troops were killed in one of these encounters.[35] "With twenty-eight deaths and seventy-five injuries in 2014, the UN mission in Mali became the most deadly UN mission that year."[36]

Given these circumstances, with Islamist militants posing threats nearly everywhere in Mali in 2014, it is not difficult to imagine how a plane full of French passengers could be brought down by insurgents on the ground. Could it be that a stand storm plus anti-French Islamist insurgencies on the ground became a perfect opportunity for militants and a perfect disaster for innocent passengers aboard Air Algérie Flight 5017 brought down over Gossi, Mali, on July 24, 2014? Less than one year later, three men, Cherif and Said Kouachi and Amedy Coulibaly and an accomplice Hayat Boumeddiene from North and West African immigrant families living in Paris attacked the French satirical newspaper, Charlie Hebdo based in Paris for cartoons that ridiculed the Prophet Muhammad. The Kouachi brothers were French immigrants described as Islamist militants with ties to ISIS and prison Islam. Amedy Coulibaly who killed a policewoman during an attack on a Jewish Kosher market in Paris was later killed. He was described as belonging to an immigrant family from Mali with ties to AQIM and prison Islam. He allegedly took hostages and demanded the release of the Kouachi brothers. His accomplice, Hayat Boumeddine apparently escaped.

AFRICA'S SLOW-MOTION DISASTERS

National response times to African disasters compared to those in other parts of the world reveal stark contrasts. This disparity became painfully clear following the Nigerian government's underwhelming response to the 276 schoolgirls abducted in Chibok, Nigeria, in April 2014. The phrase "slow-motion disasters" used in this chapter refers to differences in response times associated with the victims of terrorism in Europe and the United States compared to the victims of terrorism in Africa. Africa's slow-motion disasters harken memories of Rwanda and the haunting regret expressed by former Secretary of State Madeleine Albright and others over the massacre of 800,000 people in just 100 days in what has come to be known as the Rwandan genocide. Is history repeating itself in Africa? Only with the personal intervention of President Obama in concert with Nobel Prize and Mo Ibrahim prize winner President Ellen Johnson Sirleaf was Africa able to end its Ebola crisis of September 2014. With weeks not months to go before the disease over-flowed its then national boundaries, policy makers and medical officials checked the spread of Ebola with uncharacteristically speed in 2015. Might this outcome have been reached in 2015 without skilled and decisive leaders? Are skilled and committed leadership in place to respond to Africa's ongoing terrorist violence?

The kidnapping of 276 schoolgirls in Chibok, Nigeria, by Boko Haram terrorists in April 2014 sparked condemnation especially in Nigeria. After three years of searching (and negotiating) for their release, all 276 kidnapped Chibok girls have not been returned. Some victims may have been as young as age ten. About 83 victims were returned in 2017 but almost 100 of the schoolgirls still remain missing. Even the release of 83 girls in 2017 materialized only after the release of an unspecified number of "high-valued" Boko Haram prisoners with assistance from the international Red Cross and the Swiss government.[37] Amnesty International estimated that at least 1,500 people had been killed by Boko Haram during the first five months of 2014. A car bomb exploded in May 2014 in Nairobi, Kenya, during an attack on the Somali Parliament in the Somalia capitol with further attacks on the Somali Parliament in 2018 linked to al-Shabab (hereafter referred to as Shabab), Africa's second most deadly Islamist militant group.[38]

A year earlier in 2013, a ransom of more than one million dollars was paid to Boko Haram for the release of a French family. The incident supported rumors that terrorism in Africa had become a lucrative "growth industry." Even prominent Nigerians have not been immune from such violence as the mother of Nigeria's finance minister, Kamene Okonjo, eighty-three, was captured in late 2012. Fears in 2013 that these activities might spread to the Sahara, the world's largest desert were confirmed by rumors that the one-eyed mujahedeen veteran, Mokhtar Belmokhtar, had arrived in the area.[39] While President Obama underscored the attractiveness of Africa's investment opportunities in 2013, US businesses have been cautious. A daring attack on the Tigantourine gas facility by AQIM possibly linked to Mokhtar Belmokhtar, formerly known as the "Sheikh of the Sahel" lend support to US business concerns.[40]

WITH FRIENDS LIKE THESE . . .

US allies often fuel the very terrorism they seek to eradicate.[41] For example, President Trump's summer 2017 visit to Saudi Arabia to declare a US-Saudi alliance against "radical Islamic terrorism" ignored Saudi Arabia's controversial links to Wahhabism (Salafism), which is arguably the leading source of Islamist militancy, worldwide. Yet, without the support of the Saudis, the US-led WOT might be in even greater peril. The alliance of African states that includes Nigeria, Kenya, Mali, Cameroon, Chad, and Niger is both an asset and a liability to US interests because of (1) heavy-handed police tactics practiced in Nigeria plus failure to return all 276 Chibok girls, (2) persecution of Muslim terrorist suspects by the Kenyan state, (3) the failure to engage the enemy in Mali where US-trained troops have surrendered and retreated in the heat of battle, (4) heavy-handed police tactics used by the security forces of Cameroon, and (5) weak military forces in the physically vulnerable state of Niger. US reluctance to put "boots on the ground" in significant numbers has only worsened this concern.[42]

Post-independent Tanzania in 1960 enjoyed a reputation for honesty and moderate government thanks to its widely celebrated founding father and first president, Julius Nyerere (1922–1999). But by 2000, Tanzania, a US ally with one of the fastest growing economies in Africa, visited by President Obama in 2015, was ranked among the most corrupt countries in the world by Transparency International. Uganda, another moderate east African ally of the United States, at war with militant Islamists, remains among the most corrupt regimes in the world. To its credit, Uganda achieved political and economic stability following the tumultuous rein of President Idi Amin and decreased its high HIV/AIDS infection rate. But Uganda is a pariah state and a major embarrassment to the United States for its support of Yoweri Museveni. Mr. Museveni claims to be seventy-one but few in Uganda believe him. He has ruled Uganda since 1986 and is one of Africa's longest ruling leaders. "Elections" in Uganda are almost never described as transparent.[43]

Another US ally, Malian President Mousa Traoré, was accused of using foreign aid to build elaborate mansions for his ruling elite instead of spending it on drought relief as intended by the funding agency in 1991. Traoré was ousted in a military coup led by a military colonel named Ahmadou Sanogo on March 22, 2012.[44] According to one rumor, "Sanogo's mother is said to have fainted when she saw him on television at the head of the coup."[45] Sanogo was the beneficiary of several training trips to the United States, many of which were for English language training that enabled him to acquire a near perfect American accent. Yet, Sanogo's ouster of Traoré was both costly and embarrassing to the United States as it ended twenty years of widely heralded democratic governance in Mali, which the United States long touted as a success story in Africa.

But Mali's government suffered humiliating setbacks including inadequate ammunition during military emergencies aimed at quelling rebellions in the North, low morale among its troops and humiliating setbacks at the hands of Islamist militants. This led Mali's forces to mutiny, take control of the national broadcast station and launch a military coup that removed President Mousa Traoré in 2012. Mali's neighbors including representatives from Côte d'Ivoire, Burkina Faso, Liberia, Benin, and Niger took off in a plane for Bamako, but when they arrived at the airport in Mali's capital city they were met by protest demonstrations on the tarmac who forced them to return. The next day Mali's neighbors threatened to close its borders and block access to the central bank upon which it depended for currency, in an effort to force Mali's coup leaders to step down.[46] Sanoga stood his ground causing Mali's neighbors to impose sanctions on its fuel, cash, and food.

Sanoga then capitulated and accepted a power-sharing arrangement on April 6, 2012, that shared power with Mali's parliamentary leader, Dioncounda Traoré, who became interim-president. The new arrangement also mandated elections to be held within forty days. Given this, progress sanctions were lifted. Although the agreement was far from perfect, it helped to buy time until Sanogo and his fellow military mutineers could return to their barracks. But the military held on. Finally, on May 20, 2012, bowing to public pressure, Sanogo agreed to leave politics, turning over power to his interim-president, Dioncounda Traoré. Two days later, after agreeing to meet with a group of coup supporters, seventy-year-old Traoré was beaten within inches of his life and left for dead on the floor of the presidential palace. He was rushed to Paris for medical treatment and the situation slipped back toward chaos.[47]

The "Africa rising" period after 2000, led by Nigeria, Angola, Ethiopia, Tanzania, and Rwanda led Africa to experience brief but impressive economic gains as a result of good management, investment from China and record-high world commodity prices.[48] But bribery and corruption became widespread leading officials routinely to collect fees from prospective investors just to start a business.[49] Although these practices may be on the decline in 2018, they have survived nonetheless in Nigeria and Kenya, two of Africa's largest and fastest growing states. Kenya's level of corruption is so high that President Obama could not resist condemning it and similar state practices during a live joint appearance with Kenyan President Uhuru in the summer of 2015. Businesspersons in Kenya are regularly visited by police officers asking in Swahili for *kitu kidoko*, "a little something," where failure to oblige might result in injury or worse.[50] Citizens of US allied African states face similar treatment when forced to contend with police roadblocks (which look more like "shake-downs") ostensibly designed to check vehicle ownership documents, but which are actually designed to collect bribes. This practice is so prevalent in Nigeria, that police there give change! Is there any wonder why Islamists view police with such great disdain?

Chadian fighters possess a well-earned reputation for being effective desert fighters and loyal western allies. They are credited with checking the advance of the ever-meddlesome Muammar Gadhafy of Libya in northern Chad during the 1980s, thwarting the marauding reach of Janjaweed fighters in Darfur, Sudan, in 2007 and halting the northeastern advance of Boko Haram from Nigeria's Bornu state in 2016. Chad represents a rare bright spot in the anti-terrorist campaign in Central Africa. Chad is an example of a state that has made effect use of Muslim struggle, which Michael Scheuer describes as "defensive jihad" and Mamdani describes as "just war." With the election of President Trump, Chad curiously was placed for a time on President Trump's second list of Muslim banned states, though Chad is no longer on the list. Other western allies like Mali (not on the Muslim ban list) have had greater difficulty achieving decisive victories against elusive Islamist militants skilled at seemingly vanishing into the desert air. While contemporary Mali is roughly the size of France; Northern Africa including the Sahara is geographically larger than the continental United States. In public remarks made by President Obama following Nairobi's Westgate mall attack in 2013, Mr. Obama acknowledged African terrorists' penchant for exploiting porous borders. Such terrain may help explain Will Reno's observation that nearly all African wars after 2000 have been international.[51] Boko Haram gunmen allegedly killed polio vaccine workers in Nigeria in 2013 and bombed UN headquarters in 2011.[52]

Even the seemingly safe Island of Zanzibar off the coast of east Africa witnessed WOT violence when two male attackers riding a motor bike threw acid in the faces of two unsuspecting women tourists during the summer of 2014. Violence forced the humanitarian group Doctors without Borders to withdraw operations after their twenty-two-year mission in Somalia was forced to a close in 2013. The Islamist militant group, Shabab, unleashed a dramatic display of violence killing more than fifty people while viewing a World Cup soccer match in Kampala, Uganda, in 2010. The attack was allegedly carried out in retaliation for Uganda's role in the African Union (AU) invasion of Somalia in 2007. These events fail to resemble a dark continent that is far removed from WOT.

Days after the Westgate shopping mall attack in Nairobi, Kenya by Shabab, in September 2013, riots erupted in Kenya following the killing of Sheikh Ibrahim Ismail also known as Ibrahim Omar and three others. The victims were killed when their car was sprayed by bullets as they drove along Mombasa's palm-fringed coastal highway. Sheikh Ibrahim's predecessor, Sheikh Aboud Rogo Muhammed, "linked" to Shabab had been killed under almost identical circumstances a year earlier. Episodes like these in the WOT fought out on the streets of Mombasa by Kenyans on behalf of western interests are reminiscent of Cold War battles waged in distant African theaters that include Angola, Mozambique, Ethiopia, and Namibia.[53] Most in the United States remain unaware of their existence much less their significance. Africa's "generation Xers" may know even less about these events despite the price in blood their grandparents were forced to pay during the Cold War. However, for Kenyan Islamists like Sheikh Ismail and his followers were forced to pay the ultimate price at the hands of the police, the tragedy lives on, indeed.

A British Broadcasting (BBC) News interview of a local Muslim Imam in Mombasa, Kenya, accused the local Kenya police unit known as the Terrorist Attack Police Unit (ATPU) of targeting known Islamists in Kenya, including the slaying of Sheikh Ibrahim Omar. The ATPU has been accused of launching targeted assassinations, extrajudicial killings, torture, and renditions of Muslim terrorist suspects. Although the sheikh's allegations could not be confirmed at the time of the report, British authorities did establish that the ATUP were trained by the former colonial authority, Britain and funded by the United States. Mombasa, Kenya, suffers 80 percent youth unemployment with high rates of police presence and anti-police resentment.[54] The following is a revealing testimonial offered on behalf of a survivor of this violence.

Police are cracking down on extremism in this bustling port city [of Mombasa] but some young Muslim men say their tactics are only serving to amplify violence. When police in this bustling port city raided a mosque known for extremist sermons late last year, a 25-year-old man was among more than 100 followers trucked to a local jail and crammed into a tiny cell. He said he spent much of his three weeks in custody trying to sleep standing up before he was released without being charged. "I was treated as a terrorist" said Yassir, who gave only a nickname because he said he is required to check in weekly with police and was worried about recrimination. In that same raid, a former class-mate was shot and killed, he said. Now, the time for peaceful discussion is over, he said. Next time, he vows to respond the way he said the government does –with force. "There is no trust between the police and the Muslim community at all. It is zero said Mr. Khalifa of Muslims for Human Rights."[55]

With moto-taxis being the primary mode of transportation for ordinary citizens in northern Nigeria, one study describes how in mid-2009 "the Nigerian security forces with their long-practiced talent for making a bad situations even worse, unleashed a crackdown on Boko Haram, harassing them as they went to preach, and on the *achaba*, beating or fining them for not wearing motorcycle helmets, despite the fact that virtually no one wears them in this part of northern Nigeria."[56] These events escalated into major conflict when "between seven hundred and nine hundred people, most of them adherents of Boko Haram were killed" including boys as young as nine.[57] Mohammad Yusuf, the group's founder, was also killed in this crackdown while "trying to escape" leading his deputy Abubakar Shekau to break dozens of its members out of prison in Maiduguri and spark a brutal campaign of assassinations against government, security forces, and rival religious leaders in 2010.[58]

Back in Nigeria, bad publicity continued to haunt the Nigerian state when during a search and destroy operation for Boko Haram members in January of 2017, a Nigerian fighter jet allegedly accidently bombed a refugee camp kill-ing dozens of camp residents. The bombing also killed at least six humanitar-ian workers and wounded numerous others. As they attempted to administer first aid to the survivors, Doctors without Borders, the humanitarian charity estimated the number of deaths at over 50 with at least 200 wounded. During the same week, two suicide bombers, one of whom appeared to have been a twelve-year-old girl detonated explosives at the University of Maiduguri, where students and teachers gathered for morning prayer (*fajr*). The blast reportedly killed several people, including Aliyu Usman Mam, a veterinary medicine professor as the university prepared for exams.

The bombing may have helped persuade the United States to provide more support for the government of Nigeria's campaign against Boko Haram, as Congress approved selling the Nigerian government warplanes in January

2017 over the objections of many in Congress still troubled by Nigeria's abysmal human rights record.

Nigerian president Muhammadu Buhari secured the sale of dozens of A-29 Super Tucano warplanes from President Trump during his US visit in 2018. There is evidence that Boko Haram cooperates with AQIM and al-Shabab. However, "the alliance between Boko Haram and ISIS that was announced in early 2015 and widely discussed in the West appears to be more or less rhetorical, with little evidence for cooperation between the two terrorist organizations, although the Nigerian government under Goodluck Jonathan made use of those claims to deflect criticisms of their security forces and to attempt to obtain advanced weaponry from the West."[59]

Boko Haram violence uprooted more than 2 million people from their homes driving some to camps like Rann, where thousands of refugees have fled in little more than six months. Known as a hotbed of Boko Haram activity, the area surrounding Rann similar to the region of northern Mali had been cleared of militants months earlier. Boko Haram mounted a vicious attack on Rann in late 2016 allegedly lasting for three hours, in a display of Boko Haram force that contradicted claims by Nigerian president Muhammadu Buhari that the militants had been "technically defeated." The group's ability to escape the reach of government security forces was first witnessed in its ability to exploit hideouts in and around the Sambisa forest in Bornu state.[60]

Later the group "took refuge in the Mandara Mountains, on the Cameroon-Nigeria border, where the group was finally dispersed later that year [in 2014]."[61] The Nigerian government's use of "private military companies" (some of them mercenaries from South Africa) managed to push Boko Haram out of some of its strongholds in early 2015.[62] Although the extent of their control remains unclear to outside observers, "Boko Haram still appears to control some territory, especially in the northwest regions of Lake Chad."[63] For instance, a market woman in Kolofata in Cameroon just a few miles from the Nigerian border told a French reporter in 2016, "The prices asked by Boko Haram's wives are unbeatable. They need to sell their products very quickly, and they prefer to be paid in food."[64]

SHABAB AND ITS CONTENDERS

Similar to the September 2013 Westgate mall attack by Shabab in Nairobi, Kenya, where details of the attack were withheld for months, gunmen in Somalia reportedly attacked the Somali Supreme Court in April of 2013. But details of the attack were not released until some five months later. In a related event during the period, Shabab militants stormed the main Somali court complex in a two-hour battle that left nearly twenty people dead.

Similar to the Westgate attack, the official number of attackers and casualties were withheld by authorities. Early BBC Television News reports described how innocent civilians including women and children had been killed. The Supreme Court attack was the first by Shabab on Mogadishu, the Somali capital, since being driven out by US-backed AU forces in 2007. These attacks suggest Shabab may have been down, but not out. Lack of transparency on the part of the Kenyan state makes it difficult to provide detailed assessments of the terrorist danger.

Shabab an affiliate of al-Qaeda since 2012 only gained acceptance after the death of Osama bin Laden in 2011 who kept the group at arms-length because of its penchant for indiscriminant violence. Shabab's fighters numbering around 5,000 at its peak in 2016 have been a miniscule presence compared to the larger, better-known, and better finance ISIS. But what Shabab lacked in size and wealth was made up for in death and destruction. Its power is magnified by the relative weakness of Shabab's state opponents which include Kenya, Uganda, and the Somali provisional government. Somalia's last unified functioning government melted away with the departure of Muhammad Siad Barre, the last singularly recognized president who famously fled the country in an armored vehicle in 1991. The group targets government officials and maintains ongoing military conflicts with the provisional government of Somalia and AU troops based in Addis Ababa, Ethiopia. Like the Islamist militants of northern Mali, Shabab targets places where westerners eat, sleep, study, and shop in an effort to exploit vulnerable "soft targets" including Nairobi's Westgate mall which was viciously attacked in September 2013. Somalia and Ethiopia are longtime enemies dating to the Cold War. Ethiopia is predominantly Coptic Christian and Hebrew while Somalia is predominantly Muslim. But their differences are as much rooted in politics as they are in religion and culture.

One report characterized Shabab recruits as terrorists who kill "on a shoestring." But despite their military and political travails between 2007 and 2011, Shabab are linked to a long series of brutal attacks including one on Garissa University College in April 2015 where approximately a dozen well-armed men roamed the small college leaving "scores" dead and hundreds in need of evacuation. The Garissa attack is regarded by some as one of the deadliest attacks thus far by Shabab. According to Kenyan officials, one of the gunmen involved in the Garissa attack may have been the son of a Kenyan government official in Mandera. Lack of transparency by Kenyan government officials resulted in conflicting casualty reports in the Garissa attack. While Shabab may be known for its skill at operating on a "shoestring budget" the Garissa attack demonstrated how Shabab became proficient at (1) killing "on the cheap" (2) "dumbing-down terrorist violence," and (3) military resilience. Shabab is known for being lightly armed, highly disciplined and relatively well trained. Ruthlessly resilient and proficient at killing, the group has demonstrated an uncanny ability able to evade Kenya's superior numbers and strength. Kenyan state forces have nowhere near the skill, tenacity, or boldness of Shabab.

Driven from their base in Mogadishu by AU forces to outlying regions in southern Somalia in August 2011, al-Shabab means the youth in Arabic. It has intrigued foreign observers by its international composition suggesting an organized network far less isolated than first thought. During its brazen attack on the Westgate mall in Nairobi in 2013, western fighters (*mujahedeen*) may have been among the Shabab attackers escaping the mall along with panicking shoppers, some of whom may have come from as far away as Norway, London, or Minneapolis. The actual number of attackers in both the Supreme Court and Westgate mall attacks remains unclear. But it is clear that Shabab's opponents from within Kenya's security forces suffer poor discipline, low-morale, and rampant corruption. Samples of these unflattering images were captured on mall cameras showing Kenyan security forces carrying large plastic shopping bags full of luxury items taken from various mall stores as they casually strolled through the mall's rubble-filled ruins in the waning hours of the Westgate mall terrorist attack in September 2013.

Imagine, security forces weapons in tow, on a stroll through a glitzy upscale mall in the middle of a WOT for all the world to see! These images delivered a blow to Kenyan officials. But they also delivered a blow to their chief sponsors, the United States. The Kenyan security culprits were arrested soon after their exposure. But in addition to their corruption and poor discipline, they revealed themselves to be most inept. Kenyan state officials were unable to confirm any of the decidedly rich details provided by survivors of the nearly nonstop televised Westgate mall attack including reports that over 60 people were killed and over 100 wounded and/or injured. Eyewitnesses interviewed on BBC acknowledged the ethnic diversity of the Westgate attackers who appeared to reflect a broad mix of the marauding Shabab fighters. One Shabab fighter, Omar Hamami, a white American Muslim, and popular rapper, from Alabama joined Shabab in his words, wage "jihad." But after falling out with Shabab leaders in 2013, al-Amriki (the American) was killed by Shabab assassins.

French forces continued to battle Islamist militants in northern Mali where insurgents played hide-and-seek, awaiting the opportunity to return to commanding positions after being displaced by French troops. Some observers believe that while high-ranking al-Qaeda commanders are likely to have fled to neighboring Niger, Algeria, and Libya, low-level local fighters (*mujahedeen*) continue to hide in local desert villages to avoid encountering French forces and their allies. Islamist militants appear to prefer to wait for the right time to strike western forces in the region. They have been in no hurry to confront western forces and may be inspired by the Sahara desert's reputation for being perhaps the world's greatest conveyor of illegal weaponry. Could a mixture of local fighters remaining behind in the desert and vast supplies of weaponry have played a role in crash of Air Algérie Flight 5017 in 2014? Subsequent attacks in Mali, Tunisia, Burkino Faso, and Côte d'Ivoire suggest this may have been possible.

But not to be outdone, Boko Haram fighters were blamed in 2013 for the killing of dozens of innocent students at a Nigerian college. Boko Haran like ISIS often does not bother to claim responsibility for its attacks. Gunmen believed to be linked to Boko Haram fighters attacked an agricultural college in northeastern Nigeria in September 2013 killing more than forty students. The attackers drove into the campus of the Yube State College of Agriculture in Damaturu, the state capital. According to Musa Aliyu, whose name suggests he may be Muslim, the attackers entered college dormitories as college students slept, opening fire on them randomly in the dark. The attack was the second large-scale Boko Haram attack in less than two weeks. Hundreds of innocent civilians fled for safety in nearby Niger to avoid the carnage. Despite the area's location as a potential terrorist target, inspectors were shocked to learn how little security had been in place at the college. The governor of Yube state, Ibrahim Gaiden, issued a statement condemning the attack as "devastating, heinous, and barbaric."

One eyewitness was astonished by the violence and the absence of an obvious motive. Not a single Christian was killed. Muslims were the only victims. The eyewitness questioned how any religion could condone such acts? The distinction between Islamic and Islamist, that is, between religion and politics is what begins to answer this question, though a more elaborate explanation is offered in the following chapter. The common theme joining these episodes of violence is militant Islamism as an instrument of terror.

In vast West Africa, a new front-line in the battle against al-Qaeda, Nigeria is America's strategic linchpin, its military is one the US counts on to help contain the spread of Islamic militancy. Yet Nigeria has rebuffed American attempts to train that military, whose history of shooting freely has US officials concerned that soldiers here fuel the very militancy they are supposed to counter.[65]

AFRICA'S ANTI-TERRORISM POLITICS

Nigeria's own National Human Rights Commission estimates police kill at the rate of roughly 2,500 Nigerians per year, exceeding the number of people killed by Boko Haram militants conservatively estimated in 2013, at

2,000 people. During a recent two-day period, the Mobile Police branch of the Nigerian army—accused of shooting at least thirty young men—earned the nickname "Kill and Go." An untold number of western hostages are kidnapped in Nigeria each year. Several mostly European construction workers were abducted in Nigeria's Muslim North in February 2013 by gunmen later linked to Boko Haram. Amnesty International estimates that as many as 7,000 people may have died in government detention from brutal conditions with an additional 1,200 eliminated in extra-judicially killings, at the hands of the Nigerian security forces. At least 20,000 people have been "arbitrarily arrested, by the authorities."[66] The Boko Haram abduction of a French family including four children outside an elephant game park in neighboring Cameroon prompted militants to send a videotaped message to French authorities with the family's picture in the background reading: "We say to the president of France, we are the jihadists who people refer to as Boko Haram." A turban-shrouded man said, "We are fighting the war that he has declared on Islam."[67] African diplomacy expert I. William Zartman's pessimistic outlook on the prospects of a diplomatic resolution shows the failure of existing approaches and need for new ones.

> Africa holds a number of conflicts of different types that are rather impervious to diplomacy. . . . These contests are not contests for state control (despite IS's name) or territorial acquisition or separation, nor do they represent particular ethnic or national groups. They thrive on and promote state collapse and are conducted by nonterritorial nonsovereign bands of fanatics. They therefore constitute an additional level of difficulty beyond even the most long-lasting of the conflicts already mentioned. It is hard to see possibilities for mediation with Boko Haram, al-Shabab, or Beit al Maqdis, or other al-Qaeda or Khalifa (IS) franchises; at best, efforts other than military defeat can include deconversion of individual leaders and member, as is being tried in Nigeria.[68]

Citizens describe how Somali militants sprayed a Kenyan bus with bullets in December 2015, killing two people. But when militants demanded travelers separate themselves by religion before executing Christians, Muslim refused to identify Christians and instead shared parts of their clothing to obscure the militants' ability to single out Christians. According to eyewitnesses, the strategy worked and the terrorists departed without further incident. One eyewitnesses running away from the shots at Westgate said he could hear the attackers shouting Muslims should leave the complex. A woman hiding in the Westgate mall read text messages from her brother on how to recite the *shahada*, the Muslim declaration of faith she hoped would save her life.

AFRICA'S OTHER TERRORIST GROUPS

Militant Islamism discussed thus far in Kenya, Sudan, Somalia, Nigeria, Mali, Chad, and elsewhere in West Africa are not the only Islamist challenges facing Africans. Another wave of militant Islamists has extended this challenge to often-overlooked states such as the Central African Republic (CAR), the Democratic Republic of the Congo (DRC), and Uganda. After violence flared in 2012, the United States abandoned its embassy in CAR where one western diplomat described the situation as "extremely dangerous." CAR is sparsely populated especially outside the capital city of Bangui. Its total population is less than 5 million though territorially it is roughly the size of Texas. Christian and Muslims have lived there for centuries. But the government coup of 2012 left many dead at the hands of Seleka rebels drawn from CAR's barren North and East and neighboring states of Chad and Sudan, respectively. Seleka Muslim fighters were angered by what they viewed as betrayal and neglect by CAR's government under former President Bozizé who led them to believe they would be incorporated more fully into CAR's military (with civil service jobs for life).

Within a year of Seleka's rise, anti-Balaka primarily Christian forces from Bozizé's political networks attacked the Seleka. Some of these anti-Balaka fighters seem motivated by the need for local protection while others may have been more blatantly criminal.[69] Pope Francis met with both sides during his visit to CAR in December 2015 which had been without strong central authority since the 1990s. National elections were held in January 2016. But CAR's violent past threatened further Christian-Muslim violence if promises by its newly elected president were not kept. Like stereotypes discussed in the introduction, anti-Muslim stereotypes have been clearly on display in CAR as evident from the responses to interviews conducted by Lombard. For instance, Central Africans often described themselves as peaceful and nonviolent compared to Chadians and Sudanese who were described as quick to pull a weapon.[70] Chadians and Sudanese are mostly Muslim while most CAR citizens are Christians or proponents of traditional African religions.

Jubilant crowds poured onto the streets with news that, Michael Djotodia, CAR's self-anointed president had decided to step down on January 9, 2013, after seizing power in a military coup against former President Bozizé nine months earlier with the support of Seleka. Mr. Djotodia was summoned by regional power broker, President Idriss Déby of Chad, who admonished Mr. Djotodia (a fellow Muslim) for failing to manage the crisis and for causing widespread atrocities by the Seleka against Christians and later by anti-Balaka Christian militias against Muslims following Djotodia's departure after January 9, 2013. "Even with peacekeepers arriving violence remained widespread."[71] "Anti-Balaka forces did not share the same interests or objectives."[72] "The 'genocide card' (or more precisely verge of genocide card') was played to describe the Anti-Balaka's targeting of Muslims."[73] The crisis created a flood of Muslim refugees from CAR to nearby Chad, which Chadian President Idriss Déby simply refused to tolerate or accept.

Islamist militant violence in CAR can be divided into two types: violence against non-Muslims and Muslim struggle (*jihad*) against anti-Balaka militias. President Déby of Chad "organized the process whereby the government selected Catherine Samba-Panza, a businesswoman, lawyer and former Mayor of Bangui as new transitional president."[74] The Seleka sought revenge against Bozizé and CAR politicians before him who were viewed as gaining political power from the military muscle provided by Muslims who were recruited as mercenaries. But Bozizé failed to deliver on promises he made of civil service jobs and lucrative paychecks in exchange for mercenary support. Unsurprisingly, Christians and traditional African coreligionists resented Muslims they perceived as outsiders and therefore not "purely" Central Africans. Muslims were seen as enjoying greater physical mobility in light of their long-distant trading networks and links to tribal kinfolk in nearby Chad and Sudan. It was precisely because of these and other perceived "advantages" that Muslims were treated as strangers, foreigners, and the "other." Muslims were marginalized in their own country and ridiculed for dressing, appearing, and behaving differently from other citizens of CAR.[75]

The CAR state lacks the geographical boundaries and national sovereignty typically associated with the modern nation-state. Indeed, most important decisions related to the government and country's future are made in N'djamena, Paris, Nairobi, or New York.[76] This was evident in the waning days of the Djotodia regime in 2013 when growing opposition to Djotodia and intervention by Chadian President Idriss Déby resulted in the country's head of state, Djotodia, being flown to Ndjamena where he was forced to resign. CAR would not exist without these far-flung political connections.[77] The non-territorialized, privatized nature of the CAR state along with other factors has caused power to be associated with "mobility" as in who can and who cannot move.[78] But use of the expression "failed state" by some to describe conditions found in CAR (perhaps similar to conditions found in Somalia) may be inaccurate as such a conclusion suggest that colonialism in CAR worked perfectly smoothly and that the chaos of recent years in CAR "is a result of African stupidity/venality." But violence has always played a role in shaping the CAR state.[79]

The "Seleka's Michael Djotodia was not a legitimate leader because he took power violently . . . [the] Seleka had been ruling CAR towns and villages as fiefdoms," but without the long-term interest that a fiefdom usually entails. As a result of this, "killings, dispossession, and other violence occurred on a massive scale. With Bozizé gone, Seleka fighters moved into most of the country's west and north [but] . . . largely ignored the southeast."[80] These events met a violently bitter end with the emergence of anti-Balaka militias drawn mainly from the South. And to the extent that Seleka authoritarian rule became rationalized in the minds of its proponents, CAR's Islamism came to represent a Muslim alternative to secular authority like the idea of universal human rights promoted in the West. Mayer advances the view that [Islamists] "assert the supremacy of Islamic principles in all areas relevant for the protection of human rights, thereby providing a justification for over-riding international human rights standards by appeals to 'Islam.'" Second, "cultural traditions and religious loyalties may be invoked by political leaders and entrenched elites as pretexts for refusing to adopt guarantees for rights provided in the international norms." And third, "given the political power of conservative Islamic factions in many countries, it is very likely that the pattern of exploiting Islam to justify government policies violating rights will continue to be a serious problem."[81] These recurring actions may have been on display in CAR.

CAR's colonial history was rooted in a French version of indirect rule that exploited traditional modes of African authority similar to the system of indirect rule used by British colonialists in Nigeria. It was a history rooted in racism, stereotype, and, above all, violence as seen in the example of Georog Schweinfurth, a European traveler through Africa—from Khartoum to Mangbetu, in present-day DRC between 1869 and 1871 who wrote of his fears of cannibals. In keeping with the mores of the time, he was an avid collector of ivory tusks and human skulls (i.e., a headhunter).[82] "But to explain it he clung tightly to what he held to be an unassailable truth—that Africans were above all primitives ('dense and stupid')—and so he never managed to consider that they saw him for the head hunter and orchestrator of violence that he was."[83] Such were the mores of the times.

But colonial rule in CAR failed to grant Muslims the degree of privileges granted to Muslim authorities in northern Nigeria. The system in CAR like that in Nigeria allowed the French to solidify their rule by "piggy-backing" their authority onto the authority of traditional African rulers as a matter of convenience, especially in those instances where traditional African authority was too powerful to take-on militarily, at least immediately.[84] Such was the case of Sultan Muhammad as-Sanusi who in addition to being granted autonomy in his mountainous compound at the heart of Ndel on a rocky plateau in the North, engaged in slave raiding and transport on behalf of his patron to the North of CAR, Rabah, the Sultan of Wadai. Sanusi built an army of 20,000 and entered into treaties with the French where in exchange for granting France monopoly commercial rights was promised, 300 guns and 15,000 cartridges in a nine-month period.[85] Neither side fully held true to their commitments.[86] Nevertheless, "captives from Dar al-Kuti, Sanusi's kingdom were sold as far away as the Libyan coast."[87]

Borrowing the from Geschiere's observation (2009), Lombard describes the politics in CAR as "contests over autochthony (i.e., who belongs, who is born on the soil)."[88] This question is especially important as CAR is effectively a non-territorialized country. "That is to say, controlling a territory has never been a major objective of the government (the borders are porous not only because of a lack of capacity but also a lack of interest) and the country's politics are largely prosecuted outside the national borders—in Paris, Brussels, Nairobi, Ndjamena, New York, etc."[89] Similar to their use in contemporary Nigeria where they are a source of harassment and humiliation which drive victims into the arms of Islamist militants, roadblocks in CAR have produced similar outcomes and results. "Roadblocks are sites for negotiation," where people end up paying fees, fines, and/or "coffee money" to corrupt officials. Roadblocks make people angry. For many armed group members in northeast CAR, their experiences traversing roadblocks ultimately facilitated their radicalization[90]

> Some Muslims, whether living in the northeast or elsewhere, took the precaution of officially changing their names to Christian ones to make it easier to move around. Many southerners are convinced that a person with a Muslim name can never be a real Central African; even if the person's family has been installed on central African soil for generations, they are seen as not true natives and thus never as true citizens. As a result, they get detained and forced to pay extra fees and fines.[91]

But while non-Muslims of CAR believed Muslims were better able to move about freely unpoliced, Muslims felt they are unable to move anywhere without being hassled.[92] Graffiti appeared around this time in CAR reading: "no more mosques in CAR." In addition to this, mob violence flared throughout the state perpetrated by those known to act first and ask questions later.[93] Lynching, looting, and mob violence became widespread in CAR despite the presence of international peacekeepers. Some violence "occurred while African Union and UN peacekeepers stood nearby."[94] "The Central African Republic is nothing if not the product of encounters between people originally from elsewhere,"[95] and because of this it is an especially difficult place for determining who is and who is not a foreigner. A local assailant described the situation in the following manner:

> Ouandja Magloire confessed to/took credit for the crime. . . . They dragged the suspect and began to beat and stab him. They doused him with kerosene and set him on fire. Afterwards, they dismembered him, and it was then that Quandja grabbed a leg and bit for the photo-cameras that had been engaged to capture the carnage.[96]

"Muslims would share images of the violence against them . . . Christians would share stories of Seleka Exactions."[97] The performance aspect of Christian-Muslim violence in CAR became heightened when it occurred with cameras rolling and the possibilities of diffusing it have become popularized through means such as Facebook.[98]

These episodes reveal how although Islamist violence associated with the Seleka extracted a heavy toll, the anti-Balaka backlash from 2013 to 2017 created an even greater wave of violence moving CAR to the brink of genocidal crisis.

Moving from CAR to the neighboring African state of Uganda, an obscure rebel group (not the LRA) called the "Allied Democratic Forces," which had been hiding in the jungle of eastern DRC for years emerged after being driven from their home in Uganda. The group was formed in the early 1990s but was sidelined by the policies of Uganda's President Yoweri Museveni. Its members describe themselves as Muslims who left Uganda based on a desire to be governed by Islamic (*shari'ah*) law in 2013. But little is known of the group in the United States. France expressed concern in 2013 that it was becoming overstretched. CAR became France's fourth military intervention in ten years, following earlier interventions in Mali, Côte d'Ivoire, and Libya. By December 2013, France was forced to admit its inability to stabilize these African regions indefinitely. But when President Obama's 2013 Africa visit overlapped with a visit by former President George W. Bush, it was Mr. Bush rather Kenya's "native son" who "stole the spotlight" during brief joint appearances. Africans expressed gratitude for the humanitarian aid and personal commitment to Africa displayed by President George W. Bush. By contrast, President Obama spent less than twenty-four hours in Africa during his first term in office, although in fairness only four American Presidents (including Mr. Obama) have ever visited Africa while in office.

The case of President Obama as the first African American President may be different. Nonetheless, is there any wonder why one major media source described Mr. Obama's 2015 trip to Africa as "Obama's guilt trip?" While the United States has sent a total of four sitting Presidents on visits to Africa in its entire history, Germany's Angela Merkel visited Africa three times in 2016, alone, to promote a "Marshall Plan" for Africa amid a chorus of critics that include United States' UN ambassador, Nikki Haley, who ironically expressed opposition to Merkel's overtures to Africa in 2017 when it is the United States instead of Germany which has the deeper historical kinship with the continent.[99]

Western observers often criticize moderate Muslims for failing to denounce Muslim terrorists more vigorously. But a Boko Haram attack on an Emir during Friday prayers in Northern Nigeria in late 2014 captures the complexity of this issue. Lamido Sanusi, the Emir of the grand mosque in Kano, Nigeria, and former central-bank governor, was attacked by bombers for giving a speech critical of Boko Haram and for advising his followers to arm themselves in self-defense. The attack underscores the additional cost that moderate Muslims are forced to pay in response to terrorist violence. Yet, if former National Security Advisor and US Secretary of State Condoleezza Rice is correct in the view that the United States cannot be "the 9/11 for the world," then it must also be true that moderate Muslims cannot be responsible for policing wayward Muslims the likes of whom include Libya's Muammar Gadhafy, Iraq's Saddam Hussein, and Abu Bakar al-Baghdadi, a one-time inmate imam at the US-run prison camp known as Camp Bucca, in Iraq. Islamist militants incarcerated in Guantánamo Bay Cuba have been known to reappear on the battlefield as US adversaries after securing their release from the US-run Guantánamo Bay prison. A better remedy for ending terrorist violence in retrospect might be to eliminate the circumstances giving rise to its existence in the first instance. The United States must stop producing, arming, and supporting individuals whose long-term costs, in terms of death, destruction, and ultimately wars (e.g., as seen in the case of Baghdadi and Saddam) often outweigh any short-term benefits the United States may have accrued from such partnerships in the first instance.

THE SPECIAL CASE OF CARLOS THE JACKAL

While much is known of "black Muslim" champion, Malcolm X (d. 1965) in the United States, little is known of the Islamist once known as "Carlos the Jackal," though he is regarded by many to be the most notorious terrorist of the 1960s and 1970s. Both Malcolm X and Carlos were third world revolutionary nationalists with prison backgrounds. They espoused an ideology of Islamism with roots in the revolutionary nationalism associated with Fidel Castro, Che Guevara, and Franz Fanon, inspired as much by the principles of Islam as by the principles of Marx. This ideological background combined with the experience of prison Islam is a common feature among contemporary

Islamist militants, which perhaps warrants special mention of the man once known as "Carlos the Jackal" who may be the perfect living embodiment of this feature. The exploits of Carlos the Jackal were widely reported in the media in the 1960s and 1970s before his arrest in 1994, though little is known of his ties to Islam or Islamism. His parents were Marxists. His father was a wealthy communist lawyer who gave each of his three sons the name of the Russian revolutionary communist leader Vladimir Illych Lenin. Mamdani acknowledges similarities in the ideology of anti-western nationalism of the Cold War era and contemporary Islamist militants. There is a tendency perhaps unsurprisingly for revolutionary nationalists-turned-Islamist militants like Carolos the Jackal to treat religion as a tool of revolution instead of revolution as a tool of religion. Carolos may also be illustrative of the role of seventeenth-century allies of Islamist known as corsairs and privateers, discussed in chapter 6.

"Carlos" (Illich Ramirez Sanchez) is described as being born on October 12, 1949. Two days after visiting the African of state of Sudan for a minor testicular operation, local Sudanese authorities conspired, secretly, with French officials to arrest the Venezuelan on August 14, 1994. After being tried and convicted of murder in France in December of 1997, he was sentenced to life in prison. He apparently converted to Islam in 2001 and later appealed his sentence. He married his lawyer Isabelle Coutan-Peyre in a Muslim ceremony and published the book *Revolutionary Islam* in which he voiced support for Osama bin Laden. He apparently remains married to Isabelle Coutan-Peyre. Prior to his arrest, he was an avowed leftist member of the radical Popular Front for the Liberation of Palestine (PFLP). CNN Terrorism Consultant Peter Bergen on March 22, 2016, estimated France's Muslim population to be roughly 10 percent of the total population yet roughly 70 percent of its prison population.[100] Malcom X and Carlos the Jackal may be examples of the narrative promoted by Mamdani that third world nationalist leaders and movements once seen as "proxy wars" supported by the Soviets have been replaced by Islamists as the chief opponent of the West in the WOT.

But this idea seems more a matter of historical interpretation than one of proven fact. Mamdani's account of the roots of contemporary terror springing from the end of the Cold War in form of the Afghan jihad seems more compelling than the "culture talk" or "clash of civilizations" argument espoused by Lewis and Huntington. Nevertheless, the suggestion by Mamdani that Muslim terror begin in the mountains of Tora Bora in Afghanistan, orchestrated by the CIA in the form of the Afghan jihad ignores the long and modestly well-documented history of intermittent corsair and privateer warfare between Christian and Muslim nations detailed in chapter 6 of this study.

DISTINCTIVE FEATURES OF TERRORISM IN AFRICA

The foregoing discussion of terrorism in Africa defies popular myths and stereotypes about the importance and significance of Africa and Africans in the realm of Islamist militancy. But what more can be said about terrorism among Africans? What are its distinguishing features as compared to other instances of terrorism found elsewhere in the world? How significant is terrorism in Africa and what insights might be offered to halt its spread? How might African terrorists as seen in ISIS and al-Qaeda propaganda videos threatening the United States be avoided? This section attempts to answer these questions. Terrorism among Africans displays the following distinct features: (1) ideological fluidity, (2) rampant opportunism, (3) interregional raiding, (4) a near rather than far enemy emphasis, (5) Pan-Islamist orientation, and (6) roving fluidity.

From the outset, it is important to remember Reno's reminder that "generalizing about recent wars and their global connections in a continent as diverse as Africa is a tricky business."[101] Even the seemingly safe generalization that remote locations associated with Africa's sparse and inaccessible areas make it ideal for terrorism have been challenged by one study which asserts that getting to the area controlled by Boko Haram "is actually fairly straightforward, in good times at least."[102] But while areas in Africa as seen in the Sahel may pose a formidable physical challenge especially for outsiders, areas South of Lake Chad, the Mandara mountain region, and Sambisa forest where Boko Haram resides given the area's history of slave raiding, banditry, and weak state control, may pose a social challenge every bit as forbidding as the physical conditions of the Sahel. Yet, it is still true that "most wars in Africa since 2000 have been fought across regions rather than solely within states, and thus are inherently international wars."[103] This mostly international character of Africa's recent wars (and violence) is a product of many factors, including Africa's weak states, weak militaries, porous borders, and opportunistic political actors. Examples include "multiple armed groups inside Somalia's borders, some linked to ethnic kinsmen across borders and most pursuing global connections."[104] Others include states witnessing drug trafficking and armed clashes as seen in Guinea-Bissau.[105]

The international goals of actors in the region, whether the interventionist agendas of AU, AMISOM, or the UN, drug traffickers, or Islamists foster a degree of international-ness as unique to Africa as they are inevitable to the actors. Yet, "civilians in war zones are likely to suffer from chronic insecurity amid the collapse of effective central state authority" with many becoming refugees or internally persons displaced, driven into the arms of "an international system of humanitarian aid and crisis management," that often aggravates rather than eliminates the problem.[106] For example, CAR, described as the "world champion of hosting international peacekeeping missions," has arguably had more international interventions than anywhere else, yet remains nearly last in virtually every development indicator.[107] International peacekeepers' ability to carry out their main charge of peacekeeping as seen in their failure to eliminate violence against Muslims in CAR and their alleged involvement in commodity smuggling and teenage pregnancies in CAR and the DRC has led one expert to conclude "the primary beneficiaries of aid are the aid-givers themselves."[108]

Ideological Fluidity

The ideological fluidity of terrorism among Africans is perhaps best seen in the 2015 announced allegiance of Boko Haram to ISIS and its Caliph, Abu Bakar al-Baghdadi of Raqqa'. Recent reports suggest that a split has emerged in Boko Haram's ranks between those who continued to following Abubakar Shekau and others more aligned with ISIS, though other reports that both leaders have long since been killed. But another illustration of ideological fluidity is the near wholesale shift of at least four previously aligned al-Qaeda affiliated groups in Mali to allegiance with ISIS, prior to the terrorist attack on the Radisson Hotel in Bamako, Mali, on November 20, 2015. Unlike the US mindset during the first ten years of the WOT that seemed fix on al-Qaeda and Osama bin Laden, African terrorist groups in 2015 are far more free flowing in terms of their political allegiances.

Rampant Opportunism

African terrorist groups are heavily dependent on money generated from the ransom of kidnapped Europeans, the ransom of others including Chinese and South Koreans, drug and human trafficking across the Sahara desert, and banditry. The ambush of four US soldiers in Niger in 2017 according to some accounts resulted from a diverted mission to capture and/or kill Doundou Chefou, a terrorist leader suspected of kidnapping a US aid worker. Like other terrorist groups, African Islamist militants may have turned to kidnapping in an effort to capitalize on resources at their disposal given their location and economic circumstance. For years the Taliban of Afghanistan levied taxes on Afghanistan's large and lucrative opium-heroin trade. ISIS made similar use of petroleum revenues available to it in regions it once controlled in Iraq and Syria.

Lacking these resources, African Islamist militants with allegiance to al-Qaeda or ISIS may have turned to kidnapping, trafficking, and banditry as alternatives. Perhaps for this reason, kidnapping in the Sahel region of Africa became a lucrative enterprise for AQIM. For example, a kidnapping spree of

European tourists by AQIM emerged from 2003 to 2009 involving Osama bin Laden Afghan associates active in the Sahel who were also graduates of the Afghan jihad. These associates believed to be from the Sahel with reputations for cold-blooded killing included the likes of Abdelmalek el-Para, Abdelmalek Droukdal, Mohktar Belmohktar, and Abdelhamid Abu Zeid. Droukdal singled out France as "Islam's enemy number one."[109]

Interregional Raiding

Although some of their victims secured their release, others like a British citizen named Edwin Dyer were executed. A former member of the Armed Islamic Group, Abdelhamid Abu Zeid according to one account, was particularly well known for his cold-bloodedness. Among the few hostages who met him and lived to talk about it described him as a calculating, cerebral man, respected by his troops and devoted to his cause. The Frenchman, Pierre Cammette, held for three months in northern Mali by Abu Zeid said, he "always spoke to me in a neutral tone, without aggression. His questions were almost technical."[110] An aging French relief worker named Michel Germaneau was kidnapped in Niger and held for several months. Germaneau became sick after being denied his medication by his kidnappers who refused to accept its delivery.

He eventually died after being dragged to his death by captors as they fled a joint Franco-Mauritanian force launched along the Mali-Mauritanian border seeking his recapture.[111] Five French nationals and two other employees of the French conglomerate, Areva, and its affiliate, Satom, were kidnapped by Abu Zeid in September 2010. Three of the hostages were released including a French woman, Françoise Larribe and two non-French citizens after a generous ransom—rumored to be 10 to 15 million Euros—was paid. Meanwhile, a separate rescue effort went terribly wrong on January 7, 2011, when two young Frenchmen, Vincent Delory and Antoine de Léocour, were kidnapped at gunpoint from a restaurant in Niamey, the capital of Niger.[112]

A Near Rather Than Far Enemy Emphasis

Although this feature makes African terrorists more closely akin to bandits than terrorists, it would be a mistake to think of Islamist militants in the Sahel as simply drug smugglers as many are unwilling to engage directly in the drug trade.[113] Shabab terrorist skill at "killing on the cheap" may be a further environmental adaptation. Since being driven from their base in Mogadishu by AU forces backed by the United States when Shabab's predecessor, the Islamic Courts Union, may represent the most straightforward form of resistance authorized in the Qur'an when resistance takes the form of retaliatory but measured raiding. But the group's killing of innocent civilians, other Muslims, and other excesses go far beyond the dictums of the Qur'an, to lead even Osama bin Laden, to distance themselves from Shabab before his death in 2011. This al-Shabab to distinguish Muslims from non-Muslims in its killing after joining al-Qaeda in 2012. Shabab may be the only terrorist group denied al-Qaeda affiliation due to its violence!

The other group, Boko Haram, with perhaps an even greater penchant for excessive violence, appears to have experienced at least two splits after 2015. The first split from the original group led by Abubakar Shekau produced the splinter Ansaru. Its leader Mamman Nur is described as the mastermind of the 2011 bombing of UN headquarters in Abuja, the capital of Nigeria. Nur is a Cameroonian with significant ties to other international terrorist groups. He is also known as Abu Usamatul al-Ansari and believed to have ties to AQIM, al-Shabab, al-Qaeda Central (Majao) and other militant groups in Africa and quite possibly central Asia.[114] Another terrorist group known to have split off from Abubakar Shekau's group primarily due to the latter's excessive violence against fellow Muslims is the Islamic State of the Province of West Africa (ISIS-WA) led by Abu Musab al Barnabi, the twenty-three-year-old son of Boko Haram founder Mohammed Yusuf. Perhaps as many as 400 Boko Haram militants may have been killed in 2017–2018 from factional in-fighting. Using tactics associated with Abubakar al-Shekau's more violent Boko Haram faction, "copy-cat" motives were used to describe the kidnapping of 110 schoolgirls from the Dapchi Girls Science and Technical College in northern Nigeria on February 19, 2018. Nearly all of the girls were returned unharmed after one month on March 19, 2018, by the ISIS-WA faction of Boko Haram led by al Barnabi. A ransom in the millions was likely paid.

Pan-Islamist Ideology

Islamist militants among Africans are most likely to welcome alliances with other militant groups like al-Qaeda or ISIS out of a general commitment to Pan-Islamist ideology, but only up to a point. A similar commitment is difficult to find among ISIS as the group tends to maintain a hostile position toward others, Muslim and non-Muslim, who fail to share its ideology. African Islamists in general tend to resist this practice by forming alliances with other militants and coordinating their strategies where possible. Moreover, the dominant tendency displayed by Islamist militants among Africans is to focus greater attention on the "near enemy" of local African governments than on the "far enemy" of the West. This practice contrasts with Middle East terrorists groups like al-Qaeda and its affiliates who concentrate more on far enemy targets in the West.

Roving Fluidity

No other characteristic of terrorism in Africa is as distinctive as its roving fluidity. Unlike terrorism elsewhere in the world, terrorists in Africa strike at will only to melt away in porous surroundings, impervious to the weak state authority of the modern African state. Similar to their better-known counterparts in the Middle East, they prefer to let their bullets "do the talking" to fortify their mystique and stealth-like capacity. Geographic proximity lured Islamist militants from immigrant communities in Europe. But by the time this pattern was fully recognized it was already too late. The terrorist attacks throughout the region of the Sahel throughout the years 2015 through 2018 in Mali, Burkina Faso, and the Ivory Coast most likely by AQIM received little or no attention in the United States. This violence includes multiple attacks on the French embassy in Ouagadougou deliberately targeting the French for retaliation.

The Ouagadougou attack reflects the all too common pattern of ineffective local first responders to terrorist attacks in Africa. The boldness of the attackers launched most likely from Mali, which shares a border with Burkina Faso questions whether or not France controls the region adjacent to the Sahara desert known as the Sahel or "border" in Arabic. A terrorist attack on a tourist resort in Bamaka, Mali, was reported as late as June 2017 with little or no fanfare. A German helicopter that crashed in late July 2017 over Mali may have been the work of terrorists. Porous borders and vast barren stretches provide the perfect match for the roving fluidity of terrorism in this part of the world.

Underscoring the inconclusiveness of the WOT in Africa is the evolving challenge of Boko Haram militancy in Nigeria and surrounding areas. Although Boko Haram by 2015 changed its name to the Islamic State in the Province of West Africa, reflecting its newly acquired allegiance to ISIS and dropping some of its previously held idiosyncratic features such as publicly aired rants and taunts by its leader, Abubakar Shekau. Exploiting Africa's porous borders, Boko Haram extended its bloody campaign into neighboring Cameroon, Chad, and Niger in 2016. Capitalizing on Nigerians' deep fear of the group, Boko Haram was believed to be entrenched in the Sambisa Forest of northeastern Nigeria before Nigerian President Buhari's Christmas Day announcement that the group had been driven from its base and "technically defeated," according to Mr. Buhari.

Three women suicide bombers posing as refugees attacked a refugee camp in northeastern Nigeria in January 2016. Two of the women reportedly ignited suicide vests while a third failed to ignite her vest after allegedly recognizing her mother and sibling among the refugees in the camp. The attack killed sixty and wounded at least seventy-eight. Some observers estimate the Boko Haram refugee population to be at least 2.5 million. Nigerian officials claim as many as 1,000 women and girls were rescued from the village of

Boboshe and taken to the Dikwa camp after being used as sex slaves by Boko Haram fighters. But as of August 2017, at least 100 of the 276 Chibok girls remained missing. The Dikwa refugee camp which housed over 7,000 in 2015 reached over 80,000 in 2016. Because Boko Haram like ISIS of Iraq and Syria surrounds itself with "human shields," military rescue has been all but impossible. Islamists militants pose special threats to western authorities not unlike threats witnessed in other violent encounters with Islamist militants. One media account recently acknowledged that many western countries are financing "jihad" in regions that include Mali where al-Qaeda groups (e.g., AQIM) still predominate, although governments including the United States have been understandably reluctant to admit it.[115] President Obama announced plans to send an additional hundred troops to Niger to shore up US troop presence at a newly established drone base for unarmed Predator aircraft conducting surveillance in the region. The new base located near the Nigerian capital of Niamey illustrates the Obama and Trump administrations' desire to extend great assistance to Africa in the US-led WOT.

This chapter specifically explores (1) "A 'Good Muslim, Bad Muslim' Device"; (2) "The Mysterious Crash of Air Algérie Flight 5017"; (3) "Africa's Slow-Motion Disasters"; (4) "With Friends Like These . . ."; (5) "Shabab and Its Contenders"; (6) "Africa's Anti-Terrorism Politics"; (7) "Africa's Other Terrorist Groups"; (8) "#BringBackOurGirls"; (9) "The Special Case of Carlos the Jackal"; and (10) "Distinctive Features of Terrorism in Africa."

The following chapter examines the phenomenon of non-terrorist Muslim struggle (*jihad*).

NOTES

1. Louis Brenner, ed., *Muslim Identity and Social Change in Sub-Saharan Africa* (Bloomington: Indiana University Press, 1993), 1 introduction.

2. Brian Beary, "Terrorism in Africa," in *Global Issues: Selections from CQ Research*, chapter 3 (Los Angeles: Sage/CQ Press, 2017), 57–83.

3. Despite this chapter's discussion of terrorism as it relates to Africa over the past several years, this study as a whole examines both Muslim struggle (*jihad*) and Jihad as an instrument of terror stretching over a much longer expanse of time and beyond the strict boundaries of Africa as a continent.

4. See Elizabeth Schmidt, *Foreign Intervention in Africa: From the Cold War to the War on Terror* (New York: Cambridge University Press, 2013).

5. See Mahmood Mamdani, *Good Muslim Bad Muslim* (New York: Doubleday, 2005), 21–24.

6. Ibid., 14, 15, and 24.

7. Ibid., 50.

8. Ibid.

9. This event like so many others related to Africa received only scant coverage in the media despite considerable international attention devoted to it internationally in the news media.

10. "Air Algérie Jet Crashes In North Mali," *Wall Street Journal*, July 25, 2014. "Weather Suspected, in Algérie Plane Wreck, 116 People Feared Dead," *New York Times*, July 25, 2014.

11. Ibid.

12. Ibid.

13. Ibid.

14. "Was 2014 the Deadliest Year in Aviation History?" *The Telegraph Travel News*, December 29, 2014. http://www.telegraph.co.uk/travel/news/Was-2014-th e-deadliest-year-in-aviation-history/, also see "Is 2014 the Deadliest Year for Flights? Not Even Close," *CNN*, July 28, 2017. http://www.cnn.com/interactive/2014/07/t ravel/aviation-data/.

15. Weather Suspected, in Air Algérie Plane Wreck, 116 People Feared Dead, *New York Times*, July 25, 2014.

16. "Pentagon Asks Why a Mission Turned Deadly," *New York Times*, October 6, 2017.

17. Christopher S. Chivvis, *The French War On Al Qa'ida in Africa* (New York: Cambridge University Press, 2016), 3 and 61.

18. Ibid., 4.

19. Ibid., 93.

20. Ibid.

21. Ibid.

22. Ibid., 2.

23. Ibid., 3.

24. Ibid., 7.

25. Ibid.

26. Ibid., 152–153.

27. Ibid., 58.

28. Ibid., 58–59.

29. Ibid., 59.

30. Ibid., 63.

31. Ibid., 62.

32. Ibid., 152.

33. Ibid.

34. Ibid., 153.

35. Ibid.

36. Ibid.

37. Samuel Oyewole, "Rescuing Boko Haram's Schoolgirl Victims," *New Zeland International Review*, vol. 41, no. 1, 2016, 25–28.

38. See D. M. Anderson and J. McKnight, "Understanding al-Shabaab: Clan, Islam and Insurgency in Kenya," *Journal of Eastern African Studies*, vol. 9, no. 3, 2015, 536–557. Mohamed Ibrahim, "Somalia and Global Terrorism: A Growing Connection?" *Journal of Contemporary African Studies*, vol. 27, no. 3, 2010, 283–289.

39. See Hrach Gregorian and Ricardo Laremont, "Political Islam in West Africa and the Sahel," *Military Review*, vol. 86, no. 1, 2006, 29 and "The Danger in the Desert, Jihad in Africa," *The Economist*, vol. 26, no. 8820, 2013, 21 and Anthony N. Celso, "Al Qaeda in the Maghreb: "The Newest" Front in the War on Terror," *Mediterranean Quarterly*, vol. 19, no. 1, 2008, muse.jhu.edu/article1232388.

40. Jodi Vittori, Kristin Bremer, and Pasqale Vittori, "Briefing: The Myth of Global Islamic Terrorism and Local Conflict in Mali and the Sahel," *African Affairs*, vol. 112, no. 448, 2003.

41. "Kenyan Crackdown Strikes Anger, Militancy, Young Muslims Respond With Violence to Arrests, Killings, in Campaign Against Extremists: I Was Treated as a Terrorist," *Wall Street Journal*, February 10, 2015.

42. Edward Mogire and Kennedy Mkutu Agade, "Counter-Terrorism in Kenya," *Journal of Contemporary African Studies,* vol. 29, no. 4, 2011.

43. Difficult as it may be to imagine other states in Africa may have even worse records as seen in the state of Gabon in central Africa whose current President Mr. Ali Bongo (a Muslim) and his father Omar Bongo together have ruled for more than 30 years. Another well-known case of entrenched authoritarian rule involves African autocrat, President Hastings Kamuzu Banda, of Malawi, who was Malawi's first and for many years, only President (1963–1993). After Mr. Banda anointed himself "President for Life," he remained in office until falling ill in 1993. Hastings Kamuzu Banda (1898–1997) died at age 99. See BBC News Profile http://www.bbc.com/news/world-africa-13881367.

44. Chivvis, *The French War on Al-Qa'ida in Africa*, 67–70.

45. Ibid., 68.

46. Ibid., 67–70.

47. Ibid.

48. See Vijay Mahajan, *Africa Rising: How 900 Million African Consumers Offer More than You Think* (Upper Saddle River, NJ: Pearsons Education Inc., 2009).

49. Robert E. Edgerton, *Africa's Armies: From Honor to Infamy: From 1791 to the Present* (Boulder, CO: Westview Pub., 2002), 181.

50. Ibid.

51. William Reno, "The International Factor in African Warfare," in John W. Harbeson and Donald Rothchild (eds.), *Africa in World Politics: Constructing Political and Economic Order* (Boulder, CO: Westveiw Press, 2017), 135–155.

52. A January report identifies Mamman Nur a Boko Haram affiliate and founder of the Islamist militant Group, Ansaru, as the mastermind of the 2011 UN bombing in Abuja, Nigeria. Nur, also known as Abu Usmatul al-Ansari is described as a Cameroonian with significant international contacts. See *Boko Haram: The History of Africa's Most Notorious Terrorist Group* (Lexington, KT: The Charles River Editors, 2017), 29.

53. See Thom, *African Wars*.

54. Anneli Botha, "Political Socialization and Terrorist Radicalization Among Individuals Who joined Al-Shabaab in Kenya," *Studies in Conflict and Terrorism*, vol. 37, no. 11, 2014, 895–919.

55. "Kenyan Crackdown Stokes Anger, Militancy: Young Muslims Respond With Violence to Arrests, Killings in Campaign Against Extremists; 'I Was Treated as a Terrorist,'" *Wall Street Journal*, February 10, 2015.

56. Scott MacEachern, *Searching For Boko Haram: A History of Violence in Central Africa* (New York: Oxford University Press, 2018), 12–13.

57. Ibid., 12.

58. Ibid., 13.

59. Ibid., 14.

60. Ibid., 12–13.

61. Ibid., 14–15.

62. Ibid.

63. Ibid., 15.

64. Ibid.

65. "On Terror's New Front Line, Mistrust Blunts US Strategy," *Wall Street Journal*, February 27, 2013.

66. "Military in Nigeria Is Accused of Abuses," *New York Times*, June 4, 2015.

67. Ibid.

68. I. William Zartman, "The Diplomacy of African Conflicts," in John W. Harbeson and Donald Rothchild (eds.), *Africa in World Politics: Constructing Political and Economic Order* (Boulder, CO: Westview Press, 2017), 233–234.

69. Louisa Lombard, *State of Rebellion: Violence and Intervention in the Central African Republic* (Chicago, IL: The University of Chicago Press, originally published by Zed Publishers of London, 2016), 18.

70. Ibid., 211.

71. Ibid., 19.

72. Ibid., 18.

73. Ibid., 18–19.

74. Ibid., 19.

75. Ibid., 93–94.

76. Ibid., 24.

77. Ibid.

78. Ibid.

79. Ibid., 24–25.

80. Ibid., 16–17.

81. Ann Elizabeth Mayer, *Islam and Human Rights: Tradition and Politics* (Boulder, CO: Westview Press, 1995), 163–165.

82. Ibid., 200.

83. Ibid. For a fascinating yet chilling account of colonialism in the former Belgium Congo, see Adam Hochschild, *King Leopold's Ghost: A Story of Greed, Terror and Heroism in Colonial Africa* (New York: Houghton Mifflin Co., 2006).

84. Ibid., 73.

85. Ibid., 66.

86. Ibid.

87. Ibid.

88. Ibid., 182.

89. Ibid.

90. Ibid., 92.

91. Ibid., 93.

92. Ibid., 94.

93. Ibid., 184–85.
94. Ibid., 206.
95. Ibid., 186–87.
96. Ibid., 202.
97. Ibid., 204.
98. Ibid., 205.
99. Bob Koigi, "Merkel's Africa Visit Provides Mixed Reaction," EURACTIV. de https://www.euractiv.com/section/development-policy/news/merkels-africa-vis it-provokes-mixed- reaction/.
100. BBC News, "Jackal Book Praises Bin Laden," June 26, 2003, http://news. bbc.co.uk/2/hi/3022358.stm; Also, see Muslim Worldwide, "Famous Muslim: Carlos the Jackal," November 22, 2013, and "Illich Ramirez Sanchez, known as Carlos the Jackal, Appeals Life Sentence," *The World Post: A Partnership of the Huffington Post*, April 3, 2014.
101. William Reno, "The International Factor in African Warfare," in John W. Harbeson and Donald Rothchild (eds.), *Africa in World Politics: Engaging a Changing Global Order* (Boulder, CO: Westview Press, 2017), 150.
102. MacEachern, *Searching for Boko Haram*, "Introduction," 1.
103. Ibid., 151.
104. Ibid.
105. Ibid.
106. Ibid.
107. Lombard, *State of Rebellion*, 213.
108. Ibid., 227.
109. Chivvis, *The French War on Al-Qa'ida in Africa,* 21, 25, 30, and 31.
110. Ibid., 30.
111. Ibid., 31.
112. Ibid.
113. Ibid., 29.
114. Charles River Editors, *Boko Haram: The History of Africa's most Notorious Terrorist Group*, 29–30.
115. See "Paying Ransoms Europe, Bankrolls Qaida Terror," *New York Times*, July 19, 2014. https://www.nytimes.com/.../ransoming-citizens-europe-becomes-al-qaedas-patron.ht.

Chapter 2

Muslim Struggle (*jihad*) and Africa

This chapter explores (1) "Important Distinctions"; (2) "The Islamist Continuum"; (3) "Contemporary Episodes of Muslim Struggle (*jihad*)"; (4) "West African Resistance and Reform Movements"; (5) "The Special Case of Nigeria"; and (7) "General Features of Muslim Struggle (*jihad*)." It also identifies ways to diminish if not eliminate terrorist violence among Africans by distinguishing more carefully what we mean by the labels we use like "jihadist," "jihadism,"and "radical Islamist terrorists." Its central aim is to distinguish Islamist terrorist violence from legitimate Muslim struggle (*jihad*). While Islamist militants are inspired by Islam, they do not always adhere to the religion of Islam in a strict sense. In fact, nothing in the history of Islam or in the Qur'an or Sunnah requires an Islamist when serving in the capacity of helper (*al-Ansar*) or ally to be a Muslim. Throughout Islamic history there have been many examples of helpers or allies of the Muslim community (*ummah*) and therefore of Islam. But helpers or allies are rarely seen as believers in the same sense as the 1.8 billion Muslims that comprise the bulk of the mainstream Islamic community (*ummah*). Postmodern Islamism with its roots in the 1970s is a relatively new phenomenon described in the literature as "a generic concept referring to Muslim individuals, movements and organizations embracing Islam as an ideology and comprehensive way of life." Ideally, an Islamist seeks to establish Islamic law (*shari'ah*) as the basis for Islamic societies and states,[1] as seen in parts of northern Nigeria and Sudan in communities like Kano and Omdurman where Islamic law (*shari'ah*) prevails. Yet, despite the relatively recent emergence of postmodern Islamism, inter- and intra-religious conflict continue to exist among Africans as seen for instance in Nigeria, Mali, Somalia, and Kenya.

IMPORTANT DISTINCTIONS

One of the most common errors made by critics of Islamism has been wide-spread use of the words "jihadist" and "jihadism," to refer to a terrorist extremist instead of the term "*Khawār'ij.*" This term when used by Arabs/ Muslims denotes those who secede, rebel, revolt, or otherwise break away from the mainstream Muslim community (*ummah*) as seen in the case of ISIS/ISIL.[2] Instead of *Khawār'ij*, some westerners prefer the phrase "radical Islamic extremism." But much to the chagrin of his opponents, who flaunted its use, President Obama avoided the use of this expression. Because Muslims believe there is nothing Islamic about the words radical or extremist, many Muslims avoid their use as adjectives of Islam. Although, the intent behind using these words for many Americans may be innocent, their impact can be devastating nonetheless, as they undermine the conservative sensibilities of most Muslims and insult the religion of Islam. The more accurate and less pejorative phrase for "jihadist" is "Islamist militant" (or militant Islamist). This phrase is routinely used in the British press and therefore throughout most of the English-speaking world, though it is infrequently used in the United States for reasons that are not entirely clear. For this reason, a notation of this disparity at the very least seems warranted.

Why the distinction? "Jihad" is the Arabic word for striving or struggle. It represents an essential Islamic institution and sacred obligation for *all* Muslims, not just for Islamist militants who emphasize it. For Muslims, it may serve as a tool for mobilizing the individual or community at large, to retaliate against a perceived enemy. But the term was never meant to be used as a synonym for violence per se, though violence has most certainly been one of its many forms. Most Americans treat the word "jihadist" as though it were a synonym for terrorist. However, because all Muslims embrace Muslim struggle (*jihad*) as a sacred institution and personal obligation its use in this way is incorrect. Although this may not be the word's intended meaning, when used in this way, it nevertheless ignores the sentiments of 1.8 billion Muslims around the world. Because of this, the Islamist militant responds as though this were an attack on Islam by the opponents of Islam. Terms like "jihadist" and crusades invoke strongly negative feelings among African and other Muslims. For Muslims, words matter. Consistency between words and deeds is important. When a pattern of inconsistency occurs between one's words and deeds, the word "hypocrite," frequently used in the Qur'an, is whispered in private by Muslims.

Similar to patterns observed by Jervis in chapter 1, it is one thing when inconsistencies are the result of random error(s). But when they occur as a part of a pattern of behaviors routinely displayed over a period of time as seen for example in patterns of behavior characterized as racist, sexist,

Islamophobic, xenophobic, or homophobic, it is difficult to dismiss them as random mistakes. US policy makers are well aware of the valuable support they receive from mainstream Muslim allies like the Saudis and the Chadians without whose contribution the WOT would be difficult to sustain. Accordingly, the failure to distinguish terms like "jihadists" and "jihadism" from legitimate Muslim struggle (*jihad*) may undermine the unity needed to maintain support among allies in the ongoing WOT.

The chapter 6 discussion of sixteenth- and seventeenth-century corsairs and privateers examines Islamist militants fighting on the side of North African Muslim states, who terrorized and plundered enemy vessels at sea under the flag(s) of Muslim nations for gold and booty. They captured mostly Europeans for enslavement, ransom, and incorporation into the Muslim community (*ummah*). These corsairs and privateers are reminders of the longstanding presence of Islamist militancy as a nemesis of the West. These actions bear some resemblance to contemporary Islamist militancy among Africans. Because Muslim nations of the Mediterranean benefitted from the services of sixteenth- and seventeenth-century corsairs and privateers as promoters of the international political interests of Muslims and the broader interests of Islam, they provide vivid examples of the historical role of Islamist militancy and its links to mainstream Muslims as morally contradictory, as this may be. Christian *and* Muslim nations made similar use of corsairs and privateers and benefited from their actions and activities. But just as it is erroneous to dismiss Islamist militants during the age of empire of having ties to North African Muslim nations like Morocco and Libya (formerly Tripoli), it is equally erroneous to dismiss postmodern Gulf Coast Council (GCC) states from significant though often illicit ties to al-Qaeda and ISIS. It is equally erroneous to view Islamist militant groups as "cults" as does one non-scholarly study (2016) given the ISIS' well-known goal and experience of governing and controlling territory. While "cults" may engage in similar activities as terrorist groups, it is doubtful that the former do so at a level comparable to that of the latter.

The Islamist militant may not be a good Muslim in the strict Islamic sense. Indeed, some may be "nominal," at best. Moreover, when the Islamist militant is a practitioner of what penal expert Mark Hamm (2013) describes as "prison Islam" or serves as a fighter (*mujahedeen*) on the "front lines" in the WOT, they may be even less religiously observant.[3] Similar to situations found in comparable western settings, the Qur'anic virtues of forgiveness, tolerance, and patience are not likely to be found in great abundance among the *mujahedeen*, corsair, privateer, or practitioner of "prison Islam." Islamist militants function more as allies or "helpers" (*al-ansar*), than as fully practicing Muslims. A complicating factor for the non-Muslim observer seeking to understand this phenomenon has been the reluctance of mainstream Muslims to label another person a "non-Muslim" even when the person's behavior diverges substantially from acceptable Muslim behavior. Mainstream Muslims are reluctant to label a person a "non-Muslim" as the label may be false, leading the labeler to be guilty of slander, a sin in Islam and a crime that can be punishable by death as seen in the Charlie Hebdo executions in Paris of 2015. Because no one can know the contents of another person's heart with certainty, no one can know the relationship another person may have with his Creator. According to one study, "the Prophet Muhammad himself is supposed to have said [in a hadith] that if a Muslim accuses another professing Muslim of being an unbeliever, the accuser is the closest to unbelief."[4]

Even when attempts to do so are based on inferences derived from visible observations of the person's actions corroborated by the testimony of other observers, most Muslims believe it is unwise to declare another person a "non-Muslim." Muslims believe God (Allah) forgives whomsoever God (Allah) pleases including the sinner whose last cries for forgiveness may be heard and answered upon his or her deathbed. Hence, rather than declare a person a disbeliever (*al-Kafir*) for their seemingly aberrant behavior, observant Muslims prefer to assert (modestly) the obvious and more defensible point that the actions of Islamist militants may not be fully consistent with the teachings of Islam. Despite this moral restraint, denouncing others as non-Muslim was witnessed during the 1980s and 1990s among some Sufis of Nigeria who accused Yan Izala revivalists of being non-Muslims for their violent acts.[5] The Boko Haram practice of denouncing all persons who failed to share their beliefs provides another illustration of this behavior. The following statement by Boko Haram leader, Abubakar Shekau, provides illustration of this view.

For example, Boko Haram leader, Abubakar Shekau, according to one source claimed, I am going to kill all the imams and other Islamic clerics in Nigeria because they support democracy and constitution and therefore are not Muslims.[6]

The confession of faith, that is, belief in one God (*Allah*) and acceptance of Muhammad as his Prophet (*shahadah*) are the minimum requirements of faith in Islam. Anyone who does this with sincerity is treated as Muslim by the community (*ummah*). Also, adherence to the five pillars of Islam, namely, (1) the confession of faith (*shahadah*), (2) prayer (*siyam*) five times daily, (3) fasting during the month of Ramadan, (4) the paying of alms (*zakat*) to the needy, and (5) performing the annual pilgrimage (*hajj*) to Mecca at least once in one's lifetime are the minimum requirements for practicing of Islam. Legitimate Muslim struggle (*jihad*) is believed by some and especially Islamist militants to be an effective sixth pillar of Islam. Yet, these simple tasks achieve their ultimate legitimacy when validated by the authoritative sources in Islam of the Qur'an, the tradition (*sunnah*) and the sayings (*hadith*) of the Prophet Muhammad.

Because Islam rest on a complex system of reinforcing beliefs, customs, and laws guided by institutions, like *hijra*, *ummah* and *jihad*, the simplicity displayed in the confession of faith (*shahada*) and the five pillars of Islam can be misleading especially to the unlearned zealot unable to integrate these seemingly simple beliefs and practices into the larger more all-encompassing set of institutions with specific traditions and requirements. An Islamic scholarship derived from fourteen Islamic centuries of Islamic jurisprudence (*fiq*) in four distinct schools of law (*shari'ah*), that is, *Hanafi, Maliki, Shafi* and *Hanbali,* lend further support to the often misleading simplicity of basic Islamic belief and practice.[7] Islamist militancy may bear minimum resemblance to the five pillars of Islam. Islamic practice in the case of some Islamist militants may be minimal to non-existent and rationalized by the perceived need to promote the pressing goal of "jihad" as a matter of community survival. While embracing "jihad" may be laudable in the eyes of some, the Islamist militant often fails to remember that legitimate Muslim struggle (*jihad*) of the classical form has always been constrained by well-known limits outlined in the Qur'an and other authoritative sources. These limits include avoiding aggression, protecting innocent civilians, avoiding the killing of fellow Muslims and resisting unrestrained retaliation, or what Mamdani refers to as "just war" and Scheuer describes as "defensive jihad." The Islamist militant may provide only lip service to the Qur'anic reminder that "to kill a single human is like killing all of humanity while to save a single human being is like saving all of humanity." Boko Haram and Shabab's seemingly random violence against innocent victims, political opponents, and fellow Muslims, for example, are inconsistent with the norms and practices of Muslim struggle (*jihad*).

Of course, the word "Islamic" refers to those things related to or associated with the religion of Islam grounded in the authoritative sources of which includes the Qur'an, the traditions (*sunnah*), and sayings (*hadith*). By contrast, the label Islamist militancy may refer to a very different phenomenon. While the word "Islamic" is primarily a religious referent, the word "Islamist" is primarily a political designation. While the person identified as Islamic shares much in common with Abrahamic or Judeo Christian Islamic faiths, the Islamist militant by contrast is often hostile to these theologically related faiths as perhaps best seen in Islamist militants' vitriol against Jews in Israel, Christians in Egypt, Syria, and Iraq, and Shia Muslims worldwide. The Islamist militant is primarily concerned with promoting Islamic political goals through violence universally condemned by mainstream Muslims throughout Africa. Islamist militancy may be identified with Sunni Islam as seen in the case of Boko Haram, or Shia Islam as seen in the case of Hezbollah. But Islamist militancy's emphasis on the political as seen in Boko Haram's war with the Nigerian government, the tossing of acid in the faces of two women tourists in Zanzibar, and the tossing of acid in the faces of several American women tourists in Marseille, France, in September 2017 by an older woman described as "deranged" suggests adherence to religious orthodoxy by militants may in some instances be entirely nonexistent.

Because of this, it is difficult to see Islamist militancy having any real connection with the religion of Islam, even nominally, as these practices depart
dramatically from the teachings of the authoritative sources of Islam. Perhaps
it is no surprise that Islamist militancy among Africans is frequently associated
with young, poor, urban males often from troubled backgrounds as seem in the
case of Boko Haram leader, Abubakar Shekau. This of course says little about
the Islamist militant's quality of belief, level of sincerity, or commitment to the
Islamist cause. But these descriptions offer clues as to the socioeconomic roots
of the Islamist militant's rage. Where Islamist religious grounding is discern-
able at all, its roots may stem more from experiences in prison, the battlefields
of Syria, Iraq, or Afghanistan, and/or study under a Saudi influenced Islamic
school (*madrassa*). Such is the pedigree of the Islamist militant.

An Islamist militant can be anyone who seeks to advance an Islamic political agenda regardless of how close one adheres to Islamic religious beliefs and
practices. The notorious political assassin Carlos the Jackal captured in the
Sudan, currently serving a life sentence in France and discussed in chapter 1, is
a major case in point. For years, Islamists like the Saudis have been accused of
supporting a broad variety of Islamist activities including support for Muslim
fighters (*mujahedeen*) in Afghanistan and Iraq. The government of Qatar was
accused by the Saudis in 2017 of secretly funding Islamist militants perhaps
ironically following a visit from newly elected US president Trump. Perhaps
the greatest display of selective perception on the part of some Islamists is the
emphasis placed on some verses of the Qur'an while all but ignoring others.
While some Islamist militants emphasize passages from the Qur'an pertaining
to fighting, retaliation, and "striking terror in the hearts of the disbelievers,"
considerably less attention is devoted to equally compelling verses from the
Qur'an related to such things as forgiveness and peacemaking. The end result is
a kind of selective interpretation of Islam that ignores the Qur'an's own warning against embracing some while ignoring other of its verses.[8]

This behavior when combined with the practice of ignoring the authorita-
tive sources, relevant historical circumstances, and the informed opinions of
Islamic scholars renders an Islamic interpretation that departs dramatically
from understandings derived from fourteen centuries of Islam, knowledge
(*ilm*), and Islamic jurisprudence (*fiq*). While the Saudis are unquestionably
Islamists of the non-militant variety at home, outside "the Kingdom" of Saudi
Arabia, they represent the single largest group of foreign fighters in ISIS.
Of course, Wahhabi-Salafist doctrine remains the most recurring ideological
feature of Islamist militancy.[9] As we have seen in chapter 1, Wahhabi-Salafist
doctrines are often at the heart of Islamist terrorist campaigns supported by
Saudi money and opportunities to visit and study in Saudi Arabia virtually
free of charge as seen in the case of Mohammed Yusuf of Nigeria, founder
of Boko Haram.[10]

Western religious scholars frequently use the word "syncretism" to describe Muslim beliefs and practice that appear to combine disparate elements from distinctly different religions. But this is an inaccurate rendering of Islam. As a matter of creed, Muslims accept the divinely inspired truth of all people of the book (*ah l al-kitab*) identified as Jews, Christians, and Muslims. According to the Qur'an: "We make no difference between any of His messengers" (Qur'an 2:285). Jesus, like Muhammad, is considered a man similar to the way Jesus is perceived by Jews. Virtually all the basic teaching of the Abrahamic religions are accepted by Muslims. Such acceptance is part of what it means to be a Muslim as captured by the idea of oneness (*tawhid*) or the indivisibility of God (*Allah*) and his religion. This little-known feature in the West makes allegations of syncretism in Islam inaccurate. Yet, to the chagrin of Christians, Muslims reject the idea of a trinity.

In politically charged situations, like those found in Nigeria, Kenya, and the Central African Republic (CAR), Muslims have been known to manipulate their beliefs, practices, and even their appearances to blur their true religious identity causing a Muslim to appear religiously ambiguous or what GhaneaBassiri describes as adopting "liminal" religious identities. For example, in CAR, Muslims are known to change their names to Christian names to move about more freely and avoid the ubiquitous presence of roadblocks by security officials who in the words of one CAR Muslim "hassle" Muslims. Similar use of roadblocks in Nigeria have helped radicalize Islamists. Religious identity under these circumstances reflects a neither here-nor-there quality of ambiguity seemingly designed to enhance one's chances of surviving repression. This feature reflects the political climate of persecution faced by the fledgling Muslim community (*ummah*) of Mecca during the early years of the Prophet Muhammad. In the words of one observer of dissimulation (*taqiya*), "the greater the repression the thicker the mask."

Shia Muslims, a minority throughout the Islamic world including Saudi Arabia, of necessity make great use of the practice of dissimilation (*taqiya*) which many in the Muslim world believe is allowed by the Qur'anic verse: "*Allah* will not call you to account for what is vain in your oaths, but He will call you to account for what your hearts have earned."[11] This feature is especially valuable in bitterly violent war-torn East and West Africa. According to Shia Imam Jafar, the most noble is the one who practices *taqiya* most. Shia believe that when one fears for one's life, it is permissible to act in ways that may run contrary to one's beliefs for the sake of survival. However, it is also true that dissimulation (*taqiya*) makes it difficult for non-Muslim observers to know where one religious identity begins and another ends.

A famous saying (*hadith*) reminds Muslims: "If you see wrong, change it with you hand, if you cannot do so, change it with your tongue, if you cannot do so, change it with your heart. And this is the lowest test of faith."

In addition to this, the Qur'an states: "But indeed if any do help and defend themselves after a wrong (done) to them, against such there is no cause of blame. The blame is only against those who oppress men with wrong-doing and insolently transgress beyond bounds through the land, defying right and justice; for such there will be a penalty grievous."[12] The right to self-defense is guaranteed by the Qur'an and authoritative sources. But since this may not be clearly known by non-Muslims, its exercise may be indistinguishable from aggression. The expectation to set things right illustrates the activist nature of Islamic belief and practice based the requirement of Muslim struggle (*jihad*). It encourages believers to become involved in the life of this world rather than resort to passive asceticism. The distinction in classical Islam between the greater and lesser *jihad* wherein controlling one's passions is given greater importance than retaliating against an aggressor contradicts the stereotyped perception of Muslims as violent people.

For many in Africa, the "near enemy" takes the form of the modern African state, while the far enemy represents the guarantors of the modern African state, that is, the UN, African Union (AU), the United States, and the former colonial powers. With its strong emphasis on social justice, Eikelman and Piscatori acknowledge correctly that Marxism holds a special appeal to the world's oppressed people and to those sensitive to their suffering. But Marxism is not the only thought concerned with the oppressed[13] for the Qur'an makes frequent references to persecution, oppression, and the downtrodden (*mustada'fin*) and hastens Muslims to adopt strong measures toward combatting it. Eikelman and Piscatori make reference to the Qur'anic verse that states: "And we wished to be Gracious to those who were being depressed in the land to make them leaders (in faith) and make them heirs."[14]

But nowhere in the Qur'an are Muslims granted the license to pronounce other Muslims disbelievers and kill them at will. Nowhere in the Qur'an are Muslim given the right to kill other people of the book, that is, Jews, Christians, and Muslims simply because they hold different beliefs from their own. And nowhere in the authoritative sources are Muslims given the license to commit suicide or plant bombs that indiscriminately kill innocent victims including themselves. Other noteworthy reminders from the Qur'an state, "Oh yea believe! Stand firmly for God as witnesses to fair dealing and let not the hatred of others to you make you swerve to wrong and depart from Justice, that is next to piety: and fear God for God is well acquainted with all that ye do."[15] And on the question of tolerance toward others, the Qur'an is clear (*la ikrha fi deen*), "let there be no compulsion in religion. Truth stands out clearly from error: whosoever rejects evil and believes in God hath grasped the most trustworthy hand-hold that never breaks. And God hearth and knoweth all things"[16]

As it pertains to Islamism in Africa, nowhere in the Qur'an are Muslims given the license to kidnap innocent schoolgirls for marriage and/or enslavement as seen in the deeds, words, and actions of Boko Haram. Nowhere in the Qur'an are Muslims granted the license to invade and kill innocent people at a shopping mall as witnessed in September 2013 attack launched by Shabaab in Nairobi, Kenya. And nowhere in the Qur'an are Muslims given the right to decapitate innocent civilians as seen in Iraq in 2014 and on the streets of London in 2013. No discussion of terrorism versus non-terrorist Muslim struggle is complete without reference to the following controversial passages from the Qur'an:

> Fighting is prescribed for you, and ye dislike it. But it is possible that you dislike a thing which is good for you, and that you love a thing that is bad for you. But God knoweth and you know not.[17]

> Fight in the cause of God those who fight you, But do not transgress limits; For God loveth not transgressors.[18]

> And slay them wherever you catch them, and turn them out from where they have turned you out; for tumult and oppression are worse than slaughter; But fight them not; at the Sacred Mosque, unless they (first) fight you there; But if they fight you, slay them. Such is the reward of those who suppress faith.[19]

> And fight them on until there is no more tumult or oppression and there prevail Justice and faith in God. But if they cease, let there be no hostility except to those who practice oppression.[20]

> Therefore, when ye meet the disbelievers, (in fight) smite their necks, at length, when ye has thoroughly subdued them, bind a bond firmly (on them): thereafter (is the time for) either generosity or ransom: until the war lays down its burdens. Thus (are yea commanded): But if it had been God's Will, He could have Certainly extracted retribution from them (himself); But (he lets you fight) in order to test you, some with others. But those who are slain in the way of God, He will never let their deeds be lost.[21]

The episodes discussed in this chapter of Muslim struggle (*jihad*) contrast sharply with those involving Islamist violence examined in the previous chapter. Episodes of Muslim struggle (*jihad*) represent legitimate religious expressions in contrast to those of terrorist violence perpetrated by Islamist militants among Africans. While terrorist violence among Africans has been linked to the indiscriminate killing of innocent people, Muslim struggle (*jihad*) among Africans against injustice displays a long and brutal history. The historical record challenges the image of Muslim struggle (*jihad*) as an inherently violent, aggressive, xenophobic, anti-Western, and anti-American. Analysis of the episodes and cases discussed in this chapter reveals that more often than not it was other Africans, that is, "wayward" Muslims like the Hausa of nineteenth-century northern Nigeria whose enslavement of fellow (*Fulani*) Muslims sparked the now famous 1802 to 1804 *jihad* of Uthman dan Fodio and the establishment of the Sokoto Caliphate which still survives in contemporary northern Nigeria.

THE ISLAMIST CONTINUUM

Thus far, the discussion in this chapter has focused on differences between Islamist militancy and mainstream Islam. The decision to do so rest on the assumption that these distinctions may be among the most consequential in terms of their impact on the continued survival of the United States-Muslim alliance in the WOT. When some US officials fail to distinguish Islamist militants from mainstream Muslims through promotion of the word "jihadist," misunderstandings emerge. The word "jihadist" when used in this way undermines trust.

Despite this study's focus on terrorist violence among Africans, distinctions among Islamists based on factors other than their attitudes toward violence are also worth mentioning. Indeed, distinguishing Islamist groups on the basis of their political orientations offers insights into the unique character of Islamism among Africans. However, unlike distinctions examined thus far in this chapter, distinctions among Islamists reflect a continuum of Islamist movements rather than entities that lend themselves to strict dichotomous categorization. For example, in the Islamic world at large Islamism and Islamists in the broadest sense include persons who might wish to bring Islamic values, goals, and objectives to bear on everyday living, promote Islam as an ideological alternative to western political ideologies or install Islamic law (*shari'ah*) as the supreme law of the land. Traditionalists in Arabia promote this goal by funding mosque construction throughout the world; Islamist militants promote this goal by spreading terror.

The Seleka of CAR, Shabaab of Somalia, and Al Ansar Din in northern Mali (*Azawad*) are Islamist groups in Africa that display a consistent commitment to terrorist violence. Indirect rule by the British in northern Nigeria allowed colonial powers to "piggy back" onto traditional African authorities in colonial Africa who favored Muslims over other groups.[22] British indirect rule facilitated the survival of Islamist elites like Sheikh Ahmadu Bello in northern Nigeria, while French indirect rule favored the survival of Sultan Muhammad es Sanusi in CAR (until the French later assassinated him). Indirect rule allowed powerful Islamist interest in West Africa to benefit from colonial government preference through displays of favoritism toward Muslims that afforded Islamist elites a measure of autonomy before independence that bolstered Islamist interests for better or worse after independence in Nigeria and CAR, respectively.

Where such arrangements existed, they allowed elite Islamist interests like those of the Hausa of northern Nigeria to survive to a large degree at the expense of non-Muslim group interests as seen in the case of the Igbo of southeastern Nigeria. Even non-elite Muslim ethnic groups like the Kanuri of Chad from whence many Boko Haram members derive and northeastern Nigeria were also placed at a disadvantage, politically. This to a lesser extent appears to also apply to the Fulani although to a far lesser extent as this group over the years has largely though not entirely been absorbed by the Hausa. The Fulani represents the second largest ethnic group present among Boko Haram Islamists. Different still was the relative power position of the Muslims in northern Sudan (compared to that of non-Muslims in the South) following the 1989 coup that brought Islamists to power under the leadership of Hassan al-Turabi, "a mentor" to Osama bin Laden.

These examples illustrate the difficulty involved in generalizing about the role, power, and influence of Islamists among Africans and need to view them along a continuum of characteristics that might include their power, economic status, historical experiences, degree of Islamization, or socio-political cohesion. Despite this study's central focus on terrorist violence among Africans, the foregoing discussion demonstrates how when it comes to Islamists, level of violence is but one of many dimensions or characteristics upon which they may be evaluated. For instance, Islamists may be part of cooperating coalitions of elites as seen in the case of Hassan al-Turabi before his removal by Omar al-Bashir in 1999 or long-term stakeholders of state power as seen in the case of President Muhammadu Buhari of Nigeria and the role of Hausa Muslims in Nigerian society. Islamists, or more accurately the forerunners to postmodern Islamists before the 1970s were powerful stake-holders during periods of indirect rule under African colonialism where some Muslim groups enjoyed limited autonomy as seen in the Sokoto Caliphate of northern Nigeria and the Sanusi sultanate in northern CAR during British and French colonial rule, respectively. However, Islamists may also be the chief opponents to the African state as seen in the case of Somalia, Kenya, Mali, and Niger. Hence, no one form of Islamist sociopolitical group characteristics predominates among Africans.

CONTEMPORARY EPISODES OF MUSLIM STRUGGLE (*JIHAD*)

Several US allies have been discussed thus far representing major players in the US-led coalition against terrorism among Africans. These states in additional to the former European colonial powers include Nigeria, Kenya, Mali, Chad, Cameroon, and Niger. Other states in the region like Djibouti, Ethiopia, and CAR provide primarily logistical and intelligence support to the United States. But without these states, the WOT in Africa could not be sustained. Africa is home to over 1 billion people with Nigeria and Kenya being among the fastest growing populations in the world according to UN estimates. Other allied states in the WOT though considerably smaller in population, for example, Mali, Chad, and Niger are distinguished by their poverty, porous borders, and overwhelmingly Muslim populations exceeding 95 percent of their total populations. It is entirely conceivable that dramatic changes might very well transform these states from cooperating allies to Islamist militant havens. Such a change would be especially tragic were it to result from an entirely avoidable misunderstanding. Such a change might be hastened by a careless use of the words "jihadist" and "jihadism" that sow mistrust among WOT alliance members. This may seem like a none-issue but against the background of longstanding conflict between Muslims and non-Muslims, its potentially negative effects are both real and enormous.[23]

Former President Obama's visit to Africa in 2013 and 2015 revealed how US-African relations though respectful are far from warm. United States-Nigerian relations for example have been decidedly contentious in recent years. Nigeria and Kenya have sizable Muslim populations allowing them to wield significant regional and international influence. Their strategic geographic location in the heart of West and East Africa and growing economic potential are additionally significant factors. But Muslim Africa's current crippling pockets of poverty, political corruption, dismal human rights records, and potential for becoming the newest havens for international terrorism represent major liabilities to the United States and the West. These conditions could lead the remote regions of northeastern Nigeria and the surrounding areas of Niger and Cameroon to become net liabilities in the WOT if their governments fall into the "wrong hands." The former US ambassador to Nigeria describes the situation in the following manner: "if the country has been the 'giant of Africa,' Nigeria's current challenges politically destabilize West Africa, potentially providing a base for jihadist groups hostile to western interests, fueling a humanitarian crisis, and by example discrediting democratic aspirations elsewhere in Africa."[24]

No other state in the coalition against terrorism among Africans has been more effective than the militia fighters (*mujahedeen*) of Chad. Far from democratic, Chad is a sparsely populated, poor, and mostly desert state run by strong man Idriss Déby with a history of violent domestic divisions and serious human rights abuses. Former Chadian strong man, Hisan Habre, is currently imprisoned and awaiting trial for crimes against humanity at the International Criminal Court. Chad like other US allies in the region including Uganda, Nigeria, and Kenya are all led by strong men with spotty human rights records. Nevertheless, Chad's long record of regional achievements is especially noteworthy. For instance, during the 1980s, Chad successfully checked expansionist military pressures from Libyan dictator Muammar Gadhafy from the North. During 2006/2007, Chad successfully checked Janjaweed raiders from Sudan to its east in near genocidal attacks on communities in Darfur. To its south, Chadian President Déby intervened to avert near genocidal attacks on the Seleka of the CAR in 2013. To its West, Chad intervened to thwart the advance of Boko Haram militants in regions northeast of Nigeria at the peak of the Boko Haram reign of terror. Given this record of performance, to the benefit of US interests, why was Chad placed by President Trump in 2017 on a list of seven states whose citizens were banned from traveling to the United States is a mystery. In its most recent iteration, the Trump administration removed Chad from it Muslim banned states.

Using his status as a Muslim and reputation as a regional power broker, Chadian President Déby summoned leading CAR officials including Michael Djotodia CAR's interim head of state to N'Djamena the capital of Chad in 2013, to reprimand them for failing to manage the crisis in CAR more effectively. President Déby worried that the CAR crisis might spill over into neighboring Chad to the North to create a refugee crisis for which an already impoverished Chad could ill afford to witness. Behind the scenes, there is little doubt that powerful interests in Paris, Brussels, New York, and Washington, DC, were not also working to resolve CAR's crisis. These developments illustrate Lombard's description of CAR as a non-territorial state whose major political decisions are made outside CAR's official borders. The intervention that forced fellow Muslim Michael Djotodia to step down as interim head of state in CAR after less than one full year in office in 2013 led more vulnerable refugees to cross CAR's borders into Chad and Sudan to escape anti-Balaka (anti-Muslim) militias. Colonel Sogour Himan, deputy commander of Chadian Special Forces, describes Boko Haram as "being scared of the Chadian army," while Colonel Louis Pena, Chief of Staff of French military forces based at N'Djamena, describes them as having "undeniable" combat capacity.[25] The Chadians are not only "seasoned fighters" with a "well-equipped and well-trained" army that charges into the rumble with no fear,[26] Chad in the words of another western official "is one of the countries and armies on which we rely very strongly."[27] Based on these descriptions, the Chadian army seems to exemplify the very best of Muslim struggle and its long and established history of commitment to social justice, at least outside of Chad.

While Seleka (alliance) fighters from the Chad/Darfur borderlands who arrived in CAR in March 2012 may have seemed like fearsome protectors at least to targeted fellow Muslims, non-Muslims, and the new mobilizations from among their ranks in CAR known as "anti-Balaka" sent the Seleka and indeed all Muslims in full retreat. Although anti-Balaka militias had no central organization, they were able to mount several coordinated assaults on targets in Bangui the Capital, on December 5 and 25, 2013. Similar to cycles of violence witnessed in other African conflicts zones including Somalia in 1993 and 2011 and Rwanda in 1994 where violence spread to the Congo (DRC) to eventually ignite what some describe as "Africa's first World War," the party "at fault" typically depended on the point at which one began one's narrative. This study begins the narrative of terrorist violence in CAR with the arrival of the Seleka in March 2012. Despite their treatment up to that point as "foreigners" and "strangers" in their own land, the Seleka, by most accounts, were the primary aggressors who dawned uniforms from the start to put an end to the rule of the much-hated President Bozizé of CAR.

One rebel who joined the Seleka rebellion, Soumaine Ndodeba, accepted this narrative described by one source as a case of "cunning victimhood." But acknowledging the Seleka's role as initial aggressors in CAR, Ndodeba described how "mercenaries who had not even asked to join but [who] looted and pillaged in the group's name and would not listen."[28] Hence, in the eyes of southerners in and around Bangui, the conflict was framed as a contest between "the uncontrollable foreigners versus 'pure' Central Africans." Even Ndodeba, the Tiringoulou native who joined the Seleka, could not resist characterizing Seleka leader Nourreddine Adam as "a Chadian who grew up in Bangui."[29] Eventually, former Seleka/Muslims in CAR became the main targets of "popular justice" sparking a joint AU, UN, and French intervention campaign against the anti-Balaka. Despite CAR's Muslim struggle (*jihad*) and flight (*hijra*) against the anti-Balaka backlash, peacekeepers were the only effective barrier between Muslims and their pursuers. Muslims were randomly targeted and often killed within eyesight of UN or AU peacekeepers.

CAR's peacekeepers were arguably the greatest beneficiaries of the conflict in CAR. Their salaries were enormous by Central African standards.[30] The UN/AU peacekeeping model in CAR was itself fatally flawed for ignoring the self-interested opportunism that some peacekeepers felt entitled to exploit leading to the smuggling of CAR's valuable resources including its timber, rare gems diamonds, and gold through CAR's porous borders and largely unsealed airport. It also enabled UN peacekeepers to exploit CAR's innocent young women, a number of whom were impregnated allegedly by UN peacekeepers. Others peacekeepers from Muslim nations like Nigeria were accused of displaying favoritism toward local Muslims—an accusation that surfaced earlier during the Liberian Civil War of the 1990s, when Nigerian members of the regional military peacekeeping force known as ECOMOG were accused of favoring local Muslims combatants in Liberia. Moreover, peacekeepers from nearby Cameroon were believed to be involved in personal projects for financial gain, supporting the perception that outside peacekeepers were sometimes more interested in protecting themselves and reaping personal gain than in protecting local Muslims.

According to one local eyewitness: "All this peacekeeping is a game in order to give them time to go fishing. It's a good job, and they want it to continue."[31]

Even the French as the former colonial power cannot escape partial blame. According to another local observer, "Everyone knows that France and the French are the ones who are making Central African blood flow."[32] This accusation seems consistent with past British and French bias in favor of traditional Muslim populations in northern Nigeria and northern CAR. One Christian interviewed in CAR claimed that French peacekeepers show favoritism toward Muslims and that "people killed Christians right in front of the French [and they did nothing]."[33] Some Christians in CAR accuse the French of firing on Christians, supplying weapons to Muslims, and even infiltrating the UN peacekeepers with 250 Peulh (Muslim) fighters flown-in by helicopter and wearing Rwandan uniforms.[34] Meanwhile, the local Muslim population numbering less than 1 million has become ever more frightened and vulnerable to retaliation. This state of affairs flies in the face of one young man's description of CAR as "the world's champion of hosting peacekeeping missions."[35] Central Africans, rich and poor, educated and non-educated, often lament their country's penchant for coming in "last in the world"[36] on almost every important world measure. By 2016, CAR had more international intervention than anywhere else yet remained among the very last in terms of development indicators.[37]

Despite an upsurge in Islamist conflict in Africa, it is a mistake to view Islamism as inherently opposed to the United States, the West, or western interests in general. More often than not, Islamism and the institution of Muslim struggle (*jihad*) have served as instruments of reform aimed at Muslim rather than non-Muslim criminals. Indeed, the primary targets of Muslim struggle (*jihad*) has been wayward or corrupt Muslims, and not Christians, Americans, or westerners as widely believed in the West. The very first Muslim struggle (*jihad*) came in response to persecution of the first Muslim community (*ummah*) by the Meccans sparking the now famous flight (*hijra*) of the Prophet Muhammad and his companions from Mecca to Medina. Muslims throughout history emulate this same escape-flight (*hijra*) that culminated in Muslim struggle (*jihad*). This pattern of behavior is evident from a number of historical episodes of Islamism and Muslim struggle cited in this study. Islamism and African Muslims have been more historically deep and geographically widespread than scholars in the West have fully realized. Prominent cases of Islamism and African Muslims in the Middle East, Europe, and the Americas illustrate this point. Armed with the tool of dissimilation (*taqiya*), African Muslims with higher than average rates of literacy (in Arabic) continued to read Arabic and practice their religion as best they could despite the significant obstacles they faced.

The situation in CAR displays elements of the UN intervention in the former Yugoslavia in the early 1990s. This intervention reached a climax when at least 7,000 Muslim men and boys were executed by Bosnia Serbs under the watchful eye of UN peacekeepers in the Srebrenica massacre of July of 1995. This crisis was perhaps the first to trigger an al-Qaeda and Osama bin Laden response. Bin Laden still looked to the Sudanese Islamist Hassan al-Turabi for ideological and logistic support. Turabi may have played a direct role in sponsoring Bin Laden's first campaign against the former Yugoslavia with militant training camps established by Turabi in Sudan. A serious tragedy involving Muslims in CAR under the watchful eye of UN peacekeepers reminiscent of conflict in the former Yugoslavia may trigger a similar Islamist militant response aimed at protecting the vulnerable Muslim minority population in CAR. With many more military training camps in Africa such a response would be entirely possible. The international community has long recognized the limitations of UN peacekeeping as illustrated by peacekeeping missions in the Congo (DRC), South Sudan, Côte d'Ivoire, and Haiti. The UN's worldwide unpopularity is no less evident to Islamist militants in Africa who bombed UN headquarters in Abuja, Nigeria, in 2011.[38]

From a Muslim perspective, the common denominator in each of these events was injustice, persecution, and oppression which Muslims are compelled to resist whenever and wherever possible. African Muslim history is replete with instances of the lesser *jihad* which objective analysis reveals were neither inherently anti-American nor inherently anti-western as neither the United States nor the West were in existence at the time of their first appearance in seventh-century Arabia. African struggles were responses to injustice and oppressive more often than not involving "near enemy," that is, African rather than "far enemy" opponents. Mamdani identifies four instances of widespread "just war" before the Afghan *jihad* of the 1980s, two of which occurred in Africa. The first of these "just wars" which culminated in lesser *jihad* was the Kurdish warrior Saladin's *jihad* in response to the conquest and slaughter of the First Crusade of the eleventh century. The second was a series of the antislavery *jihad*s that began in the second half of the sixteenth century in Senegambia against the European enslavement of African Muslims. A third "just war" was the *jihad* waged by Mohammed Ibn Abd Wahhab (1703–1792) during the middle of the eighteenth century against Turkish colonialism on the Arabian Peninsula that facilitated the rise of the "House of Saud." The fourth "just war" was waged by Muhammad Ahmed of the Sudan (1844–1885) against Turko-Egyptian colonialism (see chapter 4). Ahmed declared himself Al-Mahdi or messiah. However, in addition to these widespread, "just wars" acknowledged by Mamdani prior to the Afghan jihad of the 1980s, lesser-known though no less important instances of Muslim struggle (*jihad*) involving African Muslims in Brazil,

Haiti, Jamaica, Suriname, and LaFlorida in the Americas may upon closer examination prove at least as important as the relatively short-lived Mahdi jihad in Sudan. Muslim struggle in the Americas might also be seen as possible extensions of antislavery struggles first introduced in Africa.[39]

Many of these lesser-known Muslim struggles (*jihad*) in the Americas have gone largely unnoticed by American historian unable to recognize the ethnic identities and features of African Muslims enslaved in the Americas, some of whom in rare instances managed to survive under special circumstances and locations in the Americas (e.g., Fort Musa and Fort Negro in Florida) that witnessed a concentration of Africans from Muslim backgrounds, for example, at Sapelo Island, Georgia, the low country regions around Charleston, South Carolina where rice was grown for centuries by the Baga who were Muslims from West Africa Africans among the Seminoles of northeastern Florida formed formidable fighting forces during the late eighteenth and early nineteenth centuries. Some of these instances involved enslaved Africans from Muslim backgrounds in Upper Guinea from Sufi Marabouts backgrounds as documented by Diouf (2003, 1998). Some of these Africans also came from learned Sunni Muslim backgrounds as documented by Gomez (1989, 2005), Diouf (1998), and Turner (1997). The case of the famous enslaved African Muslim, Abd al-Rahman of Natchez, Mississippi, provides a notable example. The "Prince" as he is known to slave scholars survived his American ordeal to return to Africa through the aid of the American Colonization Society (ACS) by the late nineteenth century. Others like Omar Ibn Said managed to survive their enslavement in the Americas where their reproductions of the Qur'an written in Arabic from memory earned them the attention of American slave historians.[40]

These struggles have been overlooked by most American historians until relatively recently especially in the American South where bigoted images of Africans and their progeny no doubt influenced by black myths and stereotypes undermined scholarly examinations of the history of African Muslim struggles (*jihad*) in the Americas. In addition to being largely ignored, most American historians continue to describe cases of African flight (*hijra*) and resistance (*jihad*) throughout the Americas as "slave" escapes and "slave" rebellions. Nevertheless, a fairly well-documented set of primary sources including slave testimonials, the observations of knowledgeable slave owners, court records and testimony, advertisement rewards for the return of "runaway slaves," slave ship cargo manifolds offer detailed descriptions of enslaved Africans from predominantly Muslim ethnic groups and regions sometimes described by name, ethnicity, and religion. Also, the phenomenon known as maroon escapes and settlements that survived throughout the Americas for decades especially in the Caribbean offer additionally useful evidence of Muslim struggle and the survival of Islam and Muslims in the

Americas. Many of these maroon settlements were led by African Muslims, as seen for example in the case of Francois Makandal, a Muslim learned man and Voudou priest of Haiti who led a massive "slave" resistance movement in the mid-eighteenth century which lasted at least a decade. The charismatic Makandal was eventually burned at the stake after being betrayed. He is credited with leading a major "slave" resistance movement in Haiti that appears to have been an important forerunner to the successful Haitian "slave" revolt of 1791 to 1804. This was an especially active period of resistance throughout the world of the Atlantic as important struggles for freedom emerged including the largest and most far-reaching *jihad* in Africa, the *jihad* of Uthman dan Fodio in 1802 to 1804, and the American Revolution of 1776–1777 in what would eventually become the United States. Later, a "slave" named Osman (Uthman?) of the Dismal Swamp in Virginia whose likeness widely appears in literature to represent the generic image of the "runaway slave" during the period 1850–1860 may also have been a Muslim, born in Africa. Osman and others like him were collectively referred to in the historical literature as *bozales* or blacks in the Americas who were born in Africa.

A case study discussed in chapter 5 of this study highlighting the 1835 Muslim "slave revolt" in Brazil sheds important light on this largely ignored phenomenon. For example, the largest known maroon settlement in the America known as Palmares was located in Brazil and lasted nearly the entire period of the seventeenth century from deep within the Amazon forest despite persistent efforts to destroy it by Portuguese authorities. Another famous maroon enclave of African and Native American escapees known as Esmeraldas located near present-day Quito, Ecuador, survived for over fifty years. These isolated, independent communities of fugitive Africans often from Muslim regions and ethnic groups and their Native American allies not only had ample opportunities to practice their religions in hidden enclaves away from interference from colonial authorities, many especially in what is today the US state of Florida did so with impunity thanks to three successful Seminole "Indian wars" waged against British, Spanish, and American colonial powers from areas in Florida described as "lawless" and inhabited by persons practicing "unknown" religions. The state of Florida became a US territory in 1819 and a state in 1821. But it was never fully mapped by authorities until about 1900 providing ample opportunities for native and near native persons in the region to practice their religions and cultures without interference. Closer examination of these little-known yet documented histories involving combatants born in Africa from African Muslim backgrounds may show evidence of cultural practices and beliefs related to Muslim struggle (*jihad*) rather than "slave rebellions." Finally, Mamdani's four cases cited above ignore what is perhaps the largest and most important jihad among Africans, that is, the jihad of Uthman dan Fodio of northern Nigeria (1802–1804).

The following section offers additional details regarding links between struggles (*jihad*) in Africa and their links to related activities by African Muslims and/or their progeny enslaved in the Americas.

WEST AFRICAN RESISTANCE
AND REFORM MOVEMENTS

West African resistance and reform movements may have been major forerunners to resistance and reform extended into the Americas by blacks linked to the abolitionist and the Underground Railroad. West African resistance and reform movements in the context of this study offer are noteworthy of Muslim struggle (*jihad*) among Africans. For example, one such movement, known as the Purification (*Toubenan*) movement, 1673 to 1677, led by Nasr al Din in modern-day Senegal established a model for subsequent Islamist reform movements in Africa. Abd al-Kadir and Sulyman Baal's Islamic revival/renewal (*tajdid*) movement of the Futa Toro kingdom departed from the practice of taking slaves embraced by its Arab allies to the North. The *jihad* of Sheikh Abd al-Kadir attracted wide popular support among black Africans for warning French authorities of the dire consequences associated with attempts to capture Muslims for enslavement by Christians. The Futa Toro region succeeded in recapturing a portion of its people who had previously been kidnapped for enslavement. Sheikh Abd al-Kadir blocked caravans from passing through his territory after three children were captured by the French in the Futa Torro area. A letter sent to the French Governor carrying the following warning:

> We are warning you that all those who come to our land [to trade in slaves] will be killed or massacred, if you do not send our children back. Would not somebody who was very hungry abstain from eating if he had to eat something cooked in his blood? We absolutely do not want you to buy Muslims under any circumstances. I repeat that if your intention is to always buy Muslims you should stay home and not come to our country anymore. Because all those who will come can be assured that they will lose their life.[41]

Sheikh Abd al-Kadir and others followed the practice of signing treaties with the French that banned the capture of African Muslims for sale to European Christians. Other strategies for fighting the slave trade in Africa rarely recognized by American historians include "slave suicide" (often practiced by Igbo women), 'slave redemption, self-manumission, and what one writer calls "devotion . . . at any price." These and other forms of antislavery efforts initiated by Africans challenge the myth of the docile compliant "slave" who passively awaited the arrival of well-intentioned liberal whites to rescue them from slavery on the wings of the Underground Railroad. Smaller, more vulnerable, agriculturalist like the Baga, Temne, and Bullom launched protracted antislavery "rebellions" in West Africa directed at the Mandingo, slave-owning (Muslim) elite in Moriah—a state founded in the 1720s for the benefit of traders and "Islamic missionaries." The Baga, known on both sides of the Atlantic for their rice growing skills, deliberately burned rice fields as an act of defiance against oppressive Mandingo rule.[42] Hence, the use of *jihad* by Muslims and non-Muslims alike in West Africa illustrates the wide use of *jihad* as a tool of resistance by Muslim resistance fighters (*mujahedeen*) who actively challenged oppression contrary to the contemporary image of *jihad* as a tool of anti-western, anti-American terrorism.[43] Rather than a struggle (*jihad*) aimed solely at the United States and other westerners as depicted in the media, a famous Muslim struggle (*jihad*) led by a West African maroon named Bilali (Bilali's Rebellion), son of a Muslim Freedman in Moriah, may have been mediated by Edward Wilmot Blyden, the American clergyman-turned Muslim, born in the Virgin Islands who helped found the eighteenth-century Presbyterian-based ACS. Blyden is profiled in chapter 5. Preliminary evidence suggest that Blyden may have met with representatives of Moriah and Samory to help mitigate the harsh treatment directed at the Baga and others mobilized in struggle (*jihad*) against Moriah's Muslim elite. Denunciations of Bilali's *jihad* by Moriah authorities unsurprisingly relied on rationalizations which sounded virtually identical to those that later used by white plantation owners in the US South, shaken by a loss of their "property" and fearful of reforms that might destroy the institution of slavery, altogether. But West African Muslims' success at "slave" resistance not only restricted the supply it drove up the price of "slaves" as well.[44]

The enslavement of West Africans for the flimsiest of reasons including for nonpayment of debts became so rampant that whole families were sold for "crimes" committed by a single relative.[45] Treaties with Europeans aimed at discouraging if not eliminating the enslavement of Muslims may have contributed to the relatively small number of Muslims who appeared on plantations in North as compared to South America and the Caribbean. These treaties may have also discouraged the capture and enslavement of Muslim women and children as seen in the preponderance of men of military age and background among Africans enslaved in the Americas. While historians have added significantly to our understanding of African Muslim behavior in early America attempts to link events involving Islamism in Africa to seemingly related events in the Americas, remain rare.

Europeans use of a "divide and rule" strategy to gain control over their indigenous opponents in Africa and the Americas meant Europeans honored their agreements with rulers like Abd al-Kadir only to the extent necessary. Indeed, as Muslims unity began to wane, European powers abandoned these treaties and resorted to indiscriminate capture and enslavement of vulnerable Africans. Offensive strategies included attacks on European vessels and "slave" caravans.[46] Rashid's study of *jihad* on the Upper Guinea coast of West Africa (Senegambia) alludes to links between these *jihads* and maroon villages in Africa and the Americas.[47] The founding of Freetown in what would later become the state of Sierra Leone in 1787 by the British was a powerful antislavery symbol and incentive that helped "wean the surrounding African chiefs and people from their slaving ways."[48]

Captives from a 1785 African "rebellion" were sold by their Muslim masters in Moriah to Europeans on the coast for enslavement in the Americas. The Moriah became a major slaveholding society as well as an important commercial center connecting coastal traders with the interior. One of its leaders, Fenda Modu Dumbuya, reportedly owned as many as nine villages providing nearly 100 tons of rice and 100 tons of salt annually. New captives on Moriah rice plantations were made to work on plantations before being sold to Europeans on the coast. A small number of these misfortunates were also retained as household servants, slave wives, and concubines.[49] But others wound-up toiling on plantations in the Carolinas. These Muslims are widely credited with introducing African rice technology to the Americas. But they may have contributed unwittingly to the transferred of the Islamic institutions of *jihad*, *hijra*, and *ummah* to the Americas as well.

The Tukolor Empire (1852–1864), an African Islamic theocracy, is another well-known example of Muslim struggle (*jihad*) against French colonialism in West Africa. The empire at its peak extended some 1,500 miles from present-day Senegal to Timbuktu in present-day Mali. According to one historian, "it took many years to subdue" and was one of many fierce resistance campaigns encountered against French colonial expansion in Africa.[50] The Tukolor's may have played a major role in resisting the practice of capturing its citizens for enslavement in the Americas during the Atlantic slave trade. The Tukulor were led by the Senegalese Islamic scholar, Al-hajj Umar Tall (1797–1864), who helped popularize the Sufi Muslim order known as the Tijaniyah from its capital in Dinguiraye. A series of military defeats to the French caused it to cede territory it previously controlled in Senegal to the French, leading it to retreat 300 miles east into Africa's interior. After the death of al-Hajj Umar, the empire rapidly disintegrated due to rivalries between his sons and internal military revolt.[51]

THE SPECIAL CASE OF NIGERIA

The state of Nigeria represents a special case of Muslim struggle among Africans. Not only is Nigeria the largest concentration of African Muslims, it is a microcosm of Islam and Islamism among Africans. No other African state illustrates the root causes and essential characteristic of terrorist violence linked to Islamist militants as Nigeria.[52] The roots of government corruption and oppression in Nigeria can be traced to the time of British colonialism, when Ahmadu Bello, the great grandson of Usman Dan Fodio (1754–1817), perhaps the greatest champion of Muslim struggle (*jihad*), became the first premier of Nigeria, taking office in 1954. Actively resisting the popular image of traditional African authorities as vassals tightly controlled by colonial authorities, Bello argued consistently and forcefully that northern emirs must maintain their important roles in the North and act in accordance with local government and not as overlords. Writing in his autobiography published in 1962, he expressed views that seem to diverge from Hunwick's allegation of a closely monitored, tightly controlled Muslim community in West Africa during colonialism (see "Introduction"). The roots of Islamism in northern Nigeria were present in Nigeria where leading voices rejected the passivity and quietism demanded of colonial subjects in favor of an active pursuit of Islamic goals, values, and consciousness despite the limitations imposed by the colonial system. Indeed, Bello maintained that "we must get away from the idea that they [the emirs] are effete, conservative, and die-hard obstructionists; [as] nothing could be farther from the truth."[53] With Bello's persistence and the relative size of the northern region's population, the North received the largest number of seats in the federal parliament following elections in 1959. While it is difficult to know with certainty the relative impact that Muslim struggle (*jihad*) throughout the period of colonialism may have had, it appears to have played a role in achieving Nigerian political independence in 1960. Ahmadu Bello's Northern People's Congress won the largest number of seats in the Nigerian parliament.[54]

In the words of one study, "it is impossible to understand modern-day Nigeria without considering its ethnic and regional divisions."[55] And yet, to understand non-terrorist African Muslim struggle (*jihad*) it is important to understand the Nigerian state, described by one source as "the giant of Africa."[56] Contemporary Nigeria includes 177 million people equally divided between Christians and Muslims, with Africa's largest petroleum reserves, a relatively modern army and "greater heft than any [other] African country."[57] It is a strategic partner of the United States and at times a surrogate for the United States in Africa.[58] But Nigeria is also a complex state facing a myriad of political challenges. Though it is less than 20 percent of the geographic size of the United States, Nigeria includes 36 separate states and over 250 different languages. But it has faced three separate and lethal insurgencies in the past that were never fully resolved. Nigeria's bitter insurgency in the Niger River delta, which is the leading source of its economic revenues, has challenged the state to manage its vast petroleum resources, environmental goals, and economic priorities, more effectively. But ill-advised government responses led former President Goodluck Jonathan, for example, to in-effect bribe, insurgents to stand guard over the very same petroleum reserves they once threaten to destroy. Defying international pressure against harming him, the Nigerian state under orders from President Sani Abacha executed prominent environmentalist Ken Saro-Wiwa Jr. (1941–1995), a champion of environmentalism and spokesperson for the region's Ogoni minority group, in 1995. The second major conflict facing the Nigerian state, is the inter-ethnic, inter-religious, and interregional conflict between the Muslim North and the predominantly Christian Southeast where Igbo groups continue to challenge what they perceive to be northern bias in the country's policies. Nigerian state policies according to Igbo critics promote regional inequality, corruption, and government cronyism. These conditions sparked the Igbo-initiated Nigerian civil war of 1966 to 1970.

The third major regional challenge facing the Nigerian state is the Islamist challenge in north and northeast Nigeria of which Boko Haram and its two splinter groups are a part. The Yan Izala movement led by Abubakar Gumi, a prominent Sunni imam and judge, sparked anti-Sufi violence after 1978. But even with the establishment of indirect British rule around 1903, northern Nigeria continued to witness Muslim led insurgencies that predate the emergence of the postmodernist contemporary Islamist movement linked to the 1970s, making Nigeria a pioneer in the Islamist cause among Africans. For instance, a brutal insurgency waged by Dan Makafo, described by colonial administrator Lugard, as "an outlaw from French territory," inspired others to take up arms against British colonial authority in the North. These challenges persisted throughout the colonial period in northern Nigeria where a number of them have been characterized as "Muslim Mahdists" movements, especially toward the end of the colonial period.[59] Another illustration of this phenomenon toward the end of Sir Frederick Lugard's tenure as colonial administrator over northern Nigeria (1890–1929), known as the "satiru uprising," drove British forces to raze the village of Satiru to the ground offers unmistakable evidence of the persistence of Islamist resistance and British colonialism's determination to annihilate it.

But perceived injustice and oppression rather than anti-colonialism per se were the main reasons for Muslim struggles which raged on at least as ferociously under African as they did under colonial rule. For example, deadly riots flared up in the northern Nigerian city of Kano in 1980 linked to the militant Islamist insurgency known as the Maitatsine movement. "Maitatsine" is a Hausa word given to Muhammadu Marwa, the leader of the movement which roughly translates to the "Anathematiser" or "the one who damns."[60] Marwa declared himself a prophet, made odd interpretations of the Qur'an, and rooted his movement in class and ethnic arguments against the Hausa power elite. "Riots" in the mid-1980s linked to the Maitatsine movement in Kano, northern Nigeria, killed more than 4,000 including Muhammadu Marwa and several thousand additional persons in subsequent "riots" across the country.[61] The situation had become so dire that one observer writing in 2016 concluded:

> Nigerians of all ethnicities and origins have lost any faith they may have once had in their government, justice system and security forces. The bright light of the country's vast potential has been snuffed out by thieves disguised as businessmen, military generals and politicians.[62]

The once oil-rich province of Delta state in the South allegedly witnessed the embezzlement of $250 million. Nigeria's poverty rate skyrocketed to around 28 percent in 1980 before rising to 66 percent by 1996, during the presidency of military dictator, Sani Abacha, a northerner, accused (along with his family) of looting hundreds of millions of dollars from Nigeria's Central Bank, literally by truckload according to one source.[63] These events and circumstances capture the context for the emergence of Mohammed Yusuf and Boko Haram. Boko Haram, the group described by some as "the world's most notorious terrorist group," is a by-product of legitimate mainstream Muslim struggle (*jihad*) underestimated by Hunwick and others in the West who exaggerate the impact and influence of western projects, for example, colonialism, while underestimating the resilience of African Islamist movements. But Boko Haram did not spring from a vacuum. It emerged from a rich crucible of Islamic activism and controversy in northern Nigeria to produce a potent blend of religious fanaticism, social media savvy, and cold-blooded violence.[64] The public most readily identifies the group for its 2014 kidnapping of 276 schoolgirls from their school in Chibok, Nigeria. But this atrocity may be eclipsed by more deadly ones including kidnapping of girls and boys that number in the thousands and an attack on the village of Baga (Nigeria) where as many as 2,000 people were reportedly killed.[65] These and similar actions are the by-products of an African state where, corruption is common and rarely punished and where the security services, who are typically the most visible face of the state—commit violent acts with impunity.[66]

One study describes how one Boko Haram member spotted another member being "disciplined" by security forces—known as Operation Flush II—formed to combat armed robberies and other such crimes.[67] Nigeria's police often force those it deems guilty of minor infractions to perform "frog-jumps" on the roadside or other such humiliations.[68] Perhaps the first major run-in with Boko Haram insurgents occurred on June 11, 2009, when police sought to enforce a new law requiring motorcycle riders to wear helmets.

Several members of the group were shot by police stemming from police run-ins variously linked to minor rule infractions.[69] According to police, in one such run-in, a man attempted to steal a police officer's gun while being detained causing officers to open fire, shooting the man and several others in the legs to avoid killing them. Seventeen Boko Haram members were reportedly wounded in the incident according to subsequent reports.[70] These actions bear a close resemblance to seemingly ubiquitous roadblocks used to "hassle" Muslims in CAR and similar practices found in Kenya and elsewhere that in-effect antagonize Muslims to the point of driving some into the arms of Islamist militants to fuel the very insurgency that authorities are organized to eliminate.

The rise of Mohammed Yusuf, founder of Boko Haram, may have been predicted given the Kanem-Bornu Empire's grand history and reputation in this part of Nigeria and in the shadow of the Sokoto Caliphate.[71] The region has fallen on hard times. The scrubby savannah near Lake Chad and the Sahara desert had already lagged far behind the rest of Nigeria in education and wealth around the time that Yusuf launched his movement.[72] At that time, ca. 2001, northeast Nigeria had the smallest number of students admitted to Nigerian universities, at around 4 percent of the country's total.[73] Mohammed Yusuf is believed to have been born in 1970 in Jakusko in Yobe state in northeastern Nigeria. An influential trader, Baba Fugu Mohammed from his same Kanuri ethnic group, the largest in Borno state had a reputation for taking people into his large compound. Mohammed served as a foster parent to Yusuf[74] who worked to become an influential trader, despite admitting to having virtually no formal education. He eventually made his way to Maiduguri, where he prayed at that city's magnificent mosque and came to know Sheikh Muhammad Awwal Adam Albani. Another influential acquaintance was Sheikh Ja'far who was at least ten years older and more disciplined than Yusuf. Adam may have been a graduate of the University of Medina in Saudi Arabia.

But Adam became increasing frustrated with Yusuf and publicly questioning his teaching to the point of accusing Yusuf of hypocrisy.[75] Sheikh Ja'far may have been a member of the Maitatsine movement.[76] Sheikh Adam described Yusuf as "the leader of young people." But relations between Adam and Yusuf began to cool, culminating in a formal split between the two men by 2003. Yusuf had grown increasingly more militant while Adam is described as a pragmatist.[77] Around this time, Yusuf became acquainted with another militant Islamist named Mohammed Ali who was from Bornu state. In addition to graduating from the University of Medina in Saudi Arabia, Ali along with a group of other militants from north-eastern Nigeria undertook flight/migration (*hijra*) to Medina, following a local dispute with authorities in northeastern Nigeria.[78] Although their flight/migration is described as largely peaceful, other reports emerging around this time described the members of Ali's group as Nigeria's Taliban who undertook arms training in northern Mali among the Azawad Islamist militants.[79] Yusuf for his part is known to have undertaken the pilgrimage to Mecca during this period and specifically in 2000, 2002, 2003, and 2004. Along the way, he graduated from the University of Medina in Saudi Arabia.[80] Ja'far Adam and several other older Islamists tried to convince Yusuf to renounce his militant teachings during visits with him in Saudi Arabia and Nigeria which ultimately failed.[81] Sheikh Ja'far accused Yusuf publicly of misleading Muslim youth and of hypocrisy.[82] Finally, in 2007 while Adam led dawn prayers in Kano, gunmen attacked the Dorayi Juma'at Mosque killing Adam. Another former mentor along with his wife and son were murdered later in February 2014, with Boko Haram members being the primary suspects.[83]

What conclusions might be drawn from the special case of Nigeria with its long history of oppression and Islamist activism, where Muslim struggle (*jihad*) at the institutional and individual levels are well established but where eight years of Boko Haram violence has been difficult to eliminate? If Islamists are correct in the view that Islamism is an all-encompassing way of life for many Muslims, representing a religious and moral compass and political ideology, then Islamism as way of life and moral compass has fallen short thanks to corrupt primarily Muslim officials who have benefitted personally at the expense of society as a whole. State corruption and oppression of those left behind in Bornu state among the Kanuri ethnic group are especially tragic. But other glaring deficiencies are evident in yet still unresolved tensions in the Niger River Delta, and among lingering inequalities experienced by the Igbo and other non-Muslim groups in Nigeria which sparked a civil war in 1966–1970. This last tragedy underscores the point that the Nigerian problem is not just a Muslim shortcoming, but a Nigerian shortcoming which if left uncorrected could have major spill-over effects for Africa and the international community. Boko Haram violence as unpalatable as it might be may be seen as a desperate attempt to counter the hubris and authority of the state. But doing so against Africa's largest and most powerful military and supported by the United States may be too much for Muslim struggle (*jihad*) to overcome, alone.

The rise of Boko Haram from the crucible of Muslim politics from the colonial era to the present is as much a failure of mainstream Muslim leadership as it is a failure of the Nigerian state in general. While the state fails virtually all groups, except perhaps Nigeria's elite and billionaires, mainstream Muslim leaders like former President Sani Abacha, the northerner accused along with family members of looting millions from government coffers literally by truck, has failed Nigeria's Muslims, especially among its lower classes. To the extent that conditions in Nigeria are not unique, Nigeria may offer valuable lessons to other states or regions facing similar challenges. The world during 2016/2017 experienced profound leadership crises as evident from leadership turmoil in the United States and elsewhere. Scheuer's 2005 description of the Arab/Islamic world as a vast desert wasteland, when it comes to political leadership may also apply to Nigeria.[84] President Y'ardua was weakened by brain cancer that shortened his life and presidency after prolonged absences for medical treatment in Saudi Arabia, while still in office. A successor President Goodluck Jonathan until 2016 was well known for his ineffectiveness and poor judgment both in his handling of the Niger River Delta crisis and in his failure to return the kidnapped Chibok girls. The current President Muhammadu Buhari, who took office in early 2016, appears to display elements of both Y'ardua and Jonathan with his failure to defeat Boko Haram and frequent unexplained absences from the country for medical treatment in Britain while still in office. An attempt by his wife to comment on political developments (on camera) resulted in an abrupt interruption by Buhari, an ex-military strong man, who told reporters that his wife should refrain from commenting on political matters and limit her efforts to "the kitchen and other room."

GENERAL FEATURES OF MUSLIM STRUGGLE AND AFRICA

The analysis of non-terrorist Muslim struggle (*jihad*) includes the following major features: (1) "Muslim Struggle (*jihad*) as an Alternative to Terrorism"; (2) "Africans and Muslim Struggle (*jihad*)"; and (3) "The Special Challenge of Muslim Struggle (*jihad*)." The final section of this chapter is devoted to a brief description of the general features of Muslim struggle and Africa.

Muslim Struggle as an Alternative to Terrorism

The discussion of Muslim struggle provided thus far in this study stands in sharp contrast to use of "*jihad*" as an instrument of terror. The former is on display in the behavior of Boko Haram. The latter is displayed in the case of the Muhammadu Buhari government's struggle against terrorist violence in Nigeria. From the Muslim perspective, Muslim struggle (*jihad*) is the only legitimate form of struggle. The historical record is rich with examples of Muslim struggle's legitimate use against injustice and oppression. Chapter 3 of this study examines the delicate subject of the politics of non-terrorist Muslim struggle that not only distinguishes it from terrorist violence, but also examines the proper and skillful use of Muslim struggle in solving real world problems. Thus, struggle is rarely an end in itself but rather as an opportunity for Muslims to make a positive difference in the world in which they live.

Africans and Muslim Struggle

Mamdani's inclusion of seventeenth-century Muslim struggles in Senegambia and the nineteenth-century Muslim struggle of Muhammad Ahmed, "the Mahdi" of Sudan as two of the four most widespread uses of Muslim struggle in history, is noteworthy. Not only does it place Africans at the forefront of Islamic communities who have made prominent use of Muslim struggle, it also provides a vivid reminder to Muslims worldwide of the power of faith (*iman*) and struggle (*jihad*). No other feature of Muslim struggle and Africans examined herein demonstrates the importance and significance of Islam in the lives of Africans. This of course does not mean that Africans have been the only group that has made demonstrable use faith (*iman*) and struggle (*jihad*). As a sacred obligation for all Muslims (and quite possible every human being), the contributions of Africans only underscores value of Muslim struggle (*jihad*) as a mercy to human kind. Many Muslims believe there can be no faith (*iman*) without struggle. Only three other "widespread" Muslim struggles appear to rival the record of Muslim struggle associated with Africans. These are, the eleventh-century Muslim struggle waged by the Kurdish general, Saladin, against the first Crusades, mentioned by Mamdani; the eighteenth-century Muslim struggle waged by Mohammed Abd al-Wahhab against Turkish colonial control also mentioned by Mamdani; and of course the original Muslim struggle waged by the Prophet Muhammad against the Meccans in seventh-century Arabia, not mentioned by Mamdani.

The Special Challenge of Muslim Struggle

Yet, Muslim struggle is by no means a panacea, for struggle alone provides no guarantee that one's goals will be met, one's prayers will be answered or one's objectives will be met. Again, the case of the President Buhari government in Nigeria is a notable case in point. The government's attempt to rely with Muslim struggle in its war on Boko Haram including its attempt to mobilize local Muslim militias among rural Fulani tribesmen and others has not succeeded. By contrast, the Muslim struggle over the years involving different governments in Chad represents a more successful application of the principle. Why did one Muslim struggle succeed and another fail? There is no easy answer to this question. The grace of God (*Allah*), political skill, the ability to maintain the moral high ground, recruiting effective helpers (allies) all play a role in one's successful application of Muslim struggle. Hence, until political leaders can skillfully harness these difficult to enumerate essentials

Muslim struggle in the contemporary era, successful Muslim struggle will continue to be an elusive yet important endeavor.

Mamdani admits that debates over Muslim struggle (*jihad*) increasingly center on the meaning of *jihad* or Muslim struggle. Therefore before closing, this chapter finds it useful to single out the essential features of Muslim struggle that distinguish it from terrorism. Muslim struggle must be waged in the name of God (*Allah*) and only God (*Allah*) and it must be part of what Mamdani calls "just wars" or what Scheuer calls "defensive jihads," consistent with the tradition of Islam and its Prophet. The first approach is associated with the mainstream Muslim; while the second is the approach associated with the Islamist militant. The following excerpts represent two very different approaches to Muslim struggle. "In August [2012] in a small town called Ansogo, near Gao, Majao publicly amputated a man's hand with a crude knife and no anesthesia." The same Islamist militant group had earlier "stoned a couple to death for allegedly having children out of wedlock." Most locals in northern Mali did not seem eager to adopt Islamic law (*shari'ah*). Certainly, most Tuaregs showed little desire for Islamist militancy, whether Wahhabi-Salafists, Tuareg or Arab.[85] The view of Muslim moderates displayed in the following brief quote taken from a local Muslim Imam offers an appropriately restrained distinction between moderate and militant approaches to Muslim struggle.

> "We are a country of religious tolerance" said Imam Mahamous Dicko, the head of the High Islamic Council of Mali. "Coming to any place with weapons to close bars—that's not how it's done. Stopping people playing football? That's archaic." The public even staged protests against shari'a in towns of the north.[86]

This chapter examined: (1) "Important Distinctions"; (2) "The Islamist Continuum"; (3) "West African Resistance and Reform Movements"; (4) "the Special Case of Nigeria" and (5) "General Characteristics of Muslim Struggle (*jihad*) and Africa." The following chapter examines the broader, historically significance of Africans in the establishment and spread of the institution of Muslim struggle *jihad* and in the establishment and spread of Islam. Its inclusion is intended to debunk the idea that Africans have been marginal figures in Islamic history and civilization. Chapter 3 also attempts to situate terrorist violence and other aberrant forms of behavior (*fitnah*) among Africans in their larger historical context including longstanding efforts among Africans to counter and resist them through the tool of Muslim struggle (*jihad*) aimed at diminishing if not eliminating oppression. Like efforts up to this point in this study, chapters 3 through 6 will continue to distinguish important differences between terrorist violence and legitimate Muslim struggle (*jihad*) among Africans as a precursor to offering valuable recommendations to policy makers.

NOTES

1. David Westerlund, "Reaction and Action: Accounting for the Rise of Islamism," in David Westerlund and Eva Evers Rosander (eds.), *African Islam and Islam in Africa: Encounters between Sufis and Islamists* (Athens: Ohio University Press, 1997), 309.

2. See John Alden Williams, "Khawarʿij," in John L. Esposito (ed.), *The Oxford Encyclopedia of the Modern Islamic World* (New York: Oxford University Press, 1995), vol. 2, 419–420. Just as the term "Shiite" is an Anglicized notation sometimes used to denote a member of the Shia sect of Islam the term "Karijite" is an Anglicized notation sometimes used to denote a member of a Khawarʿij movement in Islam. ISIS is widely viewed as an example of a postmodern Khawarʿij movement. For an examination of this phenomenon see Malcolm Nance, *Defeating ISIS: Who they are, How they Fight What They Believe* (New York: Skyhorse Publishing, 2016), and Jay Sekulow et al., *Rise of ISIS: A Threat We Can't Ignore* (New York: Howard Books, 2014).

3. Mark Hamm, "Prison Islam in the Age of Sacred Terror," *The British Journal of Criminology*, vol. 49, no. 5, 2009, 667–685.

4. Scott MacEarchern, *Searching for Boko Haram: A History of Violence in Central Africa* (New York: Oxford University Press, 2018), 11–12.

5. Eva Evers Rosander, "Introduction: The Islamization of Tradition and Modernity," in David Westerlund and Eva Evers Rosander (eds.), *African Islam and Islam in Africa*, 23.

6. John Campbell, *US Policy to Counter Nigeria's Boko Haram*, Council Special Report no. 70 (New York: Council on Foreign Relations), 12.

7. See Shahrul Hussain, *A Treasury of Sacred Maxims: A Commentary on Islamic Legal Principles* (Leicestershire, UK: Kube Publishing Ltd., 2016), 12–14.

8. V. Kaul, "Can Muslims be Suicide Bombers?" An Essay on the Troubles of Multiculturalism, *Philosophy And Social Criticism*, vol. 38, no. 4–5, 2012.

9. Thomas Hegghammer, "The Rise of Muslim Foreign Fighters: Islam and the Globalization of Jihad," *International Security*, vol. 35, no. 3, 2010, 53–94.

10. Mike Smith, *Boko Haram: Inside Nigeria's Unholy War* (New York: I.B. Tauris, 2016), 76–79.

11. *The Holy Qur"an*, Yusuf Ali translation, 1946, chapter 5, verse 92, 270.

12. Ibid., chapter 42, verses 41–42, 1318.

13. Some argue that Islamism has replaced communism as the ultimate ideology of dissent.

14. *The Holy Qur'an*, Yusuf Ali translation, 1946, chapter 28, verse 5, 1002.

15. Ibid., chapter 5, verse 9, 243.

16. Ibid., chapter 2, verse 256, 103.

17. Ibid., verse 216, 84.

18. Ibid., verse 190, 75.

19. Ibid., verse 191, 75–76.

20. Ibid., verse 193, 76.

21. Ibid., chapter 67, verse 4, 1378–1379.

22. For a discussion of how this works in CAR, see Louisa Lombard, *State of Rebellion: Violence and Intervention in the Central African Republic* (Chicago, IL: The University of Chicago Press, originally Published by Zed Pub., 2016), 73.

23. The Charlie Hebdo attacks in Paris in 2015 are perhaps another illustration of the seriousness of words and images especially when seen as insulting to Islam and Muslims.

24. John Campbell, *US Policy to Counter Nigeria's Boko Haram*, Council Special Report no. 70 (New York: Council on Foreign Relations), 3.

25. "Nations Turn to Chad to Fight Jihadists in West Africa," *Wall Street Journal*, January 22, 2016.

26. Ibid.

27. Ibid.

28. Lombard, *State of Rebellion: Violence and Intervention in the Central African Republic*, 190.

29. Ibid.

30. Ibid., 227.

31. Ibid.

32. Ibid., 230.

33. Ibid.

34. Ibid., 231.

35. Ibid., 212.

36. Ibid., 113.

37. Ibid.

38. Mamman Nur a Cameroonian believed to have masterminded the bombing of UN headquarters in Abuja, Nigeria, in 2011 is a founding member of Ansaru. See Charles River Editors, *Boko Haram: The History of Africa's Most Notorious Terrorist Group*, 29–30.

39. Samory Rashid, *Black Muslims in the US: History, Politics and the Struggle of a Community* (New York: Palgrave MacMillan, 2013).

40. Ibid.

41. The longer version of this letter is provided in chapter 4. See Sylviane A. Diouf, *Servants of Allah: Africans Enslaved in the Americas* (New York: New York University Press, 1998), electronic version, 27.

42. Ismail Rashid, "A Devotion to the Idea of Liberty at Any Price: Rebellion and Anti-Slavery in the Upper Guinea Coast in the Eighteenth and Nineteenth Centuries," in Sylviane Diouf (ed.), *Fighting the Slave Trade in West Africa* (Athens: Ohio University Press, 2003).

43. Ibid., 142–146.

44. Ibid., 134, 139.

45. Ibid., 135.

46. Ibid.

47. Ibid., 134–35.

48. Ibid., introduction, xi

49. Ibid., 139–40.

50. Robert B. Edgerton, *Africa's Armies: From Honor to Infamy: A History from 1971 to the Present* (Boulder, CO: Westview Press, 2002), 32.

51. Considerable information exists on the Tukulor empire. However, for a quick summary of its history, see http://www.blackpast.org/gah/tukulor-empire-1852-1864.

52. Usita G. Afoaku, "Islamist Terrorism and State Failure in Northern Nigeria," *Africa Today*, vol. 63, no. 4, 2017, 21–42.

53. Mike Smith, *Boko Haram: Inside Nigeria's Unholy War* (New York: I.B. Taurus, 2016), 65.

54. Ibid.

55. Smith, *Boko Haram*, 63.

56. John Campbell, "US Policy to Counter Nigeria's Boko Haram," *Council on Foreign Relations: Center for Preventive Action*, Council Special Report no. 70, November 2014, 3.

57. Ibid.

58. Ibid.

59. Smith, *Boko Haram*, 51.

60. Ibid., 75.

61. Ibid. Also see MacEachern, *Searching for Boko Haram*, 9–10.

62. Smith, *Boko Haram*, 60–61.

63. Ibid., 61.

64. Ibid.

65. Ibid., vii.

66. Ibid.

67. Ibid., 93.

68. Ibid.

69. Ibid., 92–94.

70. Smith, *Boko Haram*, 93. If these reports sound eerily similar to police encounters with black and brown youth in the United States, perhaps it is because they are.

71. Gilbert L. Taguem Fah, "The War on Terror, the Chad-Cameroon Pipeline and the New Identity of the Lake Chad Basin," *Journal of Contemporary African Studies*, vol. 25, no. 1, 2007, 101–117.

72. Ibid., 59.

73. Ibid.

74. Ibid., 74.

75. Ibid., 88.

76. Ibid., 77.

77. Ibid.

78. Ibid.

79. Ibid., 78.

80. Ibid.

81. Ibid., 79.

82. Ibid., 79, 88, and 89

83. Ibid., 90.

84. See Michael Scheuer, "How and How Not to Fight Terrorism," YouTube (video), March 2005. https://www.youtube.com/watch?v=E0dPy2XCst8.

85. Christopher S. Chivvis, *The French War on Al Qa'ida in Africa* (New York: Cambridge University Press, 2016), 71.

86. Ibid.

Chapter 3

Politics of Muslim Struggle
(*jihad*) and Africans

This chapter continues our discussion of Muslim struggle (*jihad*) and Africans by exploring the politics of Muslim struggle (*jihad*) hereafter referred to as Muslim struggle among Africans. No other group in human history has had more documented experience with Muslim struggle, as a group, than Africans and their progeny primarily in Africa, the Middle, Europe and the Americas (North and South).[1] The Artic and Antarctica may be the only places on earth where Muslim struggle among Africans is not known to exist. This is not to say that Africans are the only people who have immersed themselves in the experience of Muslim struggle for struggle lies at the heart of what it means to be human. The Qur'an frequently asserts that life is rooted in struggle, implying that life is full of trials and tribulations—where happiness rather than a permanent state is but a temporary respite. Terrorist violence and the state-based persecution it often seeks to eradicate, to be sure, are the trials and tribulations of our postmodern world. Yet, never were they meant to be a justification for violence, killing, and behaving unjustly toward others. Muslim struggle is the legitimate tool for responding to the challenge of persecution and oppression for Muslims and not terrorism. This chapter also introduces the Afrocentric perspective of Ivan Van Sertima and others, which despite its shortcomings reveals aspects of African history often ignored by western observers. Some ignored information by mainstream western narratives results from ignorance while others results from bigotry. For instance, most observers in the Islamic world believe divine intervention caused the elephants of would-be African invaders of Mecca to flee in 570 AD, the year of the Prophet's birth to avert a near certain defeat of the Meccans. This event is described by the Qur'an, in the chapter (*sura*) titled, "The Elephant" (*al-fil*). But the version of this event embraced in this study differs somewhat from descriptions of early Arabia offered by Afrocentric scholars who offer more boldly, provocative interpretations which though plausible are not always supported by evidence. For example, one Afrocentric scholar describes how Arabia was a Negro colony with Mecca as its capital. Another argues that Arabia was populated by Africans.[2] Yet, regardless of which view one embraces, the mainstream Muslim view or the Afrocentric view, narratives of Africans typically offered by westerners remain woefully incomplete. Although ignorance and bigotry may largely explain shortcomings in mainstream western scholarship as it relates to Africans, how might differences between mainstream Muslim and Afrocentric perspectives be explained?

Mainstream Muslim and Afrocentric perspectives may be a bi-product of the Qur'an's directive to "compete in goodness" which is what conservative mainstream Muslims and Afrocentric scholars (some of whom are Muslim) do, in effect, when they attempt to correct mainstream western views of the role of African Muslims in world and Islamic history. Differing viewpoints among Muslims have always been evident as seen in the four distinctive schools of Islamic law (*shari'ah*) and variations in the authoritative accounts of the sayings (*hadith*) of the Prophet Muhammad. Differences between the mainstream Muslim and the Afrocentric perspective is merely a reflection of this phenomenon. Yet beyond this, Afrocentric scholars arguably seem to compete with three distinct goals in mind. First, to refute myths and stereotyped images of Africans primarily produced in the West as described in the introduction of this study. Second, to refute the racism of Arabs like Ibn Khaldun also described in the introduction of this study. Third, to present bold and provocative counter-narratives to serve as antidotes to uninformed and bigoted accounts. To their credit, what Afrocentric thinkers do best is reveal important elements of the historical narrative omitted from "official" western accounts. But what Afrocentric thinkers do less well is provide credible and reliable information that seems reasonably resistant to the Afropessimist critique. This shortcoming in the Afrocentric perspective may ultimately do more harm than good. As an alternative, this chapter attempts to provide plausibly reasonable and logically sound evidence drawn from both mainstream Muslim and Afrocentric perspectives to compensate for major historical inadequacies in the literature. However, no matter the intent or perspective embraced, the ultimate arbiter of credible evidence is the individual observer. Mindful of this truism, an opportunity to determine the veracity of information about African Muslims is offered to readers primarily in sections of this chapter devoted to blacks, Arabs and Islam, and blacks in the growth and spread of Islam.

One year after the French counter-offensive in Mali and one and one-half years before the crash of the French Air Algérie Flight 5017, new violence broke out in the Malian city of Gao. On February 8, 2013, Majao fighters launched 122-mm rockets into Gao when a suicide bomber attacked a Malian army checkpoint there. The bomber was later identified as a local Arab youth who had been living in a Majao camp. Two days later street fighting between French forces and Islamist militants in Gao's tangled streets ended when a Tigre attack helicopter fired five 30-mm rounds into a house where the Islamist militant fighters were housed. The mayor of Gao fled the city for Bamako during the disturbance but not before issuing a warning with far-reaching implications. The mayor warned that "Majao had in fact never left [the vicinity], but simply shaved their beards and disguised themselves as regular citizens."[3] The mayor's remarks though heard many times before in the WOT are a grim reminder that, if left unchecked, Islamist militants are prepared to wage protracted struggle.

It is clear that terrorist violence as captured by such popular phrases as "jihadists" and "jihadism" is something different from legitimate Muslim struggle (*jihad*), hereafter referred to as Muslim struggle. It is equally clear that actions such as those linked to Boko Haram diverge from a long and celebrated legacy of successful experience with Muslim struggle among Africans and their progeny throughout the world. The implications of this are at once simple and profound. Conscious awareness of the long and celebrated legacy of legitimate Muslim struggle among Africans offers ample tools, remedies, and incentives for responding to contemporary forms of persecution and injustice without resorting to terrorist violence. African Muslims aware of this distinction struggle along the well-worn path of those who struggled before them and belong to the group the Qur'an refers to as the "rightly guided" (*al-rashidun*) ones. Western policy makers especially in the United States must be ever mindful of the distinction between terrorism and legitimate Muslim struggle, and that if trials such as persecution and oppression are unavoidable elements of life, then struggle including violent struggle may also at times be unavoidable.

This means that in its encounters with the Muslim world, US policy makers would be well advised to avoid ignoring the distinction between terrorist violence and legitimate Muslim struggle—a distinction easily lost with use of the words "jihadist" and "jihadism." Through the discussion of major historical examples of Muslim struggle, this chapter explores Muslim struggle among Africans and their progeny as an important and significant institution. Perhaps most difficult for many westerners is the need to respect the fact that Muslims have the right to determine, manage, and interpret the guidelines governing Muslim struggle. Muslims have their own Imams, sheikhs, and scholars (*'ulema*) to guide in this important endeavor. But even Muslim religious leaders face limits as Muslims believe that on judgment day, no one, that is, not the imam, not the sheikh, and not the scholars (*'ulema*) will be able to affect one's fate. Each and every Muslim faces the moral and ethical task of choosing when and how to conduct Muslim struggle mindful of the Qur'anic reminder to "fight evil with that which is best."

Failure to struggle is tantamount to a grave sin in Islam as seen in the famous saying (*hadith*), "if you see wrong change with your hands, if you cannot do it, change it would your tongue, if you cannot do it, change it with your heart, for this is the lowest test of righteousness." Major differences over the application of Muslim struggle inevitably emerge in discussions and debates between Muslims and non-Muslims. It is clear from these encounters that the West is often reticent to condone Muslim struggle where it may involve violence except in cases where the West's own interest may be at state, as seen in the US war on ISIS. But the Qur'an and the authoritative sources in Islam are decidedly less reluctant concerning the use of force in these instances. Despite western reticence to support Muslim struggle when it involves the use of violence, the historical record is replete with examples of the use of violence by western powers in response to perceived injustice, persecution, and oppression. The American War for independence against the system of British colonialism is a notable case in point. World Wars I and II against fascism and the Cold War against communism offer additional examples. But when victimized Muslims are inconsistently supported by the United States in Nigeria, Kenya, CAR, Niger, and Mali, accusations of double standards inevitably arise. Could this be a case of the adage, "do as I say and not as I do?

Black Muslim leader Malcolm X, during the US civil rights movement of the 1950s and 1960s widely denounced as a hate monger, once criticized inconsistencies that persist to this day when he asked: how can violence be justified against enemies of the United States overseas yet rejected as a tool of self-defense in the face of the killing of innocent black victims in the United States where authorities have been either unwilling or unable to protect them? When explaining his reluctance to embrace the nonviolent civil disobedience movement of Dr. Martin Luther King Jr., Malcolm X rejected the logic of encouraging blacks to take up arms to fight enemies of the United States abroad while denying them that same right to defend themselves against the violence of bigotry at home. If whites were allowed to form riffle clubs to defend their families and communities against the threat of domestic violence, then blacks should be afforded the same right, in Malcolm's view. While it is easy to dismiss Malcolm as just another black militant, this question first raised by black Muslims during the 1960s remains largely unresolved in the United States where even peaceful protests by black athletes at sporting events against police brutality are seen as expressions of anti-American dissent. Malcolm X in 1963 embraced neither the nonviolent civil disobedience of Dr. Martin Luther King Jr., nor the liberal politics of the Democratic Party. Instead, for reasons too complex to elaborate here, he supported the conservative Senator Barry Goldwater for US president based on his views related to how best to fight violent anti-black persecution while resisting pressures to join the secular Republican Party as his successor and close friend W. D. Muhammad of the Nation of Islam (NOI) movement (d. 2003) would do years later. Malcolm's stand was rare for a "black leader" at that time and an important voice missing from contemporary debates.

The United States must resist as a matter of principle the action of rejecting the possible use of violence as part of the Muslim struggle against injustice. The Muslim perspective holds that persecution and oppression must be resisted regardless of its source. This means that injustice is equally abhorrent weather it derives from actors who happen to be allies of the United States or Islamist militants such as Boko Haram. Failing to resist injustice by the state would be tantamount to repeating the same mistakes made by the United States during the period of anti-colonialism during the 1950s, 1960s, and 1970s when the United States refused to support national liberation struggles in Africa or domestic campaigns against racial bigotry in the "the Old South." Instead, the United States opposed popular democratic struggles and supported (for a time) non-democratic white minority regimes during 1950s, 1960s, and 1970s. Unsurprisingly, white minority regimes in South Africa, Rhodesia, and Mozambique eventually fell to popular African sentiments and movements. The United States was on the wrong side of history during the Cold War in Africa and because of this, it must avoid making the same mistake of believing it can control and direct popular struggles among Africans in the US-led WOT. Africa's Muslims for their part must also embrace the lessons of history and accept the fact that Muslim struggle as opposed to terrorist violence is a more effective and more normatively defensible strategy. The failure to do so will be to err on the wrong side of history as cases of Muslim struggle explored in this chapter intend to reveal. Muslim struggle when properly understood offers a demonstrably, more viable response to oppression and injustice than terrorist violence.

This chapter shifts the focus of investigation from legitimate Muslim struggle in response to *contemporary* persecution and oppression to Muslim struggle in response to *historical* persecution and oppression. The first primarily involves the struggle against colonialism and the postmodern secular state in Africa. The second primarily involves Muslim struggle against religious persecution of the kind experienced by the Prophet. Muslim struggle throughout history with its strict guidelines and limits has been a traditional response, corrective device, and resistance tool available to Muslims in the contemporary and historical eras. But its existence is overshadowed in the West when many westerners fail to distinguish terrorist violence from legitimate Muslim struggle which the West continues to benefit from, thanks to the efforts of its many African allies that include the state forces of Chad, Nigeria, and Mali in the WOT. Overlooking the value of legitimate Muslim struggle is difficult to do for those familiar with the history of Muslim struggle as a defensive response since the time of the Prophet Muhammad.

This chapter in addition to debunking a number of African myths and stereotypes emphasizes the distinction between the terrorist violence of Islamist militancy and Muslim struggle, toward the goal of better understanding the latter as a vital tool of resistance and long utilized coping mechanism among mainstream Muslims. This chapter endeavors to shine new light on more productive and sustainable ways to diminish if not eliminate terrorist violence as a response to persecution and oppression among Africans regardless of whether its source is an imperialist invader, a slave raider, authoritarian state, or Islamist militant. Legitimate Muslim struggle provides a distinct and unique tool among African Muslims that has survived largely intact with a demonstrated record of success at resisting persecution since the days of the Prophet. Understanding this and utilizing it as a defensive tool offers useful opportunities to discover alternative ways of combatting terrorist violence among Africans. But its viability in Muslim societies like Nigeria, Chad, and Mali depends on the degree to which the leaders of the Muslim struggle embrace moral standards that exceed those embraced by their oppressors/opponents. If they do not, then leaders run the risk of forfeiting the moral authority to appeal to legitimate Muslim struggle as a corrective device against persecution and oppression.

Put differently, leaders cannot call upon members of society to mobilize against the persecution and oppression condemned by the Qur'an when Muslim leaders themselves (e.g., former Nigerian president Sani Abacha) are the main sources of persecution and oppression. Evidence of this can be seen in the US reluctance to provide unlimited military support to the Nigerian state in view of Nigeria's abysmal human rights record. In addition to this, splits in the ranks of Boko Haram and the emergence of more moderate factions opposed to the killing of fellow Muslims may reflect recognition among Africans of their own moral inconsistencies and a willingness to correct past mistakes. The history and influence of Muslim struggle among Africans explored in this chapter will examine (1) "The True Meaning of *Jihad*"; (2) The *Jihads* of West Africa; (3) Blacks, Arabs, and Islam; (4) Blacks and the Growth and Spread of Islam; (5) Ziryab the Moor; (6) The Zanj Rebellion; and (7) Resisting Domination.

THE TRUE MEANING OF *JIHAD*

This chapter examines jihad as Muslim struggle rather than "jihadism" as an instrument of terror to cast greater light on events which Muslims themselves regard as instances of legitimate Muslim struggle and how the two very different conceptualizations of *jihad* render very different outcomes. There is little wonder why non-Muslims and Muslims have such different reactions to the idea of Muslim struggle. Several well-known cases of Muslim struggle among Africans are offered. This chapter is a continuation of the previous chapter on Muslim struggle. But instead of discussing episodes and cases of Muslim struggle that contrast sharply with cases and episode of Muslim terror as discussed in chapter 2, this chapter examines the Islamic institution of Muslim struggle, the role of Africans in its establishment and spread and its importance as a tool for guiding legitimate Muslim responses to the challenge of persecution and oppression.

THE *JIHADS* OF WEST AFRICA

Thornton notes correctly that "the eighteenth century witnessed a great surge of slave importation from Africa both fueled by and fueling the wars and banditry that often led to enslavement."[4] One of the earliest reactions against the slave trade by Muslims of West Africans appeared in the Purification (*Toubenan*) movement from 1673 to 1677 led by Nasr al Din in the area of modern-day Senegal as discussed in the previous chapter. But perhaps the most famous Muslim struggle/reform movement among Africans was the *jihad* of Uthman dan Fodio (1802–1804) involving the Fulani of northern Nigeria and western Chad/Niger that remains the scene of Muslim struggle today as seen in the ongoing Boko Haram insurgency.

The Fulani (or Fulbe or Puel) were a distinctive mainly pastoral people spread across the western Sudan (from *bilad al-Sudan*, or land of the blacks, in Arabic) who found themselves under growing pressure from settled agricultural populations and their rulers. They were often resented and treated as intruders, and their grazing and trading rights faced ever-tightening restriction. This plus higher taxes persecution at the hands of corrupt rulers and enslavement by elites led Fulani leaders to undertake legitimate Muslim struggle. The best-known case of Muslim struggle includes the Fulani Muslim leader Uthman dan Fodio, who struggled successfully in northern Nigeria (1802–1808).[5] Though he never completed the pilgrimage to Mecca, Uthman don Fodio was widely educated as a Muslim scholar and son of a Fulbe Muslim teacher in the northern Hausa state of Gobir. His Muslim struggle challenged political corruption among the Hausa (Muslim) ruling class, unfair taxation, and the enslavement of fellow Muslims. Hailed as an innovator, Uthman (also, Usman) is widely credited with linking the requirement of flight-separation (*hijra*) with that of *jihad* and thereby introducing elements of the very first Muslim jihad in Arabia into West Africa. Uthman's legitimate Muslim struggle established the Sokoto Caliphate perhaps the largest of its kind in Africa. It dominated in northern Nigeria until the rise of British colonial rule after the Berlin conference of 1884–1885 and the European "scramble for Africa." Uthman retired from public life shortly after the fall of Gobir in 1808 but his authority was passed on to his brother Abdullahi and son Muhammad Bello. Uthman passed away in 1817. By the time of his son Muhammad Bello's death in 1837, the Sokoto caliphate had a population of some 10 million people, larger than any other West African state before that time.

Other sheikhs emerged with the blessing of Uthman dan Fodio including Seku Ahmadu (1818–1845). The Tukolor empire of the ca. 1770s to 1864 also emerged as a major proponent of the Muslim struggle led by Fulbe (or Fulani) Muslims who rose to confront corrupt Hausa elites. A notable leader of these Muslim struggles was the Fulani leader al hajj Umar. Umar Saidu (al-Hajj Umar Tall) was born in 1796 into a family of pious Muslims. He rejected the authority of the Kadiriyya brotherhood (of Sufism), perhaps the most prominent leader in West Africa to embrace the Tijaniyya Muslim brotherhood after travelling to North Africa. He embarked on an ambitious program of travel during 1826 to 1847 during which he performed the pilgrimage to Mecca (hajj). He spent time (1830–1838) in northern Nigeria where he studied with Muhammad Bello and married one of his daughters before returning home. He built a formidable Muslim state stretching from Futa Toro to Massina from parts of modern-day Senegal to modern-day Mali and dedicated his life to the Islamization of West Africa.

The Tukolor (ca. 1852–1864) led by al-Hajj Umar Tal a member of the Fulbe ethnic group and a sheikh began preaching in Gobir following his tutelage under the Tuareg sheikh Jabril ibn Umar. The latter stressed the value and importance of *jihad*. But his preoccupation with promoting Islamization and military conquest caused him to neglect other important aspects of empire including the building of schools, mosques, and other vital institutions. Corruption returned and his practice of capturing and selling non-Muslims to Europeans in exchange for modern weaponry eventually led to his downfall as the French succeeded by supporting his adversaries one by one including members of his own family until Umar himself was eventually killed. Forced from his original home in the Futa Toro in modern-day Senegal, Umar Tal built a substantial following headquartered in Massina just south of the present-day town of Timbuktu in modern southern Mali. The rise of the Fulani (or Fuble), Tukolor (or Torodbe) Empire actually emerged before the arrival of Umar Tal. Malik Sy is described by at least one scholar as the founder of the Sisabe dynasty at about the time the Sy began to dominate the Fulani people (1690–1800). Between 1769 and 1776, the Tukolor united to establish a new Muslim state based on Islamic Law (*shari'ah*). At its peak around 1800, the Tukolor jihadist state in the Futo Toro region of modern-day Senegal represented the largest most powerful jihadist state in West Africa. Muslim Fulani Suleymaani Baal's internal jihad lasted from 1769 to 1776 and transformed the Futa Toro region in present-day Senegal to a Muslim state.[6]

To the south of the Tukolor state emerged the Mandinka empire of Samory Toure who emerged from a non-Muslim Dyula family east of the Futa Jallon.[7] As a young man in the 1860s, he emerged from a trading and military background to lead the most formidable African fighting force of its day. As noted earlier, Rogers describes Samory by the title afforded to him by the French, as the "Napoleon of the Sudan." Samory was a formidable opponent of the French and a brilliant military tactician. His Muslim struggle was unique because instead of enslaving his defeated opponents, he incorporated them into his army upon their acceptance of Islam. But he like most of his contemporaries continued to engage in the enslavement of non-Muslims. These notable examples of Muslim struggle illustrate the historical depth of this Muslim institution among Africans. Its primary objective of resisting persecution and oppression give it primacy and relevance that still exists to this day among Africans. But the fact that many of these cases of Muslim struggle occur in roughly the same geographic location as sights for contemporary terrorist violence, for example, in northern Nigeria, underscores the continued historical importance and relevance of Muslim struggle among Africans in the region.

BLACKS, ARABS, AND ISLAM

Muslim struggle or striving and sacrificing on behalf of the community to promote its interest through conquest, territorial expansion, and the defeat of rivals is not unlike similar actions undertaken by certain Christian nations during their early days of empire. The desire to solidify Muslim unity across state boundaries and diverse Muslim societies meant prominent persons from prominent Muslim families married into similarly prominent families. For example, Osama bin Laden before his capture and execution in 2011 had married into the family of Hassan al-Turabi; while Hassan al-Turabi before his death in 2016 had married into the family of Sadiq al-Mahdi, the great grandson of Muhammad Ahmad (*al-Mahdi*) and founder of modern-day Sudan. This practice illustrates the lengths to which early Muslims went to discourage conflict, disunity, and war with each other, to say nothing of terrorist violence. The Prophet Muhammad made frequent use of this device among other things to establish broad family bonds and alliances in the interest of peace and unity. The famous African Muslim sheikh al hajj Umar Tall is believed to have married the daughter of Ahmadu Bello to gain entry to the even more famous family of Uthman dan Fodio, sheikh and founder of the Sokoto Caliphate of northern Nigeria.

Muslim struggle also seeks to accommodate different though related goals that include (1) protecting the rights of minorities as seen in the struggle to promote Shia Muslim survival, (2) promoting the rights of women, (3) promoting the rights of African and other non-Arab Muslims, (4) serving as an instrument of national liberation as seen in the case of the break-away Muslim state of Moorish Spain, (5) promoting the rights of formerly enslaved Muslims as seen in the case of the Zanj struggle of southern Iraq, and (6) promoting the interests of the worldwide Muslim community (*ummah*) as seen in the seventeenth-century confrontation between Muslim and Christian nations conducted largely at sea (discussed in chapter 6). Africans played leading roles in each of these forms of Muslim struggles. Over time, African Muslims joined many others to establish the Muslim world's broad mosaic of diverse people, narratives, and cultures.

To understand Islam among Africans, one must understand the relationship between blacks, Arabs, and Islam. Long before the rise of Islam as a religion, blacks forged an unmistakable link with Arabia. Important demographic and economic factors led Southern Arabians to migrate to Ethiopia. While it is difficult to fix an exact date for these migrations, Arab migration to Africa may have begun before 1,000 BC.[8] The groups that migrated to Ethiopia from the Arabian Peninsula were many, but the Habashat and the Agazian (Gaze) may be the best known.[9] Continued contact between Ethiopians and southern Arabians became more intense and political over time. By 750 BC, the Sabeans of southern Arabia comingled with Ethiopians to form the African kingdom of Axum. Evidence of this comingling can be witnessed in *Axumite* script, a derivative of Sabaen of southern Arabia and the earliest known Ethiopian alphabet. Once dominant over the entire peninsula, the African presence in what is today Saudi Arabia is perhaps most visibly apparent among the Sabeans once known as "the Phoenicians of the southern seas."[10] While Chandler reminds us of W. E. B. Dubois's caution against drawing absolute distinctions between Arabs and blacks, while the orientalist Bernard Lewis notes that although the vast majority of unskilled slaves in premodern Middle East came from regions immediately to the North and South of Arabia and that most of these enslaved victims had a cultural level at least as high as that of their Arab masters, and by conversion and manumission were rapidly absorbed into the general population.[11] The African presence in the Arab world is perhaps most visible at present in Mauritania, Sudan, Somalia, Upper Egypt south of Cairo, Tripoli, Libya, Basra, Iraq, Yemen, and Oman in the Arab Gulf, and the Saudi Arabian cities of Mecca, Medina, and Jedda. However, the broad variety non-Arabs absorbed over time into Arab society including Turks, Europeans, and Central Asians has allowed others besides blacks to display a distinct and visible presence in contemporary Arab society.[12]

The name for Ethiopia, Abyssinia, appears in the Bible and is believed to be Greek in origin (*Aethiops*). After the rise of Axum, Africans assumed a dominant and aggressive role in Ethiopian-South Arabian relations. Around AD 195, the Ethiopian king Gadara became the most dominant figure in southern Arabia. King sent both soldiers and settlers to the region. In light of the Ethiopian occupation of Saba (southern Arabia) from AD 335 to 370, Ethiopians may be arguably responsible for implanted Christianity on South Arabian soil. A number of Sabean rulers appear to have adopted Christianity facilitating the religion's presence in early Arabia as evidenced by the presence of six Arabian bishops at the historic Council of Nicea in AD 325. Later under the leadership of *Malikkarib Yuhad'in*, southern Arabia attracted many Jews, a development which may have been associated with a rise in Jewish-Christian tensions on the Arabian Peninsula. According to one source, "Many of the first Muslim converts were Africans" [and] according to some accounts including the brilliant black writer and historian Uthman Amr ibn Bahr al-Jahiz, the Prophet himself was partly of African lineage. The Prophet's grandfather fathered ten sons all of dark complexion, one of whom was the Prophet's father, Abdullah. Historians Lewis and Gomez have corroborated this observation.[13]

Although it obviously still existed, racism seems to have been less important as a motive for enslavement by Arabs for there were slaves of all races and ethnicities in the Middle East. However, it would be a mistake to conclude that racism is nonexistent among Arabs. Ibn Khaldûn's fourteenth-century description of black thinking skills as being "close to those of dumb animals" is a case in point. An August 2007 decree aimed at abolishing Arab enslavement of blacks (yet again) in Mauritania offers and additional illustration.[14] Indeed, Saudi Arabia was one of the last modern states to outlaw slavery in the 1960s, at a time when slavery had become virtually limited to blacks. The Moorish/Arab state of Mauritania may be the only state in the modern world that still supports vestiges of black enslavement reminiscent of racist attitudes of Ibn Khaldun displayed in this study's introduction.

While race in the Arab world has been less of a serious obstacle to advancement, tribal affiliation or the lack thereof represents a more serious obstacle to social advancement in the Arab world. Perry's observation that "members of the most prestigious families in the Arab Middle East, 'tended to have slave mothers, African or otherwise' suggest that non-Arab identity may be of little or no consequence."[15] However, such a conclusion would be false. Because social status in the Arab-Islamic world is achieved through attachment to a powerful willing Arab client, Islam, or ties to an Arab patriarch, non-Arab, non-Muslim blacks in the Arab world are/were especially vulnerable to discrimination as we will see later in this chapter in the case of contemporary Iraq.[16] Tension between Islam's universalistic teachings and its application in concrete situations suggest that most Arabs were forced to modify their racial prejudices without necessarily abandoning them altogether. This behavior is most vividly displayed among some rural Bedouins in remote settings in contrast to cosmopolitan Arabs living in major cities. As Ivan Van Sertima asserts, Islam may have modified racial prejudice but it did not eradicate it.[17]

The debate over the nature of racism in the Arab/Islamic world is itself evidence of a longstanding African presence in that world. For instance, the African freedman Bilal ibn Rabah, the first Muslim caller to prayer (*muez-zin*), discussed in greater detail in chapter 4, was among the Prophet's closest and most revered companions. Enslaved Africans were frequently mentioned among the original companions of the Prophet Muhammad (*al-sahāba*). Even before the Prophet migrated from Mecca to Medina on the now famous flight (*hijra*), a number of enslaved African Muslims under the Prophet Muhammad's orders emigrated from Mecca to Ethiopia to escape persecution at the hands of the Meccans. Because of this, Ibrahim Abu Lughod argues that it is possible to view Islam as a religious belief-system as indigenous to Africa as it was to the Arab Middle East.[18] Adding to this, Robinson writes,

> On two occasions he [the Prophet] sent groups secretly across the Red Sea to the emperor's protection in Aksum, knowing that they [the Muslims] would receive a good reception as fellow monotheists. A small group went in 615 C.E. and a larger group went the following year. Over 100 went in all, representing a siz-able portion of the Muslims at the time, only two or three years after the Prophet began public preaching. Included among them were some important figures: Muhammad's daughter Ruqayya, her husband Uthman (who would become the third caliph), Muhammad's future wife Umm Habiba, and his cousin Jafar, and brother Ali.[19]

Given this history, the Prophet adopted a position of neutrality toward Christians and Jews of Ethiopia for the assistance he received from the Ethiopian king at a critical juncture in Islamic history. This position is best illustrated by the clear and direct saying of the Prophet (*hadith*) to "leave the Abyssinians alone."[20]

The freedman Zayd bin Harith, who became one of Islam's greatest generals may have been an African. Following the death of his mother, the African woman, Barakat, is said to have raised the Prophet. One of the Prophet's concubines, named Maryam, is said to have been an African.[21] Gomez and Lewis separately suggest that the Prophet in addition to being Arab may have been part African, though it is forbidden to depict physical images of the Prophet or refer his color or ethnicity as seen in the violence that targeted the satirical magazine, Charlie Hebdo, of Paris by militant Islamists in November 2015 for publishing disparaging cartoon images of the Prophet. Yet, it would be a mistake to view mention of Africans in the birth and development of Islam as an attempt to elevate Africans as a group above others as many including Arabs, Persian, Turks, Central Asians, Indonesian, Indians, Mongols, Tatars, and Chinese have made valuable contribution to the development and spread of Islam and creation of a Muslim world mosaic rather than a Muslim world monolith as explored by Gregorian.

BLACKS AND THE GROWTH AND SPREAD OF ISLAM

Islamic history offers clear evidence of the link between blacks and Islam. By the time of the Prophet's death in AD 632, Islam had reached the western half of the Arabian Peninsula. Blacks became major players in Islam's spread especially during its first decade. According to one source, "the first Muslim killed in defense of Islam was a man named Mihdja,[22] who according to one source was a Black man." Chinyelu quotes Rogers as saying "most of the [Prophet's] earliest Muslim converts were Africans" with a little more than 100 according to Robinson seeking refuge in Ethiopia before reuniting with the Prophet later on in Medina (*Yathrib*). Yet, for the sake of argument, even if one adjusts Rogers's statement to read "many" instead of "most," Rogers's observation still seems intriguing given the relatively small numbers of the early followers of the Prophet there were in Mecca. Based on historical accounts, the number seemed more likely to have been in the hundreds than in the thousands.[23] Given this logic Africans if not in the majority may have been as many as one half, one third, or one quarter of the Prophet's early followers. Another writer describes how Tarik ibn Ziad, the Muslim general who first invaded AD 711 whose name adorns the Gibraltar cliff (derived from the Arabic word for mountain Jebel and Tarik), was an African, derided by the Arab Governor Musa Nosseyr for invading without him after the Governor was first invited in 709 AD to invade by the Visogoth inhabitants of al-Andalus.[24]

Africans were pivotal to the successful Moorish conquest of Spain (*al-Andalus*) in AD 711 and to the development and spread of Islam throughout North, East, and West Africa. Indeed, one writer correctly observes that there is no time in the history of faith that Islam can be disassociated from Africans. The first convert to Islam outside the family of the Prophet was the Ethiopian and first caller (*muezzin*) to Islamic prayer, named Bilal. According to at least one hadith, Bilal was the first choice of the Prophet to be his successor. But Bilal declined and supported those who selected Abu Bakr as Caliph. When Abu Bakr by consensus was the recognized favorite within the community, he was selected to become the first successor (*Caliph*) to the Prophet. And one of the Prophet's wives was an African woman named May.

W. E. B. Dubois (1868–1963), the famous African American scholar and likely first African American to graduate from Harvard, who died in Ghana after a long and celebrated career, reminds us that Spain was not conquered by Arabs but rather by Berbers and "Negroids" who were at times led by Arabs. When Tarik the black general who crossed the straits of Hercules on April 30, AD 711, reportedly with 7,000 men, 6,700 were native Africans (Moors) and 300 were Arabs.[25] The name Gibraltar is a corruption of the words mountain (*jebel*) in Arabic and the name of the black general who crossed to conquer Spain, Tarik. Question of identity in the Muslim world in Dubois's view stems from the practice of referring to Muslims as Arabs. But obviously not all Arabs are Muslim and not all Muslims are Arabs. Therefore, a more defensible observation by Dubois is that Arabs are too nearly akin to Negros in terms of their appearance to draw an absolute color line distinguishing the two given the considerable "race mixing" that occurs in the Arab world causing the term "Arab" to have cultural value but little if any ethnic significance.[26]

MOORISH AND OTHER AFRICAN INFLUENCES

The Moors of Africa played prominent roles on the world stage. For example, Moors participated in conflicts between Rome and Carthage in North Africa. Hannibal Barca, who crossed the Alps with the aid of elephants to defeat the Romans, was a Moor. The Carthaginians used Moorish troops in their campaigns against the Romans and others.[27] Sicily was dominated by Moors and Arabs for 200 years, while the Mediterranean Island of Crete according to one source was dominated by Moors and Arabs for 125 years. The labels Berber, Moor, Arab, and Muslim were treated as synonyms by Europeans and often used interchangeably during the Middle Ages.[28]

The Moors ruled parts of Spain for nearly 800 years, from 711 to 1492. During that time, the Almoravids and their Mobt-Theim male (wearers of the veil) represented the first of two great Moorish dynasties that ruled Spain. The Almoravids ruled Spain for a little more than a century under its leader Yusuf ibn Tashifin, described as a "Black African" who presided over a joint court that governed Spain and parts of North Africa, from his based in North Africa until Tashifin's death in 1106.[29] Known as the "Empire of the two Shores" the Almoravid dynasty was initiated in 1095 by Sanhadja Berbers who practiced a form of black Judaism before becoming absorbed by the Almoravids were referred to as the *Bafour*. Sanhadja men constantly wore veils, considered a mark of privilege in Spain and forbidden to all but Sanhadja men to wear in Muslim Spain (but not in Africa). The Almoravids lasted 100 years and stretched from the Senegal River to Ebro River in northern

Spain. The tradition of the Sanhadja veil worn by men but not by women continues to exist as seen in a 2018 BBC documentary on the fabled city of Timbuktu in Mali, West Africa.[30] Afterwards, a second Moorish dynasty ruled Spain known as the Almohades. Both had a dramatic impact on Spanish life, cultural, and on all Europe for that matter. Both dynasties were led by people who originated from nearby West African areas that include Ghana, Mali, Senegal, and Songhay. While the Almoravids were known as fierce fighters, the Almohades were known as great philosophers and scholars who encouraged and scholarly debates between Averroes-Aristoteleans and orthodox Islamic thinkers like al-Ghazzali or Algazel as he was known to Europeans. While the Almoravids are described as being black African whose "blood" had been mixed with Arabs; the Almohades are described as being "pure Black" Africans. The Almohades encouraged non-theological pursuits and sparked an increase in secular approaches to knowledge that profoundly influenced western science and thinkers from Averroes to Sir Francis Bacon and the scientific method. For instance, the astrolabe may have been introduced to the world by the Moors of Spain whose skilled users according to Gomez (2005) may have played a role in Columbus trans-navigation of the Atlantic and "discovery" the New World in 1492.[31]

Consistent with the prevailing mood of *Shu'ubiyyah,* Moorish Spain prospered from its ability to harmonize the contributions of Africans, Arabs, Jews, and some Christians.[32] Such an achievement seems noteworthy given the elusive nature of peace in the contemporary Middle East. Moorish Spain also contributed mightily to the restoration of Europe in the Age of Enlightenment as known as the Renaissance. The Greeks and other Mediterranean communities benefited directly from the achievements of the Islamic world. Mediterranean Europe benefited from its unique position geographically and intellectually, while the rest of Europe languished in decline. Mediterranean Europe including Greece and Sicily enjoyed valuable access it held to the Islamic world that brought benefits to the whole of Europe. Despite these achievements, racist images of Africa and the Islamic world as described in this study's introduction persisted during this time, as by-products of European stereotypes of Africans. But the well-known cases of (1) Ziryab the Moor and (2) the Zanj "Rebellion" contradict popular stereotypes of blacks/Africans.

ZIRYAB THE MOOR

The case of Ziryab or Abu'l-Hasian Ali ibn Nafi' (789–857) described by Chandler as a Renaissance man before there was a Renaissance, demonstrates Africans's longstanding contributions to the Islamic world and beyond. Although it is not entirely clear that he was black by American standards,

Ziryab was nevertheless known as "Blackbird" because of his complexion and elegance of his voice. If he was not "black" by today's standards, he may have been part black.[33] He exercised such a strong influence over Spain's ruler that he became the standard for good taste for years to come. He rose to high favor at the Baghdad court, but was forced to flee to Spain after falling victim to the jealousy of more powerful figures in Baghdad. He is considered "the most significant of the Moorish musicians" and "the cornerstone of Spanish musical art." Among his many innovations, he is credited with adding a fifth string to the lute and founding the first conservatory of music in Cordova. He is also credited with introducing "asparagus" to Europe, along with toothpastes and underarm deodorants.[34]

He epitomized fashion and good taste in the ninth-century Arab world. Ziryab is believed to have been the first to introduce crystal tableware, creative hairstyles, and new customs in perfumes and deodorants, related to washing clothes and cooking. He is credited with introducing new food dishes which were sometimes named after himself. He introduced new fashions in dress including seasonal wardrobes displaying a greater range of colors and textures in response to changing seasons and separate courses in meals beginning with soups and ending with deserts. If he was black or part black as Lewis suggests, his contributions to the world of music join a long list of black musical innovators in the West. Also, to the chagrin of more conservative Muslims, Ziryab introduced the clean-shaven look for men and reflective of the religious laxity and material decadence of the time, made the drinking of wine more commonplace among "secular" Muslims in Spain though it is forbidden (*haram*) by the Qur'an.[35]

THE ZANJ "REBELLION"

The eighth- and ninth-century Zanj struggle against Baghdad, the Iraqi seat of power may be the forerunner to black "slave revolts" throughout Africa and the Americas. The Zanj "rebellion" (or more accurately the Zanj *jihad*) took the lives of as many as one half million people in southern Iraq and adjacent parts of Iran from 870 to 883. It also may have been an early expression of black Muslim resistance fighters (*mujahedeen*) against injustice and oppression and a glimpse of things to come in Africa and is diaspora. The word "Zanj" or "black" refers to Africans from east Africa. Gomez describes how during the ninth century AD, large numbers of enslaved Africans known as Zanj were used to cultivate sugar, drain salt flats, and drain the marshlands of southern Iraq and Kuwait. Lewis contends that black soldiers appear occasionally in early Abbasid times, and after their "slave rebellion" in southern Iraq, were recruited into the Caliph's infantry corps. Amr ibn al-'As, described in the literature as black, is also described as the "architect of Arab empire." Amr ibn al-'As conquered Egypt and became the first to introduce Islam as a political force to the African continent.

All black military units were used for a time in Egypt before being driven from Cairo by the famous Kurdish commander Saladin (*Salahu-din*) after blacks became perceived as "threatening," never to be used again.[36] Rejecting their harsh treatment in Basra where they worked to drain the salt flats of southern Iraq, and cultivate sugar in what is now western Iraq, the Zanj waged a successful insurrection that lasted for fifteen years (868–883). They sacked Basra, Iraq's major city in the south, center of the region's slave trade, and conquered the surrounding areas. The Zanj posed a serious threat to Baghdad, the seat of Muslim power for the Abbasid caliphate. The Zanj insurrection was led by an Iranian by the name of Ali ibn-Muhammad, who was an alleged descendant of Ali, the fourth Caliph of Islam. Espousing an anarchist Khawa'rij doctrine, the movement became associated with brutal atrocities. But by AD 883, the Zanj with their Arab and Persian allies were mercilessly massacred by Abbasid forces based in Baghdad. ISIS is widely regarded as a modern-day Khawar'ij movement.

The Zanj struggle raises far-reaching implications for African slave "revolts" or more accurately Muslim struggles when their chief participants involved Africans from Muslim backgrounds. Shattering the myth of Africans as docile and passive, the Zanj struggle illustrates the depth of African Muslim commitment to Muslim struggle in the quest for freedom. To the extent that African Muslims embraced the tool of Muslim struggle, they demonstrate the importance and influence of African Muslims as fighters (*muja-hedeen*) in the cause of Islam. Southern Iraqis to this day remain fiercely Shia opposed to the rule of Baghdad's longtime Sunni minority including Saddam Hussein. Before the March 2003 US invasion of Iraq, the Shia of southern Iraq along with the Kurds of northern Iraq formed the main opposition to the ruling government in Baghdad similar to the role they played centuries later under Saddam Hussein.

The natural remoteness of the swamp regions of southern Iraq helped undermine Baghdad's authority and fortify Iraq's Shia majority from the long reach of the Sunni government in Baghdad. Protection from Iraq's dense marshes made the Zanj seem nearly invincible. In the modern era, these swamps provided safe haven for Shia deserters from Saddam Hussein's military during the Iran-Iraq war (1981–1988). To minimize their constant opposition, Basra's nearby inhabitants known as the Marsh Arabs, had their swamps drained by the government of Saddam Hussein. But US and British forces largely restored the swamp marshes of modern Iraq by late 2004. In addition to being a forerunner to contemporary opposition to Baghdad, the Zanj "rebellion" of AD 870 may have been a forerunner to anti-colonial maroon (*cimarrones*) and antislavery "rebellions" that would later emerged throughout sixteenth-century America. Fugitive Africans and native Americans established quasi-independent societies in defiance of subjugation. These communities were well known and sprang up in Haiti, Jamaica, Brazil, Cuba, Ecuador, Columbia, Suriname, and Florida or anywhere African Muslims were held in bondage.

The common thread in the history of African Muslim struggle was the African determination to be free—a trait that remains alive among African Muslims who continue to struggle in the face of African terrorist violence. Lewis and others marvel at how "Blacks displayed terrifying military prowess" in the Zanj struggle of the ninth-century Iraq. But the larger more enduring message in these and other episodes of black resistance is the force behind them namely, black cultural elements that include voudou, black Judaism, black Christianity liberation theology, *and* Islam or what Jackson (2005) simply refers to "black religion." Evidence of the power of black spirituality in the service of struggle is visible in theaters as widely dispersed as the Antebellum and Jim Crow US, Apartheid South Africa, Israel, Haiti, Jamaica, Cuba, Nigeria, Somalia, and colonial Florida. Regardless of what one calls them, blacks have enjoyed a long and enduring legacy of Muslim and other struggles in the African diaspora extending well beyond the borders of Africa. The examination of Ziryab and the Zanj is not meant to suggest that all black Muslims during Islam's glorious age were glamorous trendsetters or fierce warriors. But rather, Ziryab and the Zanj represent alternative images of blacks that defy the stereotypes images and myths of Africans cited in the introduction. Blacks in Iraq similar to blacks in contemporary Africa and its diaspora maintain a unique affinity with the religion of Islam as seen in Baba Sa'eed al Basri, leader of an Islamic sect of Basra, Iraq that combines Islam with African spiritual traditions to serve as a force for change. Mr. al-Basri was one of the estimated 2–3 million black descendants of Zanj living in contemporary Iraq. Similar communities of blacks in the Middle East also can be found in Sudan, Somalia, Egypt, Mauritania, the Gulf, the cities of Jedda, Medina, and Mecca in Saudi Arabia and the city of Tripoli, Libya. Blacks in Iraq briefly attracted public notice when their leaders expressed pride and enthusiasm over Barack Obama's impending election as US president in 2008.

Black Iraqis complain of being called Abd or Abdi, the Arabic word for the N____ word. Black Iraqis despise their discriminatory treatment. Black Iraqi names continue to remind them of their past enslavement. For example, the name Abd al-Karim or servant of the Generous, Abd al-Rahim or servant of the Merciful, and Abd al-Hakim or servant of the Wise though also used by other Arabs are especially offensive when applied to black Iraqis. Jalal Diyaab, leader of the Free Iraqi Movement, sought to have black Iraqis classified as a minority (*dhimmi*), like Christians, whose rights, at least in theory, are protected. But demands by Diyaab are routinely ignored by the Iraqi government. The movement recently found an ally in the National Dialogue Front, a Sunni political party. Similar to blacks in the United States, black Iraqis according to Diyaab are welcomed as musicians at weddings and other festive occasions, but are otherwise shunned. With a 95 percent illiteracy rate, black Iraqis are typically relegated to menial jobs.

Since their successful though brief "slave revolt" (*jihad*) in the ninth century that enabled them to rule Basra for over a decade, black Iraqis over the centuries have retained their unique Muslim tradition. One of their drumming ceremonies performed at weddings begins with the invocation "there is no God but God," the Muslim confession of faith (*shahada*). Basra had been the center of the region's slave trade. However, in the dirt packed streets of Zubayr, Iraq's version of "old Harlem," an estimated 1.2 Iraqis continue to languish in despair. Although slavery was officially banned in the 1920s, black Iraqis maintain that it continued until the 1950s. On the eve of the election of Barack Obama, a January 19, 2009, CNN report, by Jill Daugherty, quotes black Iraqi, Jalāl, Thijeel, of the Movement of Free Iraqis as saying if Mr. Obama wins it will be a victory for all black people. However, an unconfirmed media report in 2014 reported that the leader of the black Iraqi community in Iraq was killed by unknown assailants. No one has been punished for this murder.

BLACKS AND ISLAM IN WEST AFRICA

The closing sections of this chapter focus more directly on jihad in West Africa. Islam's earliest arrival in West Africa arrived on the wings of world trade. The arrival of Islamic culture in the West African kingdom of Ghana is linked to Arab trading contacts introduced in the ninth century. Bornu's King Houme converted to Islam in 1086, and 400 years later, Islamists continue to control the region. Islam became the religion of the elite, the scholar, the ruler, and long-distance trader among Africans.[37] Diouf links the earliest Islamic conversions in West Africa to the early eleventh century. Robinson notes that Islam spread quickly in some areas of Africa and more slowly in other areas. Today about half the people living on the African continent profess Islam and almost 25 percent of all Muslims in the world live in Africa.[38] West Africa continues to be a stronghold of Islam. The earliest eyewitness accounts of Islam in Africa come from Arab chroniclers, including Ibn Battuta who perhaps was the greatest traveler of his era. Born in Tangier, Morocco, in 1304, Ibn Batutta died near Tangier sixty-five years later. He left home at twenty-one and traveled until he was nearly fifty, producing some of the best known first-hand accounts of Africa. His goal was to see more of the

Islamic world (*dar al Islam*) than anyone else. Setting out from his home on the holy pilgrimage to Mecca in AD 1325. Battuta's *Rihla* is perhaps the only eyewitness account of the east African city states.

Accounts of his journey across the Sahara in 1352 document the prominence of cattle and cattle herding among Africans. Describing these enterprises, he describes how he sees many wild cattle. Indeed, a herd of them can come close enough to people that herders are able to manipulate them with dogs and arrows. Regarding the people of Massufa, Battuta writes: "The people were generous to me and entertained me. . . . The clothes of its people are of fine Egyptian material . . . as for their women, they are extremely beautiful and are more important than the men." Confirming the presences of Islam in Africa, Battuta writes: "as to the former [the Massufu] they are Muslims keeping to the prayers, studying Islamic jurisprudence (*fiqh*), and learning the *Qur'an* by heart . . . [w]ith regard to their women, they are not modest in the presence of men, they do not veil themselves in spite of their perseverance in payers. . . . The women have friends and companions outside the prohibited degrees of marriage [other than brothers, fathers, etc.]. Likewise for the men there are companions among women outside the prohibited degrees. One of them would enter his house to find his wife with her companion and would not disapprove of that conduct." As early as the fourteenth century, Battuta described how: "the Blacks are the most humble men before their king and most extreme in their self-abasement before him. . . . Another of the good habits among them is the way they meticulously observe the times of the prayers and attendance at them, so also it is with regard to their congregational services and their beating of their children to instill these things in them. . . . Among their good qualities is their putting on good white clothes on Friday. If a man among them has nothing except a tattered shirt, he washes and cleans it and attends the Friday prayer in it. Another of their good qualities is their concern for learning the sublime Qur'an by heart."[39]

RESISTING DOMINATION

The charismatic Muslim leader Samory Toure led Malinke and other groups through two decades of jihad against the French. After dispatching spies to St. Louis, Senegal, to learn French rifle manufacturing techniques, Samory returned to present-day Sierra Leone and later to the present-day Côte d'Ivoire to establish his own arms industry where thousands of his Muslim supporters reproduced and manufactured French arms used to resist French imperialism in Africa. A French lieutenant later killed in battle against Samory forces wrote the following of another jihadi group, the Tukolor, "when we arrived, we were assaulted by all these people with a sort of mad boldness."[40] Amazed by the courage of the Tukulors, the officer wrote, "if instead of having the Tukulors as enemies, we could have had them with us, Africa would not have been long to take."[41] Another officer, Charles Mangin, who became a famous French general acknowledged that the Tukulor displayed "insane gallantry" against his troops.

Sheik Uthman dan Fodio (1754–1817) introduced aspects of political and military struggle that profoundly influenced subsequent antislavery campaigns in the Americas, where many of its fighters would end up.[42] Masud describes how "Shehu's [Uthman] restatement of the doctrine of *hijra* influenced a number of reform and jihad movements in Africa." "Although some of these movements did not follow up hijrah with jihad . . . their exercise of hijrah as withdrawal of political and intellectual allegiance from non-Muslim rulers constituted a very effective Islamic response to European colonialism [*sic*]."[43] Throughout the nineteenth century, West Africa was hit by a series of civil wars, drought, and famine that challenged the ability of masters to hold their slaves. Indeed, as Lovejoy observes, "by appealing directly to slaves, asking them to join the Muslim cause, Usman dan Fodio introduced ideology into slave resistance, perhaps for the first time." Thus, "adherence to Islam, as defined in terms of political support for *jihad* became a basic loyalty in the new [dan Fodio] regime." "Opposition to jihad and unbelief [i.e., disbelief]— became the justification for enslavement" in this formulation.[44] It is conceivable that other maroons who happened to be Muslim embraced this practice of self-liberation and the enslavement of those who failed to support *jihad*.

African reformers launched spirited jihads and formed prominent Islamic brotherhoods in West Africa. They advocated a return to pure Islam, adherence to Islamic law (*shari'ah*), a rejection of oppressive acts by rulers that include enslavement, corruption, abuse of power, worldliness, and the imposition of harsh taxes on their subjects. Muslim reformers in West Africa mobilized widespread support for *jihad* across a diverse specter of ethnic groups, occupations, and social classes, including the enslaved. For example, the Hausa ruling elite widely embraced the practice of enslaving Muslim commoners and selling them to North Africans for firearms and horses. West African jihads emphasized and practiced flight/separatism (*hijra*) to unite Muslims in a new and powerful community (*ummah*) committed to fighting social injustice.[45]

The examination of the Islamist militancy among Africans presented herein moves from the contemporary to the historical, through Africa, the Middle East, Europe and the Americas to help explain the role of African Muslims as (1) resistance fighters and (2) champions of the institution of *jihad*. Given this background, what the historical literature typically labels slave rebellions and insurrections were often Muslim jihads at least in the minds of the African Muslims who frequently constituted their core participants. "Plots" and "rebellions" targeted not only slave masters but also Africans who failed to join the *jihād*. This pattern of self-liberation and continued enslavement of others not part of the struggle resembles the pattern found within Uthman dan Fodio's West Africa jihad (1802–1804) and even Samory's *jihad* after 1861 which is why in the case of both, they are remembered by non-Muslims for their enslavement of fellow Africans as they are for resisting colonial aggression.

Some slave scholars dismiss the idea that slave rebellions were in fact jihads because their participants were not always Muslim and may not have always been consciously motivated by Islamic ideals and values. But whether Islamic law (i.e., *shari'ah*) requires Islamic jihads to exclude non-Muslims is considerably unclear. Four specific instances illustrate this point. First, in the Hudaybiyah pact (AD 622), Muslims and Jews of Medina crafted an alliance against the Meccans.[46] Second, a pact between Muslims and non-Muslim in the seventh century enabled the Christian King of Abyssinia to protect the earliest party of over 100 Muslims according to Robinson in their escape to Abyssinia and avoid persecution or worse at the hands of the Meccans. Third, some Shia and Sunni Muslims in contemporary Iraq have at times separately allied themselves with US forces in an effort to achieve mutually beneficial goals. Also, an alliance between the Shīa Muslim group Hezbollah and Christians in Lebanon in demonstrations aimed at forcing the government to resign in 2006 is a fourth example. Each of these instances of Muslim-non-Muslim alliances and cooperation facilitated the achievement of mutually desirable goals.

Perhaps the best illustration of successful alliances between Muslims and non-Muslims is the alliance and guardianship between the Prophet and his uncle and chief guardian Abu Talib, himself a non-Muslim. The death of Abu Tālib and the immediate danger it created for the Prophet forced him to flee Mecca for his life.[47] Thus, correctly or incorrectly, the new community (*ummah*) of fledgling Muslims and their allies set a precedent for future struggles involving Muslims and non-Muslim Africans in the Americas. Maroons were assemblies of fugitives forged together as a result of struggle and flight (*hijra*) into a new singular community (*ummah*) of like-minded persons from otherwise diverse backgrounds, united in their determination to remain free.

What conclusions might therefore be drawn regarding the politics of Muslim struggle and Africans? Muslim struggle (*jihad*) and Africans are simply inseparable. Indeed, despite the seemingly negative intent of African myths and stereotypes to marginalize and therefore alienate Africans from the religion of their ancestors, there is no time in the history of faith that black Africans or their progeny can be disassociated from the religion of Islam.[48] Blacks have played major roles in the formation and spread of Islam. Blacks were at the Prophet Muhammad's side in Islam's infancy, later development and spread. Blacks influenced Islamism in the African diaspora in ways that many are only beginning to understand. Indeed, it may be possible to argue that whenever acts of insurgency are carried forward by fighters from Muslim backgrounds or the allies of such fighters—inspired by the tactics, traditions, and ideology of Muslim struggle (*jihad*) whether in Africa or its diaspora, from the past or at present—the accurate and appropriate label for these actions is *jihad*, or Muslim struggle. Such an approach allows scholars to identify similar Islamist activities heretofore overlooked in North America and elsewhere. It also provides a way to uncover evidence of Muslim struggle heretofore overlooked largely due to ignorance. For instance, a more compelling way to account for the largely unexplained growth and appearance of Islam among blacks in the United States especially during the 1960s and 1970s might be to view it as the resurfacing of a hidden tradition explored herein and previously noted by Gardell (1996) and others.

This chapter examined (1) "The True Meaning of Jihad"; (2) "The Jihads of West Africa"; (3) "Blacks, Arabs, and Islam"; (4) "Blacks and the Growth and Spread of Islam"; (5) "Ziryab the Moor"; (6) "The Zanj 'Rebellion'"; and (7) "Resisting Domination." The following chapter examines eight cases of legitimate Muslim struggle and Africans.

NOTES

1. Although I have not mentioned persons of African descent who live and practice Islam in Australia, one such person I know personally is my colleague and friend Ameer Ali who has lived and taught in Australia.

2. For example, Chandler asserts that "Arabia itself has been populated by Black people," while Pimienta-Bey asserts, "when Muhammad was born, Arabia was a Negro colony with Mecca as its capital." There seems to be a need to qualify these remarks and provide supporting evidence for these claims. See Wayne Chandler, "The Moor: Light of Europe's Dark Age," and Jose P. Pimienta-Bey, "Moorish Spain: Academic Source and Foundation For the Rise and Success of European Universities," in the Middle Ages in Ivan Van Sertima (ed.), *Golden Age of the Moor* (New Brunswick, NJ: Transaction Pub., 1993), 151–81 and 182–247, respectively. One bit of evidence that might began to confirm these claims is one account which describes how in 536 a powerful coalition led by an Ethiopian military force placed an African named Ella Asbeba in power before returning to Africa/Ethiopia leaving behind a joint government of South Arabians and the Ethiopian military authority. This arrangement lasted until 532 when a junior Ethiopian officer named Abreba seized power before eventually being dislodged by the Ethiopians. This brief account may lend important support to the claims put forth by Chandler and Pimienta-Bey. Although Brunson and Rashidi note that Abreha passed away in 558, they also note that "no history of pre-Islamic Arabia is complete without him." See

James E. Brunson and Runoko Rashidi, "The Moors in Antiquity," in Ivan Van Sertima (ed.), *Golden Age of the Moor* (New Brunswick, NJ: Transaction Pub., 1993), 69–70.

3. Christopher S. Chivvis, *The French War on Al Qa'ida in Africa* (New York: Cambridge University Press, 2016), 127.

4. John Thornton, *Africa and Africans in the Making of the Atlantic World*, second edition (New York: Cambridge University Press, 2006), 334.

5. For a discussion of Uthman dan Fodio, see David Robinson, *Muslim Societies in African History* (New York: Cambridge University Press, 2004), 142–146, Kevin Shillington, *History of Africa* (New York: St. Martin's Press, 1995), 226–229, and David Robinson, "Revolution in the Western Sudan," in Nehemia Levtzion and Randall L. Pouwels (eds.), *The History of Islam in Africa* (Athens: Ohio University Press, 2000), 131–152.

6. See J. F. Ade Ajayi (ed.), *General History of Africa Abridged Edition VI, Africa in the Nineteenth Century until the 1880s* (Berkeley: University of California Press, 1998), 15–16, 225–228, and 239–246, 317. Also see Shilington, "History of Africa," 226–233, and David Robinson, "Revolution in the Western Sudan," 131–152.

7. For a discussion of Samory, see Shillington, "History of Africa," 231–323, and J.A. Rogers, *World's Great Men of Color* (New York: Collier Books a Div. of Macmillan Pub., 1946), 344–349.

8. S. H. Sellassie, *Ancient and Medieval Ethiopian History to 1270* (Addis Ababa, Ethiopia: United Printers, 1972), 26. Also see David Phillipson, *Foundations of an African Civilisation: Aksum & the Northern Horn 1000BC-AD 1300* (Addis Ababa, Ethiopia: Addis Ababa University Press, James Currey, an Inprint of Boydell and Brewer, Ltd., 2014).

9. Ibid., 30–31, and Brunson and Rashidi, "The Moors in Antiquity," 67–69.

10. Ibid.

11. Bernard Lewis, *Race and Slavery in the Middle East* (New York: Oxford University Press, 1990).

12. For a discussion of this phenomenon, see Bernard Lewis, *The Multiple Identities of the Middle East* (New York: Schoken Books, 1998).

13. Ibid., Brunson and Rashidi, "The Moors in Antiquity," 67–69.

14. John Sabini, *Islam: A Primer* (Washington, DC: Middle East Editorial Associates, 1990), 35, and Runoko Rashidi, *Introduction to the Study of African Classical Civilization* (Chicago Frontline International Pub., 1992), 74–75. See Brunson and Rashidi, "The Moors in Antiquity," 67–69. Human Rights Watch/Africa, *Mauritania's Campaign of Terror: State Sponsored Repression of Black Africans* (New York: Human Rights Watch, 1994), and Khaldun, *The Muqaddimah*, 59.

15. Glenn Perry, *The Middle East: Fourteen Islamic Centuries* (Upper Saddle River, NJ: Prentice Hall, 1997), 66.

16. Sabini, *Islam: A Primer*, 35. Also see Robinson, *Muslim Societies in African History*, 69–71.

17. Ivan Van Sertima, "The Moor in Africa and Europe," in Ivan Van Sertima (ed.), *Golden Age of the Moor* (New Brunswick, NJ: Transaction, 1993), 8.

18. Ibrahim Abu Lughod, "Islam in Africa," in *the World Encyclopedia of Black People*, vol. 1, Conspectus (St. Clair Shores, Michigan: Scholarly Press, 1975), 284.

19. Robinson, *Muslim Societies in African History*, 111.

20. Ibid., 112.

21. For a discussion of Zayd ibn Harith, see Chandler, "The Moor: Light of Europe's Dark Age"in Ivan Van Sertima (ed.), *Golden Age of the Moor*, 158. For a discussion of Zayd, Barakat, May and others, see Mamadou Chinyelu, "Africans in the Birth and Spread of Islam," in Ivan Van Sertima (ed.), *Golden Age of the Moor*, 360.

22. Brunson and Rashidi, "The Moors in Antiquity," 70.

23. Mamadou Chinyelu, "Africans in the Birth and Spread of Islam," in Ivan Van Sertima (ed.), *Golden Age of the Moor*, 360.

24. Chandler, "The Moor: Light of Europe's Dark Age," 161.

25. Ibid., 159, 161.

26. Ibid., 159, 162.

27. Brunson and Rashidi, "The Moors in Antiquity," 45.

28. Ibid., 45–54, and Pimienta-Bey, "Moorish Spain: Source and Foundation For the Rise And Success of Western European Universities in the Middle Ages," in Ivan Van Sertima (ed.), *Golden Age of the Moor*, 183–184, 202.

29. Ibid., 204–205, and Chandler, "The Moor: Light of Europe's Dark Age," 175.

30. Brunson and Rashid, "The Moors in Antiquity," 61.

31. Ibid.

32. *Shu'ubiyyah* represented an idea and movement prominent during the Abbassid period of Islam that resembles the diversity movement in the contemporary United States in tone and motivation. It emphasized the contributions of Persia and Persian Muslims but later the contributions of Africans and others to the achievements of Islam. Similar to the role of diversity in the United States, the movement sought to minimize the tendency of the dominant and majority group (in this case Arabs), to overshadow the contributions of smaller groups (e.g., ethnic groups) to the Islamic community (*ummah*). Like attitudes in the contemporary United States, suspicions arose over it as a potential threat to the ideas that bound the community as a whole. Hence, opposition to the idea of *shu'ubiyyah* came mainly from members of Islam's dominant (Arab) group, who saw it as a threat to the unity of the larger Muslim community. Some have compared it to ethnic nationalist movements as counterweights to larger nationalist movements in society.

33. Chandler, "The Moor: Light of Europe's Dark Age," 166–168. Also see Lewis, *Race and Slavery in the Middle East*.

34. Ibid., 168. Also see Lewis, *Race and Slavery in the Middle East*.

35. Ibid.

36. See Lewis, *Race and Slavery in the Middle East*.

37. Robinson describes the earliest Muslims as merchants and guides of camel caravans in Ghana, Mali, Songhay, and Kanem, the best-known Sahelean states from 800 to 1600 CE, who ran important networks of trade who added to the prosperity of their host societies. Even rulers who were not Muslims welcomed their presence. See Robinson, *Muslim Societies in African History*, 38–39.

38. Sylviane Diouf, *Servants of Allah: African Muslims Enslaved in the Americas* (New York: University Press, 1998), 4. Also see Robinson, *Muslim Societies in African History*, 27.

39. Said Hamdun and Noel King (eds.), *Ibn Battuta in Black Africa* (Princeton: Marcus Wiener Publishers, 1975), 1, 35, 37, 38, 39, 41, 49, 50, and 58, and David Waines (ed.), *The Odyssey of Ibn Battuta: Uncommon Tales of a Medieval Adventurer* (Chicago, IL: The University of Chicago Press, 2010).

40. Robert B. Edgerton, *Africa's Armies: From Honor to Infamy: A History from 1791 to the Present* (Boulder, CO: Westview Press, 2002), 32.

41. Ibid., 33–34.

42. Paul E. Lovejoy, "Fugitive Slaves: Resistance to Slavery in the Sokoto Caliphate," in Gary Y. Okihiro (ed.), *In Resistance: Studies in African, Caribbean and Afro-American History* (Amherst: University of Massachusetts Press, 1986), 80.

43. Muhammad Khalid Masud, "Shehu Usman Dan Fodio's Restatement of the Doctrine of Hijrah," *Islamic Studies*, vol. 25, no. 1, 1986, 74.

44. Lovejoy, "Fugitive Slaves: Resistance to Slavery." 80.

45. For a full discussion of these complex reforms see J. Fade Ajaye (ed.), *General History of Africa: Africa in the Nineteenth Century Until the 1880s* (Berkeley: University of California Press, 1998), 223–234.

46. For a brief discussion of the Hudaybiya' Pact and its historical significance, see Fazlur Rahman, *Islam* (Chicago, IL: The University of Chicago Press, 1979), 23.

47. For a brief discussion of the life of the Prophet Muhammad, see John L. Esposito (ed.), *The Oxford Encyclopedia of the Modern Islamic World*, vol. 3 (New York: Oxford University Press, 1995), 153–166.

48. Mamadou Chinyelu, "Africa in the Birth and Spread of Islam," in Ivan Van Sertima, *Golden Age of the Moor*, 360.

Chapter 4

Cases

Muslim Struggle and Africans

This chapter examines eight cases of Muslim struggle (jihad) and Africans. The cases were selected according to guidelines outlined in Robert K. Yin's *Case Study: Research and Applications: Design and Methods* (2018) and include: (1) "Bilal ibn al-Rabah"; (2) "Muhammad Ahmad"; (3) "Samory Touré"; (4) "Muhammad bin Abdulla Hassan"; (5) "Pacifico Licutan"; (6) "The Baptist Rebellion"; (7) "Benjamin Cockrane"; and (8) "Ilhan Omar"; followed by (9) a brief "Analysis" of the observations made. An additional source of guidance used in the selection of the cases has been Clifford Geertz and his groundbreaking *Islam Observed: Religious Development in Morocco and Indonesia* (1968) study. A third source of guidance in the selection of the cases used in this chapter have been works on the subject of phenomenology, including Martin Hiedeggar's *Hegel's Phenomenology of Spirit* (1988), G. W. F. Hegel's *Phenomenology of Spirit* (1977), and Syed Ameer Ali's *Spirit of Islam* (1997) for their arguments regarding the value of spiritual experience in understanding behavior based on the Islamic religious experience. Phenomenology celebrates lived experience as a valid epistemological tool. The cases in this chapter cover a broad range of experiences involving Muslim males and females, rich and poor, free and "slave," ancient and modern, Western and non-Western to capture a glimpse at how the power of Islam has affected their lives. The cases included herein seek to capture a degree of Islamic authenticity not always present in studies of Islam and Muslims and help readers already immersed in the experience to sharpen and better appreciate them.

BILAL IBN AL-RABAH

Historian J. A. Rogers, describes Bilal (c. AD 600) of Arabia as a tall, gaunt bushy-haired black Ethiopian slave who served as the first Muezzin and treasurer of Islam.[1] Bilal who was born in Mecca and died in Medina, is one of the earliest persons outside of the Prophet's family to convert to Islam. As an African in seventh-century Arabia, Bilal hailed from the ranks of those who had been enslaved. He suffered great hardship at the hands of the Meccans. Born a "slave" in Mecca he was acquired and manumitted by Abu Bakr, the Prophet's father-in-law. His mother was an Ethiopian.[2] But he is best known for the inspiration he instilled in the early companions (*sahaba*) of the Prophet Muhammad through his call to prayer (*al-azan*), which is now a regular staple in the Muslim daily diet of worship that continues to inspire (often to the point of tears) all who hear it. His characterizations of paradise (*jinnah*)—provided at the behest of the Prophet Muhammad—become the standard image of paradise (*jinnah*) adopted by subsequent generations of Muslims, worldwide. Paradise in Bilal's imagination contained *al-taba*, the Tree of life—a tree so vast the swiftest horse would take 150 years to cross its shade. The limbs of the tree are laden with every kind of good thing to eat and allegedly bent down at the slightest wish. And of course there are the legendary *houris*, the black-eyed virgins of paradise, with beautiful round bodies endowed with eternal youth and ever renewed virginity.

The call to prayer or the *azan* is one of the most recognized religious rituals on earth touching the lives of some 1.6 billion Muslims worldwide. According to the traditions of Islam, Bilal swore revenge for the suffering he endured at the hands of his former master, Omeyya. After the battle of Badr, when he spotted his former master among the captives of war, Bilal extracted his revenge by declaring to Omeyya's captors that Omeyya was the chief of the disbelievers. Omeyya and his son were killed.[3] According to at least one source, when the Prophet Muhammad was near death he first attempted to name Bilal as his successor. But Bilal later yielded to Abu Bakr who later became the caliph or successor to the Prophet Muhammad. Following Abu Bakr's relatively short-lived caliphate lasting about three years, another Arab with an Ethiopian mother, Umar ibn al-Khattab, emerged to become the second and longest lived of the four "rightly guided" caliphs or successors to the Prophet in Islam.

Both Abu Bakr and his successor, Umar ibn al-Khattab, continued to rely on Bilal who remained prominent until his death. Bilal lived to a ripe old age and amassed enormous wealth. According to Rogers, he also was able to advance his family, including his enslaved brother who secured the rare privilege of marrying a freeborn Arab woman.[4] Bilal was buried in a tomb in Damascus, Syria. So prominent is his reputation among blacks in the Americas that the black sheikh, W. D. Muhammad, son of Elijah Muhammad, during the 1970s and 1980s introduced the phrase "Bilalians" as a generic name for all African American Muslims. The significance of Bilal for Muslims worldwide is enormous as he symbolizes the triumph of the downtrodden over persecution and oppression. He is a symbol of human perseverance in the face of adversity as well as a symbol of hope. Bilal is one of several African Muslims examined in this study playing the role of resistance fighter and Islamic fighter (*mujahid*). But for Muslims Bilal is best known for being one of the earliest and arguably the closest companion (*sahaba*) of the Prophet Muhammad.

Usman dan Fodio, Sheikh, and Founder of the Sokoto Caliphate, northern Nigeria, (d. 1817)

Usman dan Fodio the powerful and influential founder of the Sokoto caliphate in the vicinity of today's northern Nigeria influenced Islamism and Muslim struggle (jihad) for years to come. By the seventeenth century this Fulani ethnic group came to acquire a distinctive presence as pastoralists spread out across much of the savannah of West Africa. The Fulani chose to remain separate from other West African groups and typically refrained from taking part in the political life of states or chiefdoms in whose areas they settled. This behavior led the Fulani to be resented as intruders leading their grazing lands and trading rights to be restricted. But Islam gave the Fulani an added sense of unity and purpose. By the early eighteenth century, a number of Fulani Muslim clans began to rival ethnic Tuaregs as leading Muslim scholars. Long before this, however, in the mountainous region known as the Futa Jalon, in the vicinity of the modern state of Senegal, Fulani pastoralists established a presence dating back to the 1500s. But in 1725 they rose in struggle (*jihad*) against nearby agriculturalists who Fulani regarded as "pagan." The immediate source of conflict was Fulani discontent over restrictions imposed on their large and growing herds and higher taxes. By 1750 the Fulani dominated the state and governed its affairs in accordance with Islamic law (*shari'ah*). The success of the Futa Jalon jihad inspired similar Muslim struggles between 1769 and 1776 in the nearby Futa Toro in what is today the lower Senegal region—waged by Fulani and Tukolor fighters (*mujahedeen*) to establish another Muslim state governed by Islamic law (*shari'ah*).[5]

The eighteenth-century jihads of Futa Jalon and Futa Toro inspired later Muslim sheikhs elsewhere in West Africa, including Sheikh Usman dan Fodio who led the now famous *jihad* (1802–1804) against perceived Hausa Muslim injustice. The Sokoto caliphate or empire was the largest single West African Muslim state of the nineteenth century. Usman dan Fodio, was the son of a Fulbe Muslim teacher in the northern Hausa state of Gobir. The Fulbe in this part of West Africa were known as the Fulani. Although he never undertook the pilgrimage to Mecca, Usman completed his studies at Agades under the influence of the revolutionary Tuareg Sheikh Jabril ibn Umar who preached and emphasized the value of Muslim struggle (*jihad*). Usman began preaching in Gobir in the 1770s. His goals were to convert Fulani pastoralists who still clung to pagan religious beliefs and practices, eliminate what he perceived as unfair taxes, and halt the enslavement of lower-class Muslims by upper-class Hausa Muslim elites. A crisis was reached in the early 1800s when the king, Yunfa, sought unsuccessfully to assassination Usman. Imitating the example of the Prophet Muhammad of Arabia, Usman combined the institution of flight (hijra) with the institution of struggle (*jihad*) to separate or flee at first to a defensible location where he could then consolidate his forces to mount a full-scale attack on Gobir around 1802. By 1808, Gobir was finally taken and a new capital and caliphate was established at Sokoto in Kebbi. Usman retired soon thereafter. By the time of his death in 1817, the Sokoto Empire stretched from Songhay in the west to Benue in the east. Active leadership over the Sokoto caliphate was passed on to Usman's brother Abdullahi and his son Muhammad Bello. By the time of Muhammad Bello's death in 1837, the caliphate or empire of Sokoto acquired a population of ten million people, larger than any other West African state before it.[6] The region, which includes parts of northern Nigeria, remains one of Africa's largest Islamic strongholds—making Nigeria with a population of 180 million (in 2017) the fourth most populous Muslim country, after Indonesia, India, Pakistan.

MUHAMMAD AHMAD

Muhammad Ahmed, known to his followers as Al Mahdi (1848–1885), was born at Khanag, Dongola, in the (eastern) Sudan in 1848, the son of a poor carpenter. His earliest experiences include service as a house boy for a French merchant in Khartoum. Unusually bright, he could recite whole chapters of the Qur'an by heart by age twelve. Muhammad was especially moved by the plight of the poor. When his teacher, Muhammed Sherif, hosted a feast celebrating his son's circumcision, Muhammad refused to touch even a morsel of food and embarrassed his teacher by underscoring the specter of guests gorging themselves with food while others of the faith went starving. Shocked by the audacity of this penniless young man, Muhammad's horrified teacher tossed him on the street making Ahmed a marked man. After considerable pleading he was eventually admitted to another school. But the event established Ahmed's reputation as a champion for the rights of the poor. Long before this incident, Ahmed was seen as a kind, dutiful, and humble servant. As the year 1300 AH of the Islamic calendar or 1881 AD of the Christian calendar drew near, rumors spread that Ahmed may have been divinely guided, with news that his name was Muhammad, and his parents' names like those of the Prophet Muhammad, were Abdullah and Aminah. Local authorities, who became increasingly alarmed by his growing popularity and growing discontent among the masses, attempted to arrest him. But Muhammad escaped with a few of his followers to an island some 240 miles up the Nile River where he established himself. Soon thereafter pilgrims from throughout Sudan journeyed to listen to his fervent prayers only to leave more convinced than ever that he was indeed the promised Messiah or Mahdi of the faithful. In response, "al-Mahdi," as he was called, vowed to free all Sudanese from the "Turks" a term of derision used to refer to all oppressors regardless of race or religion in the (eastern) Sudan which, before the creation of the South Sudan in 2011, was Africa's largest state in terms of land mass.

On New Year's day, the Mahdi sent out one of his messengers to announce that he was indeed the Mahdi who would purify religion. Shortly thereafter Raouf Pasha offered a large reward for Muhammad Ahmad, dead or alive. The Mahdi later responded by announcing a jihad against the ruling Anglo-Egyptian authorities that promised his followers four-fifths of all the wealth liberated from the oppressors. With this, his popularity grew even larger with large numbers of (non-Muslim) African recruits flocking to join his jihad. When the forces dispatched to capture him by the Pasha degenerated into open quarrel, the event was hailed a miracle by the Mahdist forces (similar to ISIS's interpretations of Turkish, Russian, and Kurdish infighting within the contemporary anti-ISIS coalition). When a large force was sent to kill the Mahdi, the force was ambushed and destroyed to a man, adding further to the belief that Al Mahdi was divinely guided. The amazing success of the Mahdist forces of the eastern Sudan became legendary not just in Africa, but throughout Europe as the Mahdi inflicted rapid and stunning victories over larger more modern Anglo-Egyptian forces led by men with names like Hicks and the celebrated British General Charles "Chinese" Gordon, whose belief in Christianity was as firm as the Mahdi's belief was in Islam.

In 1883, the British would again send troops against Africans, this time against the so-called Dervishes or fuzzy-wuzzies in the eastern Sudan, an Arabic word meaning "land of the Blacks." The Dervish army had embarked on a holy war—jihad—to cleanse the Sudan of its corrupt Egyptian rule, which profited enormously by illegally taking 50,000 slaves a year out of the Sudan, The Dervishes' divine mission to end this outage was created by a man claiming descent from Muhammad. As the reincarnation of the Prophet, he called himself the Mahdi, "the expected leader." He was a magnificent orator cut from the traditional cloth of the warrior-priest of Islam. He was also a strict Muslim. Europeans who saw him reported that he always smiled benevolently, even when he was ordering torture and death for wrongdoers.[7]

The Dervish, as they would come to be known, decapitated General "Chinese" Gordon and delivered his head to the Mahdi after staging a 321-day siege, one of the longest sieges up to that point in history. The Mahdi's "fanatical" supporters numbering of 25,000 swarmed the beleaguered

ramparts of Khartoum taking the capital and with it the seat of power in
Sudan. When Governor-General Charles "Chinese" Gordon walked calmly
to the steps of the palace, "a giant 'Kordofan Negro' ran him through with a
spear, and an officer named Nisser decapitated him with his sword. Hundreds
of soldiers stuck their spears into his body, after which it was flung up into a
tree for all to see. His head was sent to the Mahdi, who reportedly, admired
Gordon and hoped to win him over to Islam." The Mahdi was now the leader
of a rich empire 1600 miles long and 700 miles wide and true to his word he
set his people free while making their lives much easier. However, "within
six months of Gordon's death, the Mahdi was stricken with typhoid fever.
On June 22, 1885, the sixth day of his illness, he stumbled to his feet, and
summoning his last strength, shouted the Islamic creed, "La illaha illallah
Mohammed [dar] rasul Allah" and fell dead. He was only thirty-seven years
old. Victorious British forces led by British Lord Kitchener eventually reas-
serted British authority over the Sudan with characteristic brutality when in
one battle Lord Kitchener ordered the massacre of 20,000 wounded fighters
on the field.[8] Writing to commemorate the historic victories of the "dervish"
over the British, British poet Rudyard Kipling's now famous ode to the fuzzy-
wuzzies of Sudan has come to signify ridicule as well as praise—with its
recurring refrain to the "Fuzzy-Wuzzy" Muslims—as seen in the following
partial excerpt by Rudyard Kipling.

"FUZZY-WUZZY"

(Soudan Expeditionary Force)

So 'ere ' s to you, Fuzzy-Wuzzy, at your 'ome in the Soudan;
You ' re a pore benighted ' eathen but a first-class fightin' man;
We gives you your certificate, an ' if you want it signed
We ' ll come an ' 'ave a romp with you whenever you ' re inclined.

So ' ere ' s to you, Fuzzy-Wuzzy, at your ' ome in the Soudan;
You ' re a pore benighted 'eathen but a first-class fightin ' man
An' 'ere ' s to you, Fuzzy-wuzzy, with your ' ayrick ' ead of air—
You big Black boundin ' beggar—for you broke a British square!

SAMORY TOURÉ

The jihad led by the Wolof Muslim Sheikh al Hajj Umar Tal emerged the
empire of Samory Touré (d1900), Imam, and Napoleon the Sudan belonging to a non-Muslim Dyula trading family in the region of the upper Niger

basin to the east of the Futa Jalon mountain region. The Mandinka, like the Malinke, were a branch of the Mende-speaking people who formed the core of the ancient empire of Mali. Samory was born at Bissandugu in the Niger Valley of West Africa in 1830. Like others before him, he began his life in the humblest of circumstances, being the son of a poor black merchant and a female slave. Samory was not a sheikh nor was he well versed in Islamic law. When his village and tribe were suddenly invaded by Sori Bourama, inflicting death, suffering, and capture on most, his mother was captured, and unable to pay her ransom, Samory freed her by taking her place.[9] But five years later, at age thirteen, the ambitious Samory decided he no longer wished to be a slave, and escaped, killing his pursuers. He approached the king of Toron, Bitike Souane, offering him his services. The king—who was struck by Samory's splendid physique, martial bearing, and skill at throwing a spear—made him one of his personal bodyguards. From there he rose to become his counselor, thanks to his knowledge of Arabic. As a young man during the 1860s, he became the idol of soldiers. But because the king became jealous of him he returned to his native Bissandugu to become chief of his tribe.

His family engaged in the gold dust trade from Bure and cattle trade from the Futa Jalon. Under Samory's leadership, his family used their extensive Dyula contacts to import firearms from the coast to strengthen and modernize his tribe's army. As a professional soldier he built and trained a force of well-armed soldiers to protect the interests of his family. Between 1865 and 1875 Samory conquered the surrounding 'Dyula states in route to establishing a powerful Mandinka kingdom. He fostered unity and increased trade in the region. By the 1870s he extended his struggle (*jihad*) to include the Bure goldfields in the North and down the upper Niger valley toward modern Bamako. By the early 1880s he turned his trading kingdom into a huge empire, and third largest Muslim kingdom in West Africa after Sokoto and Tukolor. Samory worked to reunite the Mande-speaking people reminiscent of the ancient empire of Mali, of Mansa Musa, Kan Kan Musa, and others of that era. After converting to Islam, he played a major role in the Islamization of West African but is more widely remembered for his religious pragmatism rather than for his Islamist militancy. He created a powerful army by incorporating male captives rather than selling them of as "slaves,"—an action that no doubt engendered loyalty and respect among his followers. He imported the latest quick-loaded riffles from the Sierra Leone port of Freetown and used local ironsmith to repair and manufacture muzzle-loading guns. But Samory's empire would be short-lived. The Mandinkas had their first clash with French forces in 1881, the year that sparked what Europeans have labeled the "Scramble for Africa." The French moved to extend their colonial control from the upper Senegal to the African interior controlled by Samory. Although he is widely associated with the sale of thousands of non-Muslims "slaves" who were not absorbed by his army, his Mandinka army served as a major source of anti-French resistance in West Africa.[10] So formidable were his military skills that French commanders including Marshals Joffre and Gallieni dubbed him "the Napoleon of the Sudan," after defying French power in the region for eighteen years.[11]

Although erroneously failing to distinguish Samory's struggle from the Tukolar struggle (*jihad*) of an earlier era, one writer nonetheless captures the impression that Samory's struggle (*jihad*) left on his French opponents in the following excerpt:

> The Tukulor empire took many yeas to subdue, and their brilliant military tactician and charismatic leader, Samori Touré, led the Malinke and other troops he trained and armed through two decades of warfare against the French. Known by the British and French alike as "the African Napoleon," Samori built a highly effective army by training them to be versatile as well as showing love and devotion to his soldiers and their families . . . he sent selected blacksmiths as far away as St. Louis, Senegal, where they learned how the French manufactured their latest breech-loading riffles. Then Samori returned to Sierra Leone and further amazed the French by building his own arms factory where thousands of workers successfully reproduced them. In 1885 the French sent a large force to seize the gold fields at Boure, Samori's main source of wealth. His men not only stopped the French, they drove them away. However, when the French launched a massive invasion six years later, Samori's men could not stop them . . . "if instead of having the Tukulors as enemies, we could have had them with us, Africa would not been long to take."[12]

Samory Touré, was captured by the French while performing one of his five daily prayers. He passed away later while in captivity in ca. 1900.

MUHAMMAD BIN ABDULLA HASSAN

Muhammad bin Abdulla Hassan (1856–1921) known to his enemies as the Mad Mullah of Somaliland was a product of the vast and physically inhospitable African region known as the Horn of Africa. Somalis in this region are believed to have originated in southern Arabia and mixed over time with the people of southern Ethiopia known as the Oromo. After studying under a local sheikh, he eventually traveled to Mecca to complete the Muslim pilgrimage (*hajj*) and study under Sheikh Muhammad Saleh, his teacher in Mecca. Upon his return to Somaliland, he joined a local Sufi order and encountered much opposition. But he was as man of deep unalterable convictions who used his great poetic and oratory gifts with merciless and unrelenting fury to convince his fellow nomads to follow him in an anti-Christian and anti-colonial struggle (*jihad*). At great expense to the West and their allies who worked to oppose him, and reminiscent of Western military campaigns in Afghanistan, no less than five British military expeditions were mobilized against Muhammad Hassan of Somaliland and all five went down in defeat.

Hassan became a legend and his military exploits earned him a reputation for being the father of modern Somalia. He used both guerrilla and conventional military tactics, including the erection of fortified fortresses designed to ward off enemy invaders. Rather than a nationalist he is perhaps most accurately regarded as a religious reformer (*mujahid*). Like ISIS of today, his followers believed they were the only true believers in Allah. The principal targets of his struggle (*jihad*) were the Ethiopians, long-time opponents of Somalia. Hassan died from influenza in 1921. His forces were subdued only by the advent of modern aircraft technology introduced during World War I. Many sayings associated with al-Qaeda and Osama bin Laden were first used by the "Mad Mullah" including "I like war but you do not." "These youth love death and you love life." Hassan received most of his education in Saudi Arabia where he appears to have become a disciple of Wahhabism. Many perceive him to be a man touched by God (*Allah*). Many refer to him as Sayyid or "Master." He bears a striking resemblance to postmodern jihadists, including al-Qaeda, but few studies explore his possible influence on the Shabab.[13]

PACIFICO LICUTAN

A crowd of Malê (i.e., Muslim) fighters in San Salvador, Brazil, capital of the northeastern province of Bahia, Brazil attacked the Municipal (Council) House or city hall to free an esteemed Muslim sheikh being held there named Pacifico Licutan (d. 1835). The homes of African freedmen were used to provide space for Malê worship, meals, celebrations, and, in the eyes of authorities, "conspiracies." Many Malês, enslaved or freedmen, knew how to read and write in Arabic and passed on their knowledge to others through the medium of Arabic. Besides reading and writing, they gathered on street corners to offer their services. And while they waited for customers they busied themselves with their religious "rebellion," reading, writing, talking, sewing abadás, and Malê skullcaps, (*Kufias*), that served as uniforms of sorts. Twice daily prayers (*salah*) were organized and in some cases "masters" allowed the enslaved in Salvador to construct their own quarters for Muslim worship. An Englishmen named Stuart and another named Abraham for example, allowed James and Diego, both enslaved Africans, to construct a hut on the "masters" property. This hut was perhaps the most important Malê community center in all of Salvador in 1835. But when it came to his "master," Pacifico Licutan (d. 1835), the Muslim sheikh in San Salavador Brazil, was not so lucky. On two separate occasions when other enslaved Africans offered to pool their money to offer a fair market price for the purchase of Pacifico Licutan's freedom, his "master" despite being in need of the money, refused to "sell."[14]

Nevertheless, Pacifico Licutan, the Malê Alufá or leader, organized with other African Muslims of Bahia, Brazil to rent a room so that Muslims of Salvador Brazil might have a place to pray and meet, in peace. The majority of these "private mosques" (or *machachalis*) were located in downtown Salvador, the provincial capital of Bahia, Brazil. The exceptions to this rule were private mosques organized by Dandará and one by Vitória, two other well-known sheikhs or Malê Alufás. Alufás Manoel, Sanim, and Licutan operated in a tiny area from Ladiera da Praca to Terreiro de Jesus. Although information remains sketchy on the full range of their activities, we do know the Muslims of Bahia, Brazil met to pray, read, and write in Arabic. They also met to learn and memorize verses from the Qur'an. After the 1835 "rebellion," police officials found many papers written in Arabic. According to Reis a leading expert on Muslims in Brazil—whose work has been translated into English by Arthur Brakel—"Bahian Muslims were in no way the fierce separatists that many students of the 1835 rebellion have claimed them to be." Rather the Malê simply chose to adhere to their own Malê religious perspective and retain their own unique Africanisms in the face of Portuguese cultural encroachment. For instance, a Malê by the name of Ahuna (or Aluna) was the most wanted man in Salvador by the Portuguese, although to some he was the most beloved man among the enslaved in Salvador. The seven most important leaders of the 1835 Muslim-led "slave revolt" were Ahuna or Aluna, Pacifico Licutan, Luís Sanim, Manoel Calafate, Eselbão de Carmo (Dandará), Nicobé, and Dassulu. Another leading Alufá was Mala Mubakar, who may have been an Ahuna or bábbá mulami as the Hausa would have called him.[15]

Pacifico Licutan is described as an aged man, tall, thin, with a sparse beard and small head and ears and "perpendicular and horizontal marks on his face." He is described as "without doubt an impressive figure. He lived with his "master" a medical doctor named Antonio Pinto de Mesquita Varcella—who treated him poorly as a "slave." Pacifico Licutan was a highly esteemed alufá and a man of great power and influence within the Bahia African Muslim community of Salvador. The "rebellion" itself occurred when Licutan was incarcerated and shortly thereafter sent in handcuffs to Santo Amaro (prison). These incidents in retrospect, plus extensive eye-witness testimony at the time of the trial, sparked the Malê "rebellion" of 1835 in Salvador, Brazil. Pacifico Licutan served as a Nagô Malê sheikh. The term Nagô was originally used by the Fon, a people from the neighboring and interior African kingdom of Dahomey, to identify native speakers of Yoruba language. A Nagô "slave" known as Pompeu offered an almost perfect diagnosis of the "revolt" in Reis's view by describing how "there were no whites, no mesticos, no crioulos—there were only Nagôs and Hausas. On the night of the rebellion, one witness would recall hearing what sounded like the battle cry, 'Death to whites! Long live Nagôs!'" "Nagos and Hausas made up 81.6 percent of prisoners whose origins have been ascertained." In a familiar occurrence among Muslims in predominantly non-Muslim societies like contemporary United States and Brazil, in many cases the Male (or Muslim) of Salvador, "did not even bother to memorize the Christian names of their closest associates," or frequently and easily forget them, perhaps out of hubris or self-righteousness. When such names were mentioned by non-Muslims to Muslims, Muslims often forced themselves to pause quite deliberately and with great consternation to recall who the Muslim referred to by a Christian name, actually was.[16] The fact that this is still a common occurrence in contemporary United States underscores the difficulty some still face in recognizing Muslims even though they may be in their own midst. The practice of naming oneself for oneself and by oneself is a fundamental practice found in Muslim societies that survives to this day. Turner (2003) refers to this as signification.

While slavery may have been at the root of the 1835 "rebellion," bad treatment was cited by many, including Pacifico Licutan, as the cause. Most freedmen were far from content, as they were forced to witness the suffering of their loved ones, and tribal, and religious kinsman at the whims of the slave system. Similar to the effects of the pastoral letter (*wathiqa*) in Jamaica, Africans especially from among the freedmen engaged in transatlantic communication with their countrymen back home in Africa as brilliantly documented by Jeffrey Bolster in the study *Black Jacks* (1998). Contemporary evidence of this contact is provided by Quick who identifies Muslim mosques found in West Africa today, with names like the "Brazilian mosque." Pacifico Licutan accused of being the rebellion's leader was sentenced to one thousand lashes instead of the death penalty because he was in jail at the time of the revolt. Such minutia must have seemed bizarre to those convicted. For example, "Emerica, a female slave and companion of Dandará was sentenced to 400 lashes." The petitioners before the court called Africans barbarians who "have no place (*nao representum*) in the Political civilized world," though some whites at the time disagree with this characterization.[17]

Licutan refused to reveal the names of any of his collaborators or disciples. He even denied being a Muslim, despite overwhelming evidence to the contrary. At the same time, he maintained both his personal dignity and Malê identity for all to see –interrogators and fellow accused Africans, alike. He told the judge his name was Bilal whereupon the judge responded in a fury, saying that he knew his true African name was Licutan. The "slave" in the eyes of authorities answered with insolence by stating "it was true he was called "Licutan," but he could call himself whatever he wanted." Because of his ignorance, the Portuguese judge was unaware that Bilal was the name of the Prophet's assistant and first Muezzin in Islam. The Muslim struggle (*jihad*) was still alive in Licutan's (or Bilal's) heart despite its failure, militarily, on the battlefield. Pacifico's closest associate Louis (known to Africans as Sanim) was also of advanced age. He brought Pacifico food during his incarceration. Although Sanim could hardly speak Portuguese, several witnesses described him as a culturally versatile man and a speaker of his native Nupe, along with Nagôs and Hausa languages.[18] Contemporary Nigeria the area where Sanim was captured contains more than 250 different languages.

THE BAPTIST REBELLION

Although Muhammad Kaba, Abu Bakr al-Saddiq, and other leaders of the misunderstood "Baptist Rebellion of 1831/1832," in Jamaica remain obscure, their importance to Islamism in Jamaica and the Americas cannot be exaggerated. Afroz documents how events commonly referred to as the "Baptist Rebellion," otherwise known as the jihad of 1831/1832 wreaked havoc on the system of slavery in Jamaica and hasten the end of slavery in 1833. British abolitionism appeared three decades before the abolition of slavery in the United States in 1863. Beyond the American War of Independence in 1776 or the Patriots War as it is called in Britain and the War of 1812, British abolitionist sentiments may help explain British support for black "slave" resistance along the Georgia-Florida border (1810–1812) and support for black fugitives at the newly built British fort on the Apalachicola River in West Florida in 1816. The fort was built by the British for black fugitive "slaves" and militant Indians eager to face pro-slavery pro-settler American forces led by General Andrew Jackson. The name of the fort was later changed to Fort Negro, after Indians fortuitously decided to withdraw from its walls to make preparations for their final stand farther east in East Florida as it was known at the time. Shortly thereafter, Fort Negro was destroyed by a single "hot-shot" blast to its ammunition depot in 1818 to spark the first Seminole Indian War with the United States from 1816 to 1818, waged by Blacks and Indians seeking revenge for the Fort Negro disaster. Not only were the stated motivations of American forces led by General Andrew Jackson subject to question, Fort Negro represents a recurring dilemma in the American experience, namely, the difficulty Americans have had in recognizing black Muslim resisters.

The artillery attack on this civilian population followed by orders of General Andrew Jackson as relayed through Clinch's superior, General Edmund Pendleton Gaines. "I have little doubt of the fact, that this fort has been established by some villains for repine and plunder," Jackson wrote, "and that it ought to be blown up, regardless of the land on which it stands; and if your mind shall have formed the same conclusion, destroy it and return the stolen Negroes and property to their rightful owners." Gaines entrusted the mission to Clinch. [But] Military expediency could not justify the killings. The war with the British had ended one year and five months earlier. All across Georgia, Alabama, Mississippi and Louisiana, US power was supreme. Even so, the existence of a free nonwhite community inside Spanish Florida constituted sufficient proof, so far as General Jackson was concerned, that the fortification at Prospect Bluff was manned by "villains" bent on "rapine and plunder." [But] Accounts provided by white Americans involved in the attack inadvertently tell a different story—of people who were trying to lead peaceful lives when all was taken from them. "The force of Negroes was daily increasing, and they felt themselves so strong and secure that they commenced several plantations on the fertile banks of the Apalachicola," wrote Commodore Daniel Patterson, head of US naval operation in the region, in a report attempting to justify the attack. As white Americans saw it, Blacks growing food for themselves on foreign soil was aggression against the Unites States. The US Army and Navy units based as far apart as New Orleans and Georgia participated in the joint amphibious assault. By dawn on July 27, 1816 [they] instantly killed 270 men, women and children.[19]

The tragedy at Fort Negro and the failure to distinguish accurately black Muslim identities and motives would be repeated many times. The colonial encounter in nineteenth-century Florida may be a case in point where the various sides after a certain point could not recognize who they were fighting, much less why as perhaps seen in the tragic conflict underway in Syria. But this did not lead African Muslims or their progeny to abandon Muslim struggle (jihad) as they understood it.

BENJAMIN COCHRANE

From an Islamic perspective, the call for struggle (*jihad*) has been shown to have existed in the form of a "pastoral letter" (*wathiqa*) believed to have originated in Africa and circulated clandestinely among enslaved African Muslims in the Americas. The letter, written in Arabic, intelligible of course to most black Muslims, reminded them to remember their duty to God (*Allah*) if they wished to reach paradise. The letter independently verified by a number of important historians including Gomez, Davidson, Bolster, Diouf, Afroz, and Quick, played a key role in the misunderstood "Baptist Rebellion" of 1831/1832 in Jamaica. Africans belonging to the predominantly Muslim Mandinka (Mandingo), Fula (Fulani, Phulbe), Susu, and Hausa ethnic groups sought to preserve their Islamic beliefs and practices in secret.[20]

A wealthy English traveler residing in the British West Indies by the name of Mrs. A. Carmichael is reported to have written in 1833 that although: "it is a commonly received opinion in Britain, that negroes are professed idolators . . . there is not a trace of idol worship among them [in Jamaica]. . . . I am convinced there is not a negro, old or young, who could not tell that one God made the world, and created mankind; and that He is all Powerful and all Seeing."[21] Accounts by Bryan Edwards, provide an additionally revealing description of African Muslims enslaved in Jamaica.

> An old and faithful Mandinka servant, who stands at my elbow while I write this, relates that the natives practice circumcision and that he himself has undergone that operation; and he has not forgotten the morning and evening prayer which his father taught him. In proof of this assertion he chants in an audible and shrill tone, a sentence that I conceive to be part of the al-Koran, 'La Illa illa illa! (i.e., La Ilaha Illahhah, there is no god but Allah) which he says aloud at first appearance of the new moon. He relates, moreover, that in his own country Friday was constantly a strict fasting [day]. It was almost a sin, he observes, on that day to swallow his spittle; such is his expression."[22]

The narrative in a letter written by Jamaican magistrate Robert Maden below offers additional evidence of the surviving legacy of Islam among blacks in the Americas despite the forced baptism of enslaved blacks during centuries of enslavement. British Magistrate Robert Maden in a letter written to J. F. savory, Esq., of Jamaica on March 30, 1835 wrote:

> I had a visit one Sunday morning very lately, from three Mandingo Negroes, natives of Africa. They could all read and write Arabic; and one of them showed me a Koran written, from memory by himself—but written, he assured me, before he became a Christian, I had my doubts on this point. One of them, Benjamin Cockrane, a free negro . . . was in the habit of coming to me on Sundays. . . . His history is that of hundreds of hundreds of others in Jamaica. . . . Cockrane says his father was a chief of the Mandingo country. I (Madden) have not the time to give you an account of his religious opinions; but though very singular, they were expressed with infinitely more energy and eloquence than his sentiments on other subjects. He professed to be an occasional follower of one of the sectarian Ministers here, and so did each of his two friends, I had my doubts thereupon, I expressed them to my wife . . . and told her to prepare for a demonstration of Mohometanism. I took up a book, as if by accident, and commenced repeating the well-known . . . [passages]. In an instant, I had a Mussalman trio, long and loud, my Neophytes were changing their names with irrepressible fervor, and Mr. Benjamin Cockrane I thought, would have inflicted the whole of the perspicuous book' of Islam on me, if I had not taken advantage of the opportunity for giving him and his companions reproof for pretending to be that which they were not.[23]

"The Abrahamic heritage of Islam and Christianity enabled the Muslim slaves to secretly practice Islam, while outwardly professing Christianity and maintaining membership of the local Christian churches by paying regular dues at the rate of 3 pence each."[24] An enslaved Mandinka (Mandingo) assigned to Magistrate Robert Madden, named Abu Bakr al-Saddiq provided evidence in two autobiographical pieces written in Arabic that he was the son of a learned family in Islamic Jurisprudence from the city of Timbuktu. So strong was his Islamic teaching that even after thirty years of enslavement in Jamaica, Abu Bakr al-Saddiq still knew the Qur'an and was able to produce a written copy from memory.[25] While Abu Bakr expressed bitterness toward enslavement and oppression he did not lose faith in Islam contrary to the claims of Waves of Immigrant (WOI) theorists who believe that African Muslims in early America abandoned their (African) Islamic faith as a result of their conversion to Christianity and the rigors of enslavement. African Muslim enslaved in Jamaican, Muhammad Kaba, aged seventy-six years displayed such unshakable faith in Islam that British Magistrate Robert Madden amusingly wrote, "so much for the old African renunciation of faith."[26]

ILHAN OMAR

Ilhan Omar, thirty-four, defeated forty-four-year-old incumbent Phyllis Khan to become the Democratic Party representative to the US Congress from the Minneapolis area. She represents a liberal democratic district that includes most of Minneapolis. Ilhan Omar was born in Somalia and immigrated to the United States along with her family at age twelve. Before arriving in the United States she spent four years in a refugee camp in Mombasa, Kenya. She is quoted as saying she was disappointed to encounter racial and economic inequality and religious intolerance upon arriving in the United States; she states, "our democracy is great but . . . fragile." These and other challenges led Ms. Omar to get involved in politics while still a teenager and to fight for hers and other communities across the state of Minnesota. She is the mother of three children and earned a degree in political science and international studies at North Dakota State University. Before winning a seat in the US Congress, Representative Omar worked in local politics for ten years. When she first arrived in the United States she lived for a time in Arlington, Virginia where she studied English. Although the struggle for Ms. Omar and her family to come to America was long and arduous her challenges in some respects are only just beginning. For instance, appearing on "the Rachel Maddow Show," on MSNBC in December of 2016, Ms. Omar described how a cab driver who picked her up on the night of December 8, 2016 from the Omni Shoreham hotel in Washington, DC, called her ISIS and threatened to remove her hijab. She is quoted as saying "I am still shaken by the incident," and expressed astonishment at the boldness of how some people have become in "displaying their hatred toward Muslims." As the only Muslim woman in the US Congress and only one of three Muslims serving in the US Congress, Ms. Omar faces many more battles to be sure. But her election to the US Congress reminds us of the growing visible presence of Muslims in the United States, our rising social diversity, and the challenges that they continue to bring.

ANALYSIS

Although four of the eight cases of Muslim struggles examined in this chapter are set in Africa, the case of Bilal ibn al Rabah, captures the important role of Africans in the institution of Muslim struggle (*jihad*) and among members of the original companions (*sahaba*) of the Prophet. The four other cases of Muslim struggle outside Africa display the effects that black enslavement and immigration have had in facilitating the cultural and political dispersal of African Islamists throughout the world. Because many of the Prophet's original companions in Africa played noteworthy roles in a seventh-century Arabia close to "the horn of Africa," the case of Bilal ibn al-Rabah is included herein. Even in contemporary Saudi Arabia, Muslims from African backgrounds continue to comprise a recognizable part of the communities of Jedda, Medina, and Mecca in Saudi Arabia in part due to the influence of the Muslim pilgrimage to Mecca and the generations of Africans who have come to live in Saudi Arabia. For this reason, the case of Bilal, widely believed to have been a member of the Prophet's inner circle of a half dozen or so persons, is included. Some credit Bilal with being the first male, nonmember of the Prophet's own family to accept Islam. Brazil's so-called "Muslim led slave rebellion of 1835" based on primary source court testimony is the other example of Muslim struggle involving Africans outside Africa. Its inclusion underscores the importance of Islam and Muslim struggle among Africans beyond Africa attempting to cope with sociopolitical circumstances beyond their immediate control. This case joins three others of Muslim struggle (jihad) among the progeny of Africans living in Arabia and the Americas who even with their wide separation from Africa remained true to their Islamist duties, beliefs, and values. Nearly all the original cases of Muslim behavior associated with the Prophet are narrated by one or more primary sources, though the veracity of some may be more or less accurate.

This chapter examined eight cases of Muslim struggle, including: (1) "Bilal ibn al-Rabah"; (2) "Muhammad Ahmad"; (3) "Samory Touré"; (4) "Muhammad bin Abdulla Hassan"; (5) "Pacifico Licutan"; (6) "The Baptist

Rebellion"; (7) "Benjamin Cockrane"; and (8) "Ilhan Omar"; followed by (9) a brief "Analysis" of the observations made. The following chapter turns attention to eight cases of "jihadism" as an instrument of terror as found among Africans. Both chapters demonstrate the importance of Africa and of Africans in the worldwide Islamist challenge with Africa and Arabia at the center of this international and increasingly influential experience.

NOTES

1. See Bernard Lewis *Race and Slavery in the Middle East* (New York: Oxford University Press, 1990), 25, and J.A. Rogers *World's Great Men of Color* (New York: Collier Macmillan Pub., 1972), 143–47.

2. Bernard Lewis *Race and Slavery in the Middle East* (New York: Oxford University Press, 1990), 25.

3. J. A. Rogers *World's Great Men of Color*, vol. 1, (New York: Collier Books, a division of Macmillan Pub., 1972), 143–47.

4. Ibid., 146–147.

5. See Kevin Shillington, *History of Africa,* Revised Edition (New York: St. Martin's Press, 1995), 226–27.

6. Ibid., 227–29.

7. Robert B. Edgerton *Hidden Heroism: Black Soldiers in America's Wars* (Boulder, CO: Westview Press, 2002), 209.

8. This case is based on J. A. Rogers, *World's Great Men of Color*, vol. 1, 295–309.

9. J. A. Rogers, *World's Great Men of Color*, vol. 1, 344.

10. See Kevin Shillington, *History of Africa*, revised edition, 230–232.

11. See J. A. Rogers *World's Great Men of Color*, vol. 1, 344–349.

12. Robert B. Edgerton *Africa's Armies: From Honor to Infamy A History from 1791 to the Present* (Boulder, CO: Westview Press, 2002), 32–34.

13. See Douglas Jardine, *The Mad Mullah of Somaliland* https://archive.org/details/TheMadMullahOfSomaliland and also see Roy Irons's *Churchill and the Mad Mullah of Somaliland* http://www.pen-and-sword.co.uk/Churchill-and-the-Mad-Mullah-of-Somaliland/p/4167/.

14. João José Reis, *Slave Rebellion in Brazil: The Muslim Uprising of 1835 in Bahia*, translated by Arthur Brakel (Baltimore: The Johns Hopkins University Press, 1993), 93–141, and 146–86.

15. Ibid.

16. Ibid.

17. Ibid.

18. Ibid.

19. T. D. Allman, *Finding Florida: The True Story of the Sunshine State* (New York: Atlantic Monthly Press, 2013), 85–90.

20. Sultana Afroz, "The Jihad of 1831–1832: The Misunderstood Baptist Rebellion in Jamaica," *Journal of Muslim Minority Affairs*, vol. 21, no. 2 (2001): 227–243.

21. Ibid., 228.
22. Ibid., 227.
23. Ibid., 228–29.
24. Ibid., 229–30.
25. Ibid.
26. Ibid., 236

Chapter 5

Cases

Terrorism and Africans

The previous chapter explored cases of Muslim struggle and Africans by putting a human face on this essential Islamic institution. This chapter seeks to extend this task by putting a human face on the phenomenon of terrorism and Africans by examining (1) "Anatomy of the 'World's Deadliest Terrorist Group,'" followed by brief discussions of eight cases of terrorism and Africans that include: (2) Boko Haram survivors, (3) Michael Adebolajo and Michael Adebowale, (4) Zubayr Ahmed Abdi Godane, (5) Abubakar Shekau, (6) Iyad Ag Ghaly, (7), Mokhtar Belmokhtar, (8) Mohammed Yusuf, and (9) Ahmed al-Faqi al-Mahdi and closing remarks devoted to (10) an analysis. Along the way, a deeper, more thorough, examination of the historical roots and politics of Boko Haram violence will be offered based on what is known of the group. Because so few details are known about the inner workings of what some describe as the "world's most dangerous terrorist group," portions of this chapter focus on Bauer's investigative work on Boko Haram. Despite the value of Bauer (2016) and Smith's (2016) journalistic accounts, it is prudent to remember that journalism is but the first draft of history.

ANATOMY OF "THE WORLD'S DEADLIEST TERRORIST GROUP"

Nigeria and Boko Haram captured world attention with the largely unsuccessful #BringBackOurGirls campaign aimed at mobilizing public support for the 276 kidnapped schoolgirls of Chibok Nigeria in April 2014. At least 100 of the original Chibok schoolgirls still remain at large, though one estimate suggests that since then the number of women and children captured by Boko Haram may have risen to thousands.[1] As deadly as the group has been, very little is known about Boko Haram, including how it is administered, what its long-term goals are, who finances it, and how it reaches some of its decisions.[2] While this study stops short of fully answering these questions, it nonetheless provides additionally useful information about the group. In fact, we may know more about the leaders of North Korea than we do about the leaders of Boko Haram, including the group's inner workings, modes of recruitment, and strategies. The United States cannot afford to ignore the terrorist violence of Boko Haram. If it does it may be forced to witness its own blood being spilled as witnessed in an ambush of Green Berets in Niger in 2017.[3]

Few states combine the complexity and contradictions found in Nigeria. For instance, a 2017 study attempting to capture these features described the Nigerian state as a "conglomeration of 514 ethnic groups and 190 million inhabitants," whose changes are "pulling North and South Nigeria further and further apart."[4] The South with it significant middle class displays a collective gaze oriented toward North America while the North displays a collective gaze oriented toward Saudi Arabia and the Sudan.[5] The depth of northern Nigeria's Muslim world orientation has been consistently underestimated if not overlooked as seen in Hunwick's 1997 book chapter reference discussed in the introduction of this study. Indeed, the failure to recognize Boko Haram's origins in the mainstream Islam of northern Nigeria with its links to Saudi Arabia has led some to overlook the rise of Islamist militancy among West Africans. Indeed, what began as a small prayer/study group in northeastern Nigeria evolved to become an army which at its peak may have included as many as 50,000 armed soldiers. The Boko Haram movement appears to have displaced as many as seven million persons, enslaved thousands and killed an estimated 20,000 people.[6] While 59 percent of the population in southwest Nigeria suffers extreme poverty, 76 percent of the population of Nigeria's predominantly Muslim North suffers extreme poverty. Ironically, as noted in the preface, most casualties of war in Nigeria and elsewhere in Africa have been caused most immediately by sickness and hunger than by bullets and grenades.[7]

Boko Haram has gone through many metamorphoses. For example, it was first simply known as "Yusifiyya" after its namesake and founder Mohammed Yusuf, but it mushroomed from a small group of orthodox Muslims and militants led by its charismatic founder, Mohammed Yusuf, to what it is at present. At first at least, Yusuf failed to fashion himself as an imam who had studied rather than as a man of the people.[8] Unlike others in Nigeria at the time, he had a special appeal to the youth and rallied against depravity and corruption. He began preaching in his father-in-law's barn and formally broke with the Izala Islamic reform movement of Nigeria, whose full name translates to the Society for the Elimination of Heresy and Reestablishment of the Sunna, in 2000. An ambitious senator, Ali Modu Sheriff, who was a member of the Nigerian parliament and son of a wealthy entrepreneur, allied himself with Yusuf to win gubernatorial election in May 2003. The senator's support added to Yusuf's appeal. Both men saw secular law as corrupt and Islamic law (*shar'iah*) as the only alternative. Around this same time the movement began to branch out.[9]

An even more important figure influencing Yusuf at this time was Mohammad Ali an Islamist who studied Islam in the Khartoum, Sudan where he became a follower of Osama bin Laden. Ali followed bin Laden to Afghanistan and returned to Maiduguri, allegedly with three million dollars, where he met Yusuf and worked to incite violence in Nigeria. Before this, Yusuf had preached nonviolence, but this changed after meeting Ali.[10] The group attacked security forces, stole their weapons, and over-ran guard stations in surrounding areas, with one episode lasting ten days. After mounting a two-day siege on "Camp Afghanistan" most of Yusuf's followers were killed including Mohammed Ali, bin Laden's alleged ambassador. Yusuf reportedly fled to Saudi Arabia in the aftermath of the Camp Afghanistan siege to devote himself to religious studies. But he returned two years later under the auspices of the governor of Yobe state.

Together with survivors of "Camp Afghanistan" they formed the militant core of the "Yusuf" movement and vowed revenge against the Nigerian state.[11] Although the law was rarely enforced, Nigerian state officials singled out and stopped members for failure to wear motorcycle helmets (similar to state roadblocks targeting Muslims in CAR). But Yusuf's men refused to cooperate leading to a scuffle and eventually a confrontation that left three killed and seventeen injured—though details of the incident vary widely. Yusuf issued an ultimatum in an open letter to state authorities. When the deadline expired without event, the group attacked using everything they could, from bows and arrows, knives, hoes to firearms to attack police stations, police officers' homes, and military armories. They also set fires to churches, stormed the central prison to free inmates and killed thirty-two police officers by cutting their throats. In the end, reinforcements were called in and Yusuf was publicly executed outside a police station.[12]

Yusuf's successor, Abubakar Shekau, became the new Boko Haram leader. It is perhaps no coincidence that in a region and continent associated with slavery, "slaves" became the foundation upon which Boko Haram attempted to erect its empire. Moreover, women and girls, according to one eyewitness account, became the currency with which Boko Haram leaders bought the loyalty of subordinates. The emirs decide who is allowed to reproduce with whom. Women have become mere receptacles for Boko Haram genes.[13] Although "Afghanistan" was the name they called their first encampment before it was destroyed by security forces and Yusuf's subsequent flight (hijra) to Saudi Arabia, the movement was modeled after the great Kanem-Bornu Islamic state of the classical Islamic period. Kanem-Bornu occupied a territory that now overlaps with the modern state of Chad, northeast Nigeria and small parts of northern Cameroon, Niger, CAR, and southern Libya. The Fulani and Kanuri were among the group's first victims, and were the predominant ethnic groups in Boko Haram. Due to the prevalence of slavery in the region, men and women display scarified faces so that in the event of abduction, the victim's tribal affiliation might be recognized by fellow tribesmen and returned to their home(s).[14] Acknowledgment of this practice among Africans enslaved in the Americas is carefully explored by the American historian Michael A. Gomez.[15]

An important factor in the rise of Boko Haram is the fact that "for a long time, Nigeria's centers of power did not take Boko Haram seriously." Thousands die every day in Nigeria's big cities as the victims of robbery and "street gang" violence in Lagos."[16] But this all changed when Shekau assumed leadership of Boko Haram. The movement became decidedly more violent when "on August 26, 2011, a twenty-seven-year-old mechanic, Mohammed Abdul Barra, drove into UN headquarters with a truck full of explosives. The explosion killed twenty-five UN employees and more than a hundred people were injured."[17] A Cameroonian with substantial international ties named Mamman Nur, also known as Abu Usmatul al-Ansari, a founding member of the Boko Haram splinter group, Ansaru, is believed to be the mastermind of the UN bombing in Abuja, the Nigerian capital in 2011.[18] Boko Haram has the capacity and stated goal of attacking Western interests, which some believe could be achieved with a simple and modest leadership/ideological realignment.[19] This realignment may already be in the offing given the group's announced allegiance with ISIS and rise of Boko Haram splinter groups by 2015, including Ansaru, led by Mamman Nur.[20] Shekau, who remains a divisive leader, enjoys legitimacy based on his ethnic origins as a Kanuri and grassroots credentials as Mohammed Yusuf's former second-in-command. Any leadership change would likely see Khalid al-Barnawi assume operational control and Mamman Nur assume ideological control.[21] "Boko Haram is a force both to be recognized and feared" and while it lacks the capacity to subdue the Nigerian state headquartered in Abuja, it retains the capacity to inflict massive insecurity in the North." One source who interviewed many of the insurgency's surviving victims concludes: "Boko Haram is a force both to be recognized and feared" and while it lacks the capacity to subdue the Nigerian state headquartered in Abuja, it retains the capacity to inflict massive insecurity in the North."[22] Four factors lend credence to this rather dire observation.

First, competing political factions seeking to win the hearts and minds of Nigeria's Muslims since the 1970s and 1980s like the Maitasine movement,

(Maitasine in Hausa means one who curses) led by Muhammad Marwa, have made Islam a force to be reckoned with. Second, Nigerian state authority remains weak to nonexistent in the northeast where its role resembles an occupation force more than a protector. Third, Boko Haram is not the only actor which benefits from the tragedy. Nigerian officials who exploit the tragedy to wrest more military aid from the West; secular politicians who seek to curry favor from the state based on fear; elites with affinities to the militants who channel support to them for a price, freelancers among the state security forces who peddle their services for a price, South African mercenaries in state-sponsored "security companies" who quietly earn handsome fees, and Boko Haram leaders rumored to have received millions in ransoms in 2018 alone, have all benefited. When one considers the enormous cost of logistics and maintenance for Boko Haram hostages, while supporting a fighting force which at its peak has been estimated to number around 50,000, it goes without saying that others, including supports outside the region, for example, AQIM and ISIS, have profited enormously from the Boko Haram insurgency.

The Nigerian military has "often acted with more cruelty than Boko Haram" by randomly shooting people, plundering, and setting houses of suspects and their neighbors on fire.[23] Perhaps most revealing is the fact that "attempts to weaken Boko Haram have ultimately made it stronger."[24] The fallacy of Hunwick's 1997 suggestion that West African Muslims may have been "cut off" from other Muslims on the continent from 1860–1960 is undermined by evidence of deep-rooted ethnic, religious, and historical kinship bonds among Boko Haram fighters, as seen in the following excerpt.

Many followers of Boko Haram are Kanuri, including Yusuf and Shekau. The Kanuri are the descendants of a people whose empire, the Kanem-Boru Empire, once stretched from the oases of southern Libya to Cameroon. Their elites were the first to bring Islam to Nigeria in the eleventh century. . . . Humans were the most important commodity the Kenem-Bornu had. In the competitive struggle with other West African states, owning more slaves meant having more power. Slaves were the oil of West Africa. . . . The Kanen-Bornu Empire, lasted for more than a thousand years and disappeared only at the beginning of the twentieth century, when Germany, Great Britain, and France divided the territory among themselves. Still, also under colonial domination, the Kanuri managed to preserve their identity. The second strongest group among the Boko Haram fighters is the Fulani. They too, once had a powerful empire, the independent Sokoto Caliphate, which only in 1903 was conquered by the British. Only a small minority of Kanuri and Fulani support Boko Haram, but those who have joined the group hope for a return of the glory of earlier days.[25]

As a testament to their early success, "just six months after their [2014] offensive began, the Boko Haram fighters had conquered nearly the entire

Kanuri tribal homeland" and now ruled a territory the size of Belgium with a population of 2 million.[26] Helping to fuel Boko Haram terrorist violence are the Nigerian security forces who often feel greater loyalty to local patronage networks than to the public interest. Recently, "ten generals from the North were convicted of passing attack plans along to Boko Haram." Similar to police corruption in other societies, "police often become hired thugs or sometimes even contract killers. Again and again, officers are accused of selling the identities of informants to Boko Haram."[27]

> Sani Abucha [*sic*], the last soldier-president of Nigeria, died only in 1998 of a heart attack while in the company of three Indian prostitutes. Abucha [*sic*] had stolen 4.5 billion dollars from the state and had ruthlessly persecuted political opponents. For example, he had the writer and civil rights campaigner Ken Sarowiwa put to death [by hanging] in 1995. The parties that took power after Abucha's [*sic*] death tried to tame the military to prevent any further coups. Year after year, the government has reduced the military budget, further to achieve this goal. . . . At the end of 2014, the police force had to apply for credit.[28]

For these reasons, the United States has been reticent to support Nigerian security forces. Although it did assist the government of Goodluck Jonathan with combat helicopters, in the search for the kidnapped Chibok girls in April of 2014, again and again the United States turned down requests for military aid.[29] Only with the election of current president Muhammadu Buhari (a former military officer and head of state) did the United States extend military assistance.[30] Even with this assistance, the main burden in the battle against Boko Haram is still carried out by the neighboring states of Chad, Niger, and Cameroon.[31] This provides little comfort to states facing formidable challenges of their own from Boko Haram. Similar to the Nigerian security services, "Cameroon's army is also known for its brutality." For example, "the Cameroonian army attacked the city of Gwoza, the former Boko Haram headquarters, and killed more than seventy civilians."[32] This attack may have been in retaliation for Boko Haram's kidnapping of the Cameroonian deputy prime minister's wife, freed months later after paying a ransom reportedly in the millions of dollars.[33]

But Abubakar Shekau, who holds the title of supreme emir (*amir ul-Aam*) of Boko Haram, in reality, may only be a figurehead with real power residing in Boko Haram's emirs.[34] The group's six emirs suggest that the group may be led by at least six different Boko Haram factions.[35] At least one faction has complained that Shekau shows favoritism toward fellow Kanuri tribal members.[36] In addition to this, the potent Ansaru faction has criticized Shekau's faction for killing innocent fellow Muslims. Reflecting its international ties, facilitated by the forces of globalization, eyewitnesses have reported spotting whites working with Boko Haram in and around the Sambisa forest.[37] These reports appear to confirm additional reports of Boko Haram fighters being spotted in Iraq, Syria, and Libya.[38] This and other evidence disputes the myth of Africa as a "dark continent" far removed from the outside world and reveals the reality of Boko Haram as a deadly international force. The following cases of terrorist violence offer specific instances of terrorism among Africans.

Boko Haram Survivors

Bauer's *Stolen Girls* (2016), based on field studies conducted in northeast Nigeria and translated from German, offers a chilling account of Boko Haram survivors.

For example, Sadiya, thirty-eight, was a market woman and mother of five who was held hostage by Boko Haram for nine months in the Sambisa forest. Like so many other kidnap victims, she was forced to marry one of her abductors. She was expecting a child from the man she was forced to marry. Another victim Sadiya was only in the ninth grade and was fourteen when she was abducted with her mother and was forced to marry one of her abductors. Batula, forty-one, a market woman and mother of nine was the older sister of fourteen-year-old Sadiya. Batula was held hostage for nine months in the Sambisa forest. She was pregnant with her youngest child at the time of her abduction. Rabia, thirteen, the daughter of Batula was only in the fifth grade at the time of her abduction. She was abducted along with her mother and forced to marry. Sakinah, thirty-three, served as a midwife. She was the mother of six and hid for several weeks in the mountains but was held hostage for two months. Her oldest daughter, only eleven years old at the time, died when separated from her mother while fleeing Boko Haram. Isa, twenty-three, a goat trader, was Sakinah's cousin who fled with Sakinah's husband into the mountains where they hid for several months. During this time they buried Sakinah's oldest daughter. Rachel, twenty-one, Sakinah's half-sister who worked as a farmer was held hostage for several weeks by Boko Haram.[39] These are but a few of the tragic stories produced by the Boko Haram nightmare.

Michael Adebolajo and Michael Adebowale

British authorities witnessed the very thing they apparently feared most when Islamist militants returned to Britain in 2013 to engage in "home grown" terrorist violence. In the words of twenty-nine-year-old Michael Adebolajo, "I wished the bullets had killed me," as he lay wounded in London awaiting arrest for the gruesome execution of British soldier, Lee Rigby, whom he had just killed minutes earlier. "Please let me lay [*sic*] here," he moaned as a paramedic assessed his wounds. Michael Adebolajo came to Britain from a conservative Christian immigrant family from Nigeria. He grew up in Rumford on the border between London and Essex. Both Michael Adebolojo and his co-defendant Michael Adebowale, twenty-two, had been Christians who reverted to Islam as young adults. Adebolajo accepted Islam while studying toward a degree in politics at Greenwich University. He reportedly said "I saw Operation Shock and Awe and it disgusted me. . . . Every one of those bombs was killing people."

Michael Adebowale, twenty-three, and the younger of the two assailants experienced a troubled youth. While Adebolajo entered his teenage years absorbed in political and religious debate, by age fourteen Adebowale had already entered a life of crime, gangs, and drugs. Adebowale is described as being the victim of bullying. Running a flat described as a "crack den" Adebowale and two of his associates were attacked by a professional fighter and addict named James Lee, who had come to Adebowale's flat to buy crack. But after a dispute broke out between Lee and his potential buyers, Lee launched a ferocious attack that plunged a knife in the neck of one associate, cut the second associate, Faridon Alizada, "to pieces," in a futile attempt to defend the group, and stab Adebowale twice before taking flight. Following this event, Adebowale had not been seen for months and upon his reappearance, he identified himself as Muslim.

By this time the older Michael Adebolajo had been expelled from his politics degree program at Greenwich University to become immersed in anti-Western protest as part of the Al-Muhajiroon movement in Britain. The group led by Omar Bakri Mohammed in 2003 had been banned by Britain's counter-terrorism laws, forcing Bakri to flee London in 2005. He is believed to be living in Lebanon. Adebolajo appears to have reverted to Islam at a meeting in south London where the group, Al-Muhajiroon, maintained a considerable presence in Greenwich. Adebolajo received a fifty-one-day jail sentence in 2006 for assaulting a British police officer. He resurfaced again in 2009 during another anti-British demonstration and again in October 2010 when he and four other men ended up in a court in Mombasa, Kenya after attempting unsuccessfully to join Islamists in Somalia. Adebolajo was deported by Kenyan authorities back to Britain to become one of a stream of foreign fighters largely from the West attempting to slip into Somalia by moving secretly across the Kenyan border. A friend of Adebolajo's, Abu Nusaybah, told BBC *Newsnight* that Britain's MI5 intelligence agency had "harassed" his friend.

The founder of the community organization known as "Street," Abdul Haqq Baker, himself an Afro-British Muslim in London, told the BBC's

Panorama that before Street lost its funding, members of its team had identified Adebolajo as a possible threat. In a film documentary of the murder of Lee Rigby, Abdul Haqq Baker describes how his organization believes it may have been able to help avert Adebolajo's murder of Lee Rigby and in the process assist other troubled youth under the spell of older extremist sheikhs. But unfortunately, we may never know whether or not Street could have made a difference. Lee Rigby was randomly murdered by Michael Adebolajo and Michael Adebowale after he was mowed down by a vehicle, stabbed, and nearly decapitated in broad daylight on a busy public street in London. His murder represents one of the most brutal episodes in the seventeen-year-long WOT.

According to one Woolrich woman, "Michael was more scary [*sic*] than the others [on the stall]—he had quite an encroaching presence." "When I saw the footage of him ranting [he] was familiar to me from his preaching in Powls Street." Eight months before Woolrich, Adebowale is believed to have been among the two hundred people who protested outside the US Embassy in London as part of the worldwide demonstrations against a film mocking Islam and its Prophet. The murder of Lee Rigby and its aftermath were captured in a rambling monologue by Adebolajo recounting why he had just killed Rigby in retaliation for the killing of innocent Muslims in the Middle East. His confession made to a random woman bystander lasted long enough for the police to arrive to wound and apprehend the meat cleaver-wielding Adebolajo. The episode was captured in its entirety on video. Both men were tried and found guilty in January 2014 for the murder of Rigby.[40] Michael Adebowalo, the younger of the two assailants was described by the assistant police commissioner as hitting, spitting, and throwing water on police.[41] Both men admitted killing the soldier Lee Rigby, but Adebolajo argued that it is not murder because "I am a soldier of Allah" and "this is a war." Adebolajo also apparently mentioned to British officials that he loved al-Qaeda.[42] Adebolajo sustained a wound to his upper left bicep while Adebowole sustained wounds in his thumb, abdomen, and thigh. While he was being treated by paramedics, Adebolaljo reportedly said, "your government is all wrong. I did it for my God. I wish the bullets had killed me so I can join my friends and family."[43] The case of Michael Adebolajo and Michael Adebowale provides further evidence of non-Arab Islamist militants born in the West (Europe) from the progeny of African Muslims. Not only do these militants pose a significant challenge to their home countries (as perhaps best seen in France), they are also an increasingly significant part of the group the media labels "foreign fighters" in the ranks of ISIS and other militant groups who manage to reach ISIS training camps in Syria and Iraq and return to the West to carry out attacks.

Zubayr Ahmed Abdi Godane

The attack on the Westgate Mall in Nairobi, Kenya in September 2013 is believed to have marked the transformation of Shabab from a national to an international insurgency whose driving force was its emir Ahmed Godane, also known as Zubayr. Godane led a successful internal purge that placed him firmly in control of the Islamist militant organization. Born in the breakaway region of Somaliland in 1977 and a member of the Isaaq clan which dominates the north but is in the minority in the rest of the country, Godane went to school in Hargeisa, won scholarships to study in Sudan and later Pakistan. He is believed to have traveled to Afghanistan from Pakistan to receive military training. Though he went on to become one of the most wanted terrorists in the world. He is known to have become a quiet, pious, lover of poetry. Godane according to at least one observer led a very devout life.

Godane was perceived to be a quiet charismatic leader, who never smiled, with a reputation for being a no-nonsense person who spent most of his time alone writing poetry. Godane is believed to have used Somali poetry to mobilize and rally people to political causes. He places himself in the tradition of the Somali warrior poet to rally Somali clans against outside forces. He employs a cadence in his speeches that is especially appealing to young people. He praised the Nairobi attack on the Westgate Mall in an audiotaped message released days after the four-day long attack and siege. Speaking in a Somali language recording shared on Twitter and posted on several websites, Godane congratulated the Westgate Mall attackers and attempted to justify their actions as retaliation for the presence of Kenyan soldiers in Somalia as part of an African Union peacekeeping mission. Godane would rationalize Shabab attacks in east Africa as deliberate attempts to torment Kenyans and others who participated in the African Union (AU) invasion force that drove Shabab from Somalia in 2011. It was also retribution against the West that he accused of supplying and supporting the AU invasion that killed innocent Muslims to pave the way for Western mineral firms.

Gordane is believed to have held operational and organizational control over Shabab's 5,000 fighters believed to include dozens of westerners. Godane did not believe the West could endure a prolonged war in Somalia and promised a bloody and prolonged struggle if western states and their clients chose to remain in Somalia. Godane first became linked to terrorism in October of 2003 when he joined Al-Ittihad al Islamiya (AIAI). He is accused of involvement in the murder of a British couple, Dick and Enid Eyeington, who ran a school in Somaliland. He later moved to the south and climbed the ranks of the armed wing of the Islamic Courts Union, a grassroots movement that controlled Somalia during part of 2006. When the United States backed the Ethiopian invasion of Somalia to oust the Islamic Courts, Shabab reinvented itself as the nationalist, Muslim resistance force committed to defeating foreign Christian occupation. By 2008 Godane become emir, succeeding Aden Hashi Ayro, who was killed in a US missile strike.

Although Godane sought to move al-Shabab closer to al-Qaeda, Osama bin Laden declined an initial offer of a formal alliance with Shabab according to documents found in Osama bin Laden's Abbottabad compound. Bin Laden is believed to have warned Godane to govern well and to be careful not to harm Muslims in his attacks. Survivors of the Westgate Mall attack in Nairobi, widely reported how al-Shabab separated Muslims from non-Muslims before executing its victims, an action that has come to distinguish al-Qaeda from ISIS sponsored terrorist attacks. After bin Laden's death, Godane is believed by Western intelligence to have been accepted into the al-Qaeda fold in 2012 and to have pledged allegiance to the group. Under Godane, Shabab ventured outside of Somalia for the first time with suicide bombings in Kampala, Uganda that killed seventy-four people in 2010. Shabab also moved to control almost all of southern Somalia and suffered a string of setbacks at the hands of the African Union Mission in Somalia (AMISOM). Evidence of internal rifts emerged in Shabab as seen in the case of the American jihadi, Al-Amriki, who submitted a letter to senior al-Qaeda leader Ayman al-Zawahri criticizing Godane as autocratic and secretive. Godane responded by launching a bloody purge of the Shabab ranks, including the elimination of the American jihadi Omar Hammami and Ibrahim Al-Afghani—a friend and one-time mentor, and cofounder of Shabab. Like Gadane, Al-Afghani was also a member of the Isaaq clan. Amniyat is a special clandestine division of Shabab, secretly loyal only to Godane and involved in intelligence gathering, fund raising, assassination, and suicide attacks. It has been described as an organization within an organization and most likely to survive Shabab. US officials announced the assassination of Godane in September 2014. President Obama and high-ranking US military officials frequently point to the killing of high-ranking terrorist leaders like Gadane as proof of the success of the military drone program over conflict zones in Africa and the Middle East. While there is no reason to doubt the accuracy of this claim, there is reason to believe that like the US prison at Guantánamo Bay, Cuba, the campaign of killing or detaining "high value" targets like Godane may produce larger numbers of terrorists than it destroys. In the words of a Muslim-world insurgent, "you may kill us by the ones but we are born by the thousands."

Abu Mansur Mukhtar Robow, who was an elusive, charismatic Islamist militant and senior commander in Shabab, surrendered to Somali government authorities on August 13, 2017 following a "falling out" with Shabab's leader in 2013. He had conducted secret talks with government officials after orchestrating hit-and-run attacks on Ethiopian forces and weak Somali forces. Ethiopian forces invaded Somalia in 2006 forcing Shabab to retreat underground for a time. Robow, who had a $5-million bounty on his head, is described as fearing for his life. The Trump administration quietly dropped the $5 million reward for his capture because Robow had entered into secret talks with Somali government officials. His defection has led some to speculate that Shabab may be more divided and at war, internally, than many had previously believed.

Abubakar Shekau

Abubakar Shekau is leader of the Islamist militant group, Boko Haram, which in the Hausa language means Western secular education is sinful and therefore forbidden. Declared dead on at least two different occasions, Shekau came to lead Boko Haram in 2009 after serving in the group's number two position. The group was founded by Mohammad Yusuf, who was killed brutally by government forces while in police custody.[44] Since the killing of Yusuf, Shekau has presided over the killing of roughly 6,000 people according to the Council on Foreign Relations.[45] Some believe that even Yusuf was afraid of Abubakar Shekau. Boko Haram violence includes bombings in central Nigeria and an attack on Christian churches in northeastern Nigeria killing eighty-six; the suicide bombing of UN headquarters in Abuja, killing twenty-three in 2009, and an attack on a boy's school in northeastern Nigeria in November 2014 killing over forty students. The group's atrocities in 2011 include bombings in Damaturu and Potiskum killing sixty-five, and Christmas-day bombings across Nigeria in 2011 killing thirty-nine. Gun and bombing attacks in Kano killed up to two hundred in January 2013. A Maiduguri market attack in February 2012 left thirty people dead. Suicide bombings at churches in June 2012 left twenty-one dead. And attacks in Plateau state left dozens dead, including two politicians appearing at a funeral for the victims.

Shekau was described as the quiet one who walked silently to meet fellow disciples in a house by the railroad tracks, declining to greet other men on the street. But when he became agitated—over taking up arms against the government, or about his hatred of Christians and Jews—it was no use arguing with Abubakar Shekau."[46] But a junior disciple was forced to learn this fact the hard way. The disciple would be "locked in his room by Mr. Shekau for a week with no food or water in the 100-degree heat, he barely survived."[47] Believed to be in his late thirties or early forties, Shekau was born in a remote village on the border with Niger, in Yobe State in Nigeria. According to one account, when he was a young boy, his father took him to a Qur'anic school, run by a mallam, or learned man, in Maiduguri, who remembers him as the most troublesome of all his students. According to the mallam's son, Baba Fanani, Shekau "argued with the mallam all the time," and showed signs of drifting toward militant Islamism even back then,.[48] After eleven years of study at his Quranic school, not once did school officials ever see the boy's parents visit him. Some in Maiduguri believe this "abandonment" explains in part the harshness that Shekau developed.[49]

Fighting between Boko Haram and Nigerian government troops in Baga left two thousand people dead and possibly many more. Local officials describe how government troops set fire to dwellings in Baga in an attempt to smoke-out Boko Haram militants. Eyewitnesses described how the Nigerian military clashes with the group in fierce gun battles that lasted for hours with almost two thousand homes being burned in the process. According to Governor Kashim Shettima of Bornu state "The Boko Haram militants "are everywhere . . . there is no place that is insulated from their presence."[50] As noted earlier, a May-2013 attack in the fishing town of Baga left many dead. An attack on a school in Yube resulted in the killing of thirty children. Killings at a mosque outside Maiduguri left forty-four dead in 2013 while additional attacks on a private school in 2014 produced further casualties.[51] A Boko Haram attack on a prison in Nigeria in March 2014, captured on video, left hundreds of Nigerians dead by heavy-handed government tactics, including aerial bombing of escaping prisoners some of whom may have been Boko Haram conscripts pressed into service by the group, who ended in prison and were eventually shot while trying to escape. Some of the bombed escapees may have been randomly imprisoned months earlier during government sweeps for Boko Haram supporters. These victims were often non-Muslims knowing little about the group or its ideology.

Three North Korean doctors traveling without a security escort in 2013 were killed by Boko Haram militants. Since the killing of Osama bin Laden in Abbottabad, Pakistan, bin Laden's assassins are believed to have gained access to his compound/residence by posing as healthcare workers seeking to administer critically needed vaccines to children, as depicted in Hollywood renderings of the event in the movie *Zero Dark Thirty*. Boko Haram is blamed for killing at least 792 people in 2012 alone.[52] The group demanded the release of imprisoned members from its ranks in exchange for the release of the French family kidnapped in neighboring Cameroon.[53] On June 1, 2014 Cameroon's communications ministers reportedly said "two Italian priests and a Canadian nun, kidnapped" in a region rife with Boko Haram militants two months earlier had been freed.[54] In what might be seen as the Nigerian government's version of religious profiling, Abubakr Ari, a Quranic teacher wearing traditional Muslim attire, and others like him were forced to flee across the Nigerian border for their lives. These refugees describe how civilians were killed by soldiers undeterred by the distinction between militants and innocent civilians.[55] Boko Haram released nearly fifty hostages originally captured in northern Cameroon that included Chinese petroleum workers and the wife of a top Cameroonian government official. Judging from their names, the Cameroonian official and his wife appear to be from Muslim backgrounds like many of the residents in the region.

Conflicting reports in the US media claim that Shekau had been killed, wounded, or otherwise marginalized by a split in the ranks of Boko Haram. A split between Shekau and Abu Musab al-Barnawi (supported by ISIS) may have been validated by a YouTube-video appearance by Shekau during the summer of 2016, months after his absence, leading many to believe he had been killed. Although only one of the originally 276 kidnapped schoolgirls has been rescued by Nigerian authorities, the remaining girls are believed to be alive and probably with Shekau rather than with al-Barnawi's faction. The principal reason for Boko Haram's split into competing factions is criticism of Shekau's violence against fellow Muslims that has been strongly denounced by ISIS and others.[56]

Iyad Ag Ghaly

Iyad Ag Ghaly is a Tuareg and leader of Ansar Dine. Dine and other Muslim militants are key players in an intermittent insurgency in northern Mali. The main Islamist groups in Mali are, Ansar Dine, the Movement for Unity and Jihad in West Africa (Majao), al-Qaeda in the Islamic Maghreb (AQIM), the Signed-in-Blood-Battalion and the Islamic Movement for Azawad (IMA). Ansar Dine is described as a "home grown" movement that seeks to establish Islamic law (*shari'ah*) across Mali. Its full and formal name is Harakat Ansar al-Dine or "movement of defenders of the faith." By contrast AQIM is described by the BBC news service and other Western media outlets as "the North African wing of al-Qaeda." AQIM is believed to have derived from the bitter (and second) civil war in Algeria involving the Islamic Salvation Front, or by French acronym, FIS, during the early 1990s. Since then the group has evolved to become a more internationalist Islamist organization. It emerged in early 2007 after the feared-Algerian Salafist group—Group for Preaching and Combat (GSPC)—also aligned with Osama bin Laden's international network. The group attracts members from Mauritania, Morocco, Mali, Niger, and Senegal. AQIM with its expressed aim of liberating Malians from the French colonial legacy, is known for kidnapping westerners for ransom and drug trafficking. "Kidnapping is such a lucrative industry for extremists in western Africa, netting them tens of millions of dollars in recent years, that it has reinforced their control over northern Mali and greatly complicated plans for an African-led military campaign to take back Islamist held territory."[57] In a campaign to impose a strict Salafist form of Islamic (*shari'ah*) law, the Muslims of northern Mali have reportedly banned festivals, dances, and music and carry out amputations as punishment for theft.[58]

Majao is a splinter group of AQIM formed in mid-2011. In contrast to the scope of AQIM whose focus is the Sahel and the Maghreb regions, Majao's focus places emphasis on spreading jihad to West Africa. Majao's first major operation emerged in October 2011 with the kidnapping of three Spanish and Italian aid workers in the town of Tindouf. The hostages were freed in July 2012 reportedly after a handsome ransom was paid. Although Majao contains many Tuaregs in its ranks, it is believed to be led by a Mauritanian, named Hamada Ould Mohamed Kheirou. France launched a military offensive on January 11, 2013 to drive out the militants. Prior to that, Muslim militants controlled the key towns of Kidal and Gao, widely regarded as the center of Mali's drug trade. Ansar Dine's influence operated mainly in Mali's northwest where it would capture the historical city of Timbuktu and proceed to destroy many of that city's (Sufi) artifacts of historical if not of religious significance. Sufis are looked down upon by Wahhabi-Salafis and mainstream Muslims as being considerably less than pure.

Ansar Dine split in January 2013 when the IMA, led by Al-ghabass Ag Intalla, an influential figure in Kidal, was formed. Al-ghabass Ag Intalla split from Ansar Dine due to the former's rejection of terrorism. IMA claims to champion the cause of the people of northern Mali who have long felt marginalized by the government based in far-off Bamako in the country's south, since Mali gained political independence from France in 1960. AQIM joined forces with Ansar Dine to impose a harsh form of Islamic law (*shari'ah*) across Mali. Unconfirmed reports allege that AQIM has provided training for Boko Haram militants in Nigeria. The signed-in Blood-Battalion led by the notorious one-eyed Muslim militant, Mokhtar Belmokhtar, is believed to enjoy close ties Ansar Dine, Majao, and others. Belmokhtar is rumored to have joined the administration of Gao after it was seized by Majao. These Muslim militants support the Saudi-inspired Wahhabi-Salafi sect of Islam, making them unpopular among Mali's majority Sufi Muslim sect. The implications of the broad and complex mix of quixotic jihadi groups raises many implications for Islamism in this part of Africa. For example, not only does it raise interesting questions related to the downing of Air Algérie flight 5017 in 2014, the rumor that Boko Haram may have trained in the area may explain one eyewitness victim of the November 30, 2015 attack hearing some of the terrorist fighters speaking English during the attack. This is significant because the region is almost exclusively French speaking with Boko Haram and Nigerians being the closest English speakers for miles. The suggestion that militant Islamists remain active in the area challenges earlier French claims to the contrary. French claims seem all the more suspect given a stream of deadly terrorist attacks witnessed in Paris, Nice, and Normandy during 2015/2016 from terrorists with ties to immigrant North- and quite possibly West Africans in France.

Mokhtar Belmokhtar

Mokhtar Belmokhtar (1972–present) is the Algerian leader of the Islamist group known as al-Murabitoun. He was tried in abstencia, found guilty and sentenced to life in prison in 2004. He was also found guilty of terrorism in 2007 and murder in 2008. He became a battle-hardened veteran of the Islamist freedom fighters (*mujahedeen*) of Afghanistan against Soviet occupation in 1991. He lost his left eye while mishandling explosives during this campaign. He is also a veteran of the Armed Islamist Group (GIA) from 1993–1998 in his native Algeria and later a member of the GSPC. He served as the military commander of AQIM from 1998 to 2012. He is credited with leading a daring raid in January 2013 on the Tigantourine gas facility in Algeria killing thirty-nine and taking eight hundred hostages before being driven out by authorities after losing twenty-nine fighters. He left AQIM following a dispute after the group stripped him of the title: "Emir of the Sahel." This led him in 2012 to form al-Mulathameen or the "Masked Brigade" which he led from 2013 to 2014. Libyan authorities announced that he had been killed in Libya while leading the group known as al-Mua'qi'oon Biddam or the "Those who Sign in Blood Brigade," in 2015. Like other leading Islamists, he is/was an elusive figure. His actions defy simple classification. He has been an active combatant in terrorist theaters from Afghanistan to Algeria, from Chad to Mali and from Niger to Mauritania. He may have been involved in Islamist terrorist attacks in Ouagadougou, Burkina Faso and Abijan, Cote d'Ivoire as late as 2016. Reflecting the ideological fluidity of African terrorist groups he is believed to have formed ties with Ansar Dine, Majao, AQIM, and others in the northern Mali region known as Azawad containing Tuareg and Arab tribes hostile to the central government of Bamako to the south. The tribes of Azawad have engaged in the slave trade resulting in the enslavement of Africans from the south for centuries. Like other leading terrorists profiled in this study, Belmokhtar is rumored to have been killed on numerous occasions. For instance, Chadian officials announced his death in 2013; while Libyans announced his death from a French airstrike in 2014. But US officials have been unable to confirm these allegations.[59]

A group led by Mokhtar Belmokhtar claimed credit for attacking a French-owneduranium mine in Arlit, Niger and is rumored to have played a quasi-governing role in Gao, Mali after an Azawad group claimed control of the town in 2013. He is described as being a smuggler of illegal drugs and contraband cigarettes, an arms dealer, and a human trafficker . He is said to have been known by several different aliases, including the "Marlboro Man," "the Uncatchable" and "the One Eyed." The US government declared al-Murabitoun a terrorist organization in 2013. Beyond its daring military exploits, three factors explain the success of Belmokhtar's al-Murabitoun: (1) porous desert borders separating sparsely populated states; (2) weak state militaries (e.g., Niger) responsible for governing these states; and (3) over-stretched French military forces responsible for protecting this region from terrorism. But the region contains five different African states and former French colonies whose total geography may exceed the area of France by several times. This area includes the states of CAR, Niger, Chad, Burkina Faso, and Mali previously discussed. Some sources list AQIM as the most lucrative of the al-Qaeda "franchises" due to its prolific pace of kidnapping and equally prolific success at collecting lucrative ransoms. Most of its victims have been westerners caught in the wrong place at the wrong time. Yet, little or no mention has been devoted to Mokhtar Belmokhtar or his affiliated groups, publically, in the United States.

Those tempted to suggest that the United States has little interest or involvement in the region must remember that the US government has been the main trainer and financier of Mali's government troops who suffered at least one humiliating defeat and several smaller setbacks (including one involving UN troops), from 2014 to 2016, inflicted by Azawad forces linked directly or indirectly to Mokhtar Belmokhtar. This undoubtedly was the result of the Obama administration's refusal to leave a large military footprint in the region. While the merits of this strategy continue to be debated in the United States, the prospect of a sharp and successful reversal of Western fortunes in the region by an untested Trump administration who has promised to bomb the sh___ out of ISIS seems unlikely. It remains to be seen if Republican Party policies will fare any better than Democratic Party policies in this lawless (Azawad) region of Africa. Republican Party critics blame former secretary of state Hillary Clinton and President Obama for covering up the lethal attack on the US Embassy in Benghazi to protect former president Obama's reelection bid in 2012. The attack on the nearby US embassy in Benghazi, Libya (in North Africa) killed US ambassador Christopher Stephens and three members of his staff in 2011.

The region of the Sahel, the Sahara, and the Azawad area of Mali remain a challenge to the West—a challenge for which Mokhtar Belmokhtar seems to have prepared for in advance, as evidenced by his taking of four wives from among the local tribes. He married four Berber and one Tuareg women from prominent families in northern Mali in an obvious bid to forge tribal loyalties among the tribes in the region. This, for a man who if not for his militant Islamists exploits might easily have been seen as an outsider, cannot be overlooked. He also named one of his sons after Osama bin Laden. His lucrative success derived from his many varied operations seems to have helped seal his acceptance, loyalty, and support among the tribes in Azawad. British and French special forces have been mobilized in the search for Mokhtar

Belmokhtar. A European bounty of €100,000 and a US bounty of $5 million have been placed on him.[60]

Mohammed Yusuf

Mohammad Yusuf (1970–2009), also known as Ustaz Mohammed Yusuf, is founder of the Islamist group, Boko Haram in 2002, whose formal name means "People Committed to the Propagation of the Prophet's Teachings and Jihad" (*Jama' atu Ahlis Sunna Lida' awati wal-Jihad*). Yusuf was born in the village of Girgir in Jakuso in Yobe State, Nigeria. He studied in Medina, Saudi Arabia, and became a Salafi. His ideas were strongly influenced by Sheikh ibn Taymiyyah though he was a student of Shukri Mustafa, founder of the Salafi movement in Egypt during the 1960s. Egypt's Salafis were an offshoot of the Muslim Brotherhood of Egypt. He is described as having four wives, twelve children, and supporting a lavish lifestyle including the driving of a Mercedes Benz.

Although Boko Haram is described by local citizens as meaning Western education is forbidden, the group forbids Muslims from taking part in any political or social activity associated with Western society, including voting in elections, wearing shirts and trousers, or receiving a secular education. The group was only designated a terrorist group by the United States in 2013. After returning from Medina, Yusuf established a mosque and an Islamic school (*al-madrassa*). The group's goal is to establish an Islamic state. Most of the group's members are drawn from the Kanuri ethnic group. Kanuris are easy to identify by Nigerians for their facial marks and heavy Hausa accents. The group declared Abu Musab al-Barnawi the new leader of Boko Haram replacing former leader, Abubakar Shekau, who disputes this and is still at large. Nigerian president Muhammadu Buhari declared the Boko Haram "technically defeated." Given the group's cache of money and weapons Mr. Buhari's announcement may be premature.[61] However, the case of Mohammed Yusuf may add further evidence that calls into question Hunwick's assertion cited in chapter 1 that Muslims in West Africa during the colonial period were "cut-off" from co-religionists in the rest of the Muslim world with the narrow exception of African Muslim performing the annual Muslim pilgrimage to Mecca (hajj) and traveling to undertake language study. While the case of Mohammed Yusuf most certainly reflects both these exceptions, it also reflects the experiences of hundreds if not thousands of other Nigerian and African Muslims before and after colonialism as seen in generations of Africans currently living in Jedda, Medina, and Mecca.

The case of Mohammed Yusuf is neither unique nor isolated. Yet, notwithstanding the colonial and/or African state monitoring systems alluded to by Hunwick, the transformative and rejuvenating impact of Yusuf and other

African Islamists in the spread of Salafi (Wahhabi) among Africans can no longer be denied. Salafist ideas and dogma have been readily available since their introduction in eighteenth-century Arabia especially to those venturing to travel to Saudi Arabia to access the kingdom's abundant literature and influential scholars. No amount of surveillance is capable of halting its spread as seen in the case of Salafist influence in Nigeria. Although it may be readily apparent to most, the best remedy for a bad idea is a better idea, delivered on the wings of persuasion and fashioned by the evidence of results.

Ahmad al-Faqi al-Mahdi

Mr. al-Mahdi was convicted and sentenced to nine years on September 27, 2016 as a co-perpetrator of the war crime of intentionally directing attacks against historic monuments and buildings dedicated to religion, including nine mausoleums and one mosque in Timbuktu, Mali in June and July of 2012. Time spent in detention since his arrest by the ICC, in pursuit of a warrant for his arrest issued on September 18, 2016, will be deducted from his nine-year sentence. Mr. al-Mahdi was born in 1975 in Agoune, 100 kilometers west of Timbuktu, Mali. He is believed to have been a member of the Islamist group Ansar Dine, described as mainly a Tuareg movement associated with AQIM who worked closed with the leaders of both groups. It was alleged that until September 2012, he was the head of "Hisbah," the group established to monitor morality and vice, established in 2012. He was also allegedly associated with the work of the Islamic Court of Timbuktu and participated in executing its decisions. At his trial he admitted his guilt and offered an apology for his actions. The court hoped this case would serve as an example to deter others involved in such actions.[62]

ANALYSIS

The terrorist attack on January 15, 2016 on the Splendid Hotel in downtown Ouagadougou, in Burkina Faso represents an important episode and escalation in the WOT in Africa and symbolizes the state of militant Islamist terrorism in contemporary Africa. It delivers us back to the starting point of chapter 1, with the mysterious case of Air Algérie flight 5017 in Ouagadougou, the airport of departure for flight 5017 in March 2014. The attack was launched in retaliation against the French which if one accepts the official explanation of events provided by Paris should never have happened because the terrorists according to French authorities had been driven from the region by 2013. The Splendid Hotel was a four-star hotel frequented by westerners in general and UN personnel in particular. The 2016 attack on the Radison Hotel in Bambako, Mali, killing twenty is officially regarded as an isolated episode of Islamist violence against Mali. But it may be too early to know with certainty whether the attacks were part of a series of attacks beginning with the mysterious crash of Air Algérie flight 5017 which departed from Ouagadougou airport in route to France with a scheduled stop in Algeria in March 2014.[63] Four terrorist attackers at Ouagadougou killed twenty-six and injuring fifteen beginning with two car bomb explosions at a hotel's entrance followed by gun battles between militants and the authorities on the streets. When one of the hostages fled next door to the nearby Yibbi Hotel he was pursued by the attackers and killed.

All four attackers were killed two of whom may have been women. The attack included an attack on a nearby Western restaurant on Friday evening, January 15, targeting westerners believed to have been dining before catching flights back to Europe. The victims came from eighteen different countries including France, Switzerland and Canada. A US missionary was also among the victims. French and US troops assisted local forces a in the rescue operations. According to one eyewitness, the militants touched the feet of downed victims to determine if they were still alive before shooting at them again. The attacker torched the hotel leaving some of the survivors to come close to suffering smoke inhalation. Another eyewitness, described how first responders did little in the critical early hours of the attack to either rescue victims or fight the fire which may have burned on for hours. Eyewitnesses described how authorities seemed to come and go doing little of substance until the fire was eventually brought under control the next day.

The Ouagadougou attack reflects the all-too-common pattern of local emergency personnel's inability to respond efficiently and effectively to terrorist crises. The boldness of the attack launched most likely from Mali which shares a border with Burkina Faso calls into question whether France truly controls of the region adjacent to the Sahara desert known as the Sahel, or border in Arabic. Porous borders and vast barren stretches played important roles in the attack. BBC reports describe how AQIM claimed responsibility as revenge "against France and the disbelievers." Media correspondents on the BBC news have described how AQIM seemed to convey the message that it is able to strike anywhere in the Sahel at any time. This statement contradicts France's earlier claims to have pushed back militant Islamist from controlling in the region of the Sahel.

Boko Haram by 2015 changed its name to the Islamic State in the Province of West Africa West Africa reflecting its newly acquired allegiance to ISIS and dropping a few of its previously held idiosyncratic features including publicly aired tirades by its leader, Abubakar Shekau. But its tactics continue to evolve. For example, exploiting Africa's porous borders it extended its bloody campaign throughout Nigeria and into neighboring Cameroon, Chad, and Niger in 2016. Capitalizing on Nigerians' deep fear of the group it is well entrenched in its hide-out in the Sambisa forest of northeastern Nigeria where it comes and goes with impunity. Despite the valuable support of the Chadians, Boko Haram atrocities continue to escalate. For instance, suspected members of Boko Haram attacked a camp named Dikwa for Nigerians and other West Africans made homeless by Boko Haram in the small town of Daloria. Three women suicide bombers posing as refugees attacked the camp in northeastern Nigeria in January 2016. Nigerian authorities have alleged that two of the women ignited suicide vests while a third failed to ignite her vest after allegedly recognizing her mother and sibling in the camp. The attack killed sixty and wounded at least seventy-eight. Some estimate the Nigerian refugee population to be at least 2.5 million, thanks to Boko Haram violence. Nigerian officials claim as many as 1,000 women and girls have been rescued from the village of Boboshe and taken to the Dikwa camp after being exploited as sex slaves. But as of February 2016 Nigeria's over 200 Chibok girls are still missing. The Dikwa camp, which reportedly housed 7,500 people in September 2015, now holds 80,000. Boko Haram and ISIS of Iraq and Syria surround themselves with civilians who serve as "human shields."

In closing it seems appropriate to ponder over reasons for the recent rise in terrorist violence worldwide which arguably might be described as world war III, in effect. A prominent body of scholars (closely linked to the media and US government) accuse the Saudis of creating a monster in the world of Islam. They accuse the Saudis of exporting a rigid, bigoted, patriarchal, fundamentalist strain of Islam known as Wahhabism (Salafism) that has fueled global extremism and contributed to terrorism, leading one scholar to accuse the Saudis of being both "arsonists and firefighters." In addition to this, the Saudis are accused of supplying more foreign fighters, (2,500) to ISIS, than anyone else with the possible exception of Tunisia and Libya in Africa, which includes, a number of black and brown Arabs, similar to the profile displayed among the September 11, 2001 attackers.[64] Claiming that "Americans like to have someone to blame—a person, a political party or country," former US ambassador to Syria and Algeria, Robert S. Ford, maintains that "it's a lot more complicated than that."[65] Indeed, the twentieth-century ideologies of most influential among modern jihadists, like Sayyid Qutb of Egypt and Abul Ala Maudidi of Pakistan, reached their militant, anti-Western views without much help from the Saudis.[66] Proponents of this view while acknowledging Saudi influence also point to equal if not more influential factors that include repressive secular governments in the Middle East, local injustices and divisions, the hijacking of the internet for terrorist propaganda, and American interventionism in the Muslim world as significant factors responsible for the rise of terrorist violence among Africans.

Similar arguments explaining terrorist violence among Africans and their progeny can be traced to heroic African Muslim figures of the past like Francois Makandal of Haiti or Uthman dan Fodio of Nigeria? But they can also be traced to influential contemporary Muslims like Malcolm X and Jamil al Amin in the United States and Abdullah Hakim Quick of South Africa. What does the history of Africans and Muslim struggle (jihad) examined in this study tell us about the Islamist challenge among Africans? What do the historical and contemporary episodes of Africans and Muslim struggle (jihad) tell us about the role and significance of the Islamist challenge among contemporary Africans? And finally, what do the cases of Muslim struggle (jihad) and jihad as an instrument of terror described in this study tell us about the contemporary Islamist challenge among Africans and Muslims worldwide? Answers to these questions underscore the critical importance of the Islamist challenge among Africans and others.

This chapter has explored: (1) "Anatomy of the World's Deadliest Terrorist Group," briefly discussed eight cases of terrorism and Africans including (2) "Boko Haram Survivors"; (3) "Michael Adebolajo and Michael Adebowale"; (4) "Zubayr Ahmed Abdi Godane"; (5) "Abubakar Shekau"; (6) "Iyad Ag Ghaly"; (7) "Mokhtar Belmokhtar"; (8) "Mohammed Yusuf"; and (9) "Ahmed al-Faqi al-Mahdi"; and (10) offered a brief "Analysis." The following chapter examines the Islamic institution of flight (hijra) and the role it played in the dispersal of African Islamist influence from Africa to the West.

NOTES

1. Wolfgang Bauer, *Stolen Girls: Survivors of Boko Haram Tell Their Story*, translated by Eric Trump (New York: The New Press, 2017), 16.
2. Ibid.
3. Ibid., 17.
4. Ibid., 22.
5. Ibid.
6. Ibid., 23.
7. Ibid., 127.
8. Ibid., 25.
9. Ibid., 26, 28, 29.
10. Ibid., 35.
11. Ibid., 35–36.
12. Ibid., 41.
13. Ibid., 34.
14. Ibid., 54.

15. Michael A. Gomez, *Exchanging Our Country Marks: The Transformation of African Identities in the Colonial and Antebellum South* (Chapel Hill: The University of North Carolina Press, 1998).

16. Bauer, *Stolen Girls*, 57.

17. Ibid., 58.

18. Charles River Editors, *Boko Haram: The History of Africa's Most Notorious Terrorist Group*, 29 and 30.

19. Ibid., 31.

20. Ibid., 30.

21. Ibid., 31.

22. Ibid.

23. Ibid., 58.

24. Ibid.

25. Ibid., 68–69.

26. Ibid., 86–87.

27. Ibid., 72–73.

28. Ibid., 73.

29. Ibid.

30. Ibid.

31. Ibid., 74.

32. Ibid., 123.

33. Ibid., 86.

34. Ibid., 90.

35. Ibid., 89.

36. Ibid., 90.

37. Bauer, *Stolen Girls*, 97.

38. Ibid.

39. Ibid., on pages that are un-numbered.

40. Dominic Casciani, "Woolowich: How Michael Adebolajo Became a Killer?" *BBC News Magazine*, December 19, 2013, http://www.bbc.co.uk/news/magazine-25424290.

41. BBC News, "Lee Rigby Murder: Map and Timeline," December 19, 2013, http://www.bbc.co.uk/news/uk-25298580.

42. BBC News, "Lee Rigby Murder Trial: Michael Adebolajo 'Is a Soldier of Allah,'" December 2013, http://www.bbc.co.uk/news/uk-25301907.

43. BBC News, "Lee Rigby Trial: Killing 'Cowardly and Callous,' Court Hears," November 29, 2013, http://www.bbc.co.uk/news/uk-25153273; Duncan Gardham, "Counter-terrorism Projects Worth 1.2 m Pounds Face Axe as Part of End to Multiculturalism," February 11, 2011, *The London Telegram*, http://www.telegraph.co.uk/news/politics/8319780/Counter-terrorism-projects-worth-1.2m-face-axe-as-part-of-end-to-multiculturalism.html.

44. "In Nigeria, Militant Raises His Profile Through Terror," *Wall Street Journal*, May 14, 2014.

45. Ibid.

46. "Jihadist's Fare Taunts Nigeria From Shadows: Fear Leader is Behind Kidnappings," *New York Times*, May 19, 2014.

47. Ibid.

48. Ibid.

49. Ibid.

50. "Civilians Caught in Nigerian Battle," *New York Times*, April 22, 2013.

51. Heather Murdock, "Nigeria's Boko Haram Threatens Oil Refineries, Muslim Clerics," *Voice of America*, February 20, 2014. Also see "Deadly Attacks tied to Islamists Militants Shake Nigeria," *New York Times*, March 3, 2014.

52. "3 North Korean Doctors Are Killed in Nigeria," *New York Times*, February 11, 2013.

53. "Family Freed by Militants in West Africa," *New York Times*, April 20, 2013.

54. "Three Kidnapped Missionaries Are Freed in Cameroon," *New York Times*, June 2, 2014.

55. "In Nigeria, 'Killing people Without Asking Who They Are," *New York Times*, June 6, 2013.

56. "Boko Haram Leader Is Wounded in Airstrike, Nigeria's Military Says," *New York Times*, August 8, 2016.

57. "Kidnappings Fuel Extremists in West Africa," *New York Times*, December 13, 2012.

58. "French and Malian Forces Retake Timbuktu," *Wall Street Journal*, January 20, 2913.

59. Missy Ryan, "The US Still Doesn't Know if its Killed the Legendary One-eyed Militant," *Washington Post* (online edition), February 17, 2016.

60. See https://www.rewardsforjustice.net/english/mokhtar_belmokhtar.html. Also see http://www.bbc.com/news/world-africa-21061480.

61. This case was based on the report, BBC News, "Who are Nigeria's Boko Harm Islamist Group?" November 24, 2016, http://www.bbc.com/news/world-africa-138 09501.

62. See the International Criminal Court, "Situation in the Republic of Mali," The Prosecutor v Ahmad Al Faqi Al Mahdi, updated October 7, 2016. Also see Prosecutor v. Ahmad al-Faqi al-Mahdi, *Harvard Law Review*, May 10, 2017 https://harvardlawre view.org/2017/05/prosecutor-v-ahmad-al-faqi-al-mahdi/.

63. Since these attacks several terrorist attacks have occurred in Cote d'Ivorie. Burkino Faso and Mali Between 2016 and 2017 presumably carried out by al-Qaeda in the Islamic Maghreb (AQIM).

64. For a detailed discussion of this, see "Both Arsonists and Firefighters: Saudis Promote Jihadist Ideology Yet also Fight Terrorism," *New York Times*, August 26, 2016.

65. Ibid.

66. Ibid.

Chapter 6

Flight (*hijra*) to the Americas

This chapter explores the essential Islamic institution of flight (*hijra*) to improve our knowledge and understanding of the Islamist challenge in historical perspective. It includes sections devoted to: (1) "Muslim flight"; (2) "The Elusive Atlantic"; (3) "In the Shadow of 1492"; (4) "Jihad and Hijra by Other Means"; (5) "Other Avenues of Flight"; and (6) "Analysis." The assumption that "jihad" and therefore Islamist militancy first reached the United States with the September 11, 2011, attacks implied in the title of Pipes' *Militant Islam Reaches America* (2002) and other misperceptions in the WOT are debunked in this chapter. Terrorist violence had long-since reached the Americas as evidenced by the first bombing of the World Trade Center bombing in New York in 1993 planned and implemented by Osama bin Laden from his first base in the African nation of Sudan. Other pre-September 11, 2001, attacks include occupation of a US Federal building, in Washington, DC, by Hanafi Muslims in 1977 and the assassination of an Iranian diplomat by a "Black Muslim" posing as a mail carrier in 1979 who escaped to Iran and presumably survives underground. The assailant gave an identity concealing television interview to ABC News during the 1990s. Other attacks include the Muslim led "slave" uprising" (*jihad*) in Brazil of 1835, the Muslim-led conspiracy and insurgency led by Muslim leader Francois Makandal of Haiti in 1758, and the Muslim-led "coup d' etat" (*jihad*) against the government of Trinidad in 1989. These episodes provide evidence of the presence of Islamist militancy throughout the Americas reflecting the now famous line by the Last Poets of the 1970s proclaiming "the revolution will not be televised!"

The Island nation of Trinidad may supply more militant Islamists per capita to al-Qaeda and ISIS than any other location on earth. The earliest recorded encounter with Islamist militants in the United States involved a splinter group of the Nation of Islam (NOI) movement in San Francisco dubbed the Zebra killers by the press in 1974–1975. The second earliest episode involved the Hanafi Muslims, a small Black Sunni Muslim group that occupied a US federal building taking hostages and shooting unarmed innocent civilians in Washington, DC, in March of 1977. The third involved the assassination of an Iranian dissident by an indigenous Black Shia Muslim in Washington, DC, in 1979. Each marked a significant episode of Islamist violence despite the fact that they are routinely ignored by journalists and public officials. It is important to note that these major episodes as precursors to the September 11, 2001, attacks involved the progeny of African Muslims in the United States rather than foreign Arab terrorist as is often assumed.[1] These and other misperceptions are what I elsewhere label "multicultural blind spots" in our understanding of Islam in the Americas. This chapter uncovers a few of them.

The New World's earliest Muslims and Jews were drawn from the ranks of explorers, conquistadors, refugees, and New World trade financiers. Fleeing the persecution of the Spanish Inquisition (1492–1614), crypto-Muslims and crypto-Jewish refugees, or those who chose to keep their true religious identity a secret, emigrated from Europe seeing refuge in North Africa and the New World. Long before the rise of the post-modern Islamic revival (*tajdid*) during the 1970s, or the tragic events of September 11, 2001, Muslims and Jews posing as "New Christians" reached the New World and settled in areas that would later become part of the United States. Indeed, the prominent slave historian Michael A. Gomez, reminds us that "Christopher Columbus crossed the Atlantic . . . and with him came Islam"[2] to offer further support to the idea that Americas' earliest Muslims reached the New World long before September 11, 2011. The progeny of this first Muslim flight (*hijra*) to the Americas survived to form the nucleus of the Muslim community (*ummah*) that persists in the United States to this day. Others including Muhammad (2000) argue African Muslims arrived in the Americas long before Columbus in the fourteenth century when the predecessor of Mansa Musa (described by some as the richest man in the world) from the African kingdom of Mali crossed the Atlantic.

MUSLIM FLIGHT (*HIJRA*) TO THE AMERICAS

Despite their historical significance, the arrival of Islam, Muslims, and jihad to the New World remains largely hidden and woefully under-examined by scholars. For example, Harvey acknowledges that because *Moriscos* or "New Christian converts from Islam" (*Neuvos Cristianos convertidos de Moros*) were nearly always unwilling converts, "it is highly probable that Islam remained embedded in their souls."[3] While *Morisco* "is what they were forced to become; Muslim is what they remained underneath."[4] If Harvey is correct in this view, it seems all but certain that Muslims in the New World were no more *Morisco* than Jews were *Marrano*, the bigoted Spanish term used for Jews at the time, which means pig, swine, or filthy persons. Other evidence supports this view. For example, Spanish Muslims (*Moriscos*) who escaped to the Americas continued to speak of themselves as Muslims (*Muslimes*). "Moro and morisco were names that other people had for them, not the name they used for themselves."[5] Spanish authorities banned heretics and "New Christians" from entering the Americas, but "the attempt to screen or filter slave imports was ineffective."[6]

By the sixteenth century when Europeans reserved slavery for Africans, Senegambians brought to Spain from West Africa became known as *ladinos* or "Europeanized" slaves. Most Ladinos were forcibly baptized though most had been previously Muslim. Using primary sources, Diouf documents how *ladinos* became the first slaves sold in the New World. Klein corroborates this view by describing how "ladino slaves who accompanied their masters on voyages of discovery and conquest to the Atlantic Islands and the New World," became "the first Black inhabitants of America."[7] We may never know "the physical characteristics such as dark skin or frizzy hair" of refugees from Spain in that the native inhabitants of the Iberian Peninsula and the African invaders of AD 711 had nine centuries to intermingle. The chief defenders of Moorish Spain were African Berbers who covered a broad range of people, and enslaved Africans who crossed into Granada, Spain's southern-most province, "right up to the end of Muslim times [1492] and almost certainly later."[8] Given this history, it is no surprise to find that *Moriscos*, *Ladinos*, and *Bozales* (African-born blacks) in Spain's vast New World colonies as these mostly "New Christians" became the principal targets of the Spanish Inquisition. These practices predate the Muslim ban of 2017 in the United States. But they also display a long-term fear of Muslims. Just as political turmoil in Africa, Syria, and Iraq forced Africans, Middle Easterners, and others to migrate to the West, political turmoil on the Iberian Peninsula drove the first mass migration of Muslims from the Old to the New World.

Decades of dispute and warfare between Portugal and Spain for control of the waters off the coast of Africa culminated in the Treaty of Alcoçovas in 1479–1480, which gave control of the Canary Islands to Spain. This treaty allowed Portugal to gain (1) navigational rights to the seas around Guinea, (2) the right to supply Spain with slaves, and (3) control over Maldria and the Azores. Fourteen years later at the behest of the Pope, Spain, and Portugal signed the Treaty of Tordesillas of 1494 that established a north-south line drawn through the Atlantic Ocean somewhere between the forty-first and forty-fourth meridian, and fifteen hundred miles west of Cape Verde Island dividing the continent of South America. Everything west of the line was ceded to Spain, and East of the line, including Africa and Asia, was ceded to Portugal.[9] This treaty continues to define in significant ways the geography and identity of contemporary Latin America.

Illustrating what Cornel West would later described as "religion in the service of empire," Africans from predominantly African Muslim ethnic groups like the Wolof, Djola, Mandinka, and Baga, along the Guinea coast became some of the first enslaved Africans to arrive in the New World. By the 1450s Portuguese control of the largely unpopulated Canary Islands, Sao Tome, Cape Verde Islands, the Azores, and Madiera enabled these islands to serve as launching pads for Portuguese slave raids along Africa's Guinea coast. At their closest point, the Canary Islands are a mere sixty-seven miles off the coast of West Africa. Ironically, these same routes represent the reverse avenues used for the contemporary illegal trafficking of Africans into Europe and the illegal trafficking of illicit drugs from Colombia via Africa into Europe. The first large-scale slave revolt in the New World occurred on Christmas Day, 1522, when ethnic Wolof (Muslims) working at a sugar mill owned by a son of Christopher Columbus, revolted in Hispaniola. Similar revolts occurred four years later in Colombia, where the town of Santa Maria was razed to the ground. Enslaved Africans also revolted in Mexico in 1523, 1537, and 1546; in Puerto Rico in 1527; and in Venezuela in 1552. Because African Muslims played major roles in many of these revolts, the Spanish crown adopted numerous decrees designed to ban the importation of Muslims into the New World.[10] These early historical events reveal how the arrival of African Muslims in the New World was accompanied by the specter of both fear and great dread by colonial authorities throughout the Americas.

Notwithstanding the Muslim defeat in Spain in 1492 or the Spanish Inquisition that followed, it is doubtful that Islam completely disappeared from Spain and its vast Diaspora after surviving in Iberia for eight centuries. Several factors seem to support this view, including Spain's Islamophobia (i.e., anti-Muslim bigotry), Muslim participation in most, if not all of the major sixteenth-century slave revolts in the New World, and a seemingly endless string of Spanish decrees aimed at keeping Muslims (i.e., moors) from reaching the Americas. These factors suggest Spain must have doubted its erstwhile efforts to halt Muslims from reaching the New World. Muslim flight (*hijra*) to Central and South Americas contrasts sharply with idyllic images of immigrants at Jamestown, Virginia. Arriving in the Americas mainly as captives, desperados, and refugees, America's early Muslims were often found among the exiled, corsairs, and maroons. But historians have largely ignored this important exodus. The case of the Muslim Imam and collaborator, Ali Sarmiento, who secured safe passage for himself and his family to Spain's vast empire as described in the following original document is revealing.

By this royal deed [data] granted by our holy and royal Council with our accustomed mercy, and confirmed by us and our sacramental religion, Ali Sarmiento and all his descendants may and can enjoy the liberty and freedom which their forebears enjoyed, to the satisfaction of the said Ali Sarmiento, because he was very obedient and truthful to his sole King, and no less fidelity have we found in him in matters which concern us, and thus, by reason of his merits, we give him frank and free liberty through all our potentates [*sic*] by land and by sea, to live and travel without hindrance, whether going, returning or staying, or in any further return journeys he may make whether in our own days or after them . . . let him live and maintain his state in whatsoever religion or law may be his will. Given in our royal Alcazar of the Alhambra of Granada; sealed with our royal seal, on May 22 of this present year of 1499.[11]

While pressures on them to emigrate began to grow after the fall of Granada in 1492, Muslim expulsion from the Iberian did not occur all at once. For instance, it was not until 1496 that King Manuel of Portugal announced in a royal decree the ban of all Moors from Portugal. Similarly, it was not until 1609 that the Spanish King Philip II expelled all remaining Moors from Spain, by special decree. According to at least one study, fully one half million Moors (or *Moriscos* as their descendants were called) left Spain between 1492 and 1610. Yet, few studies in the West examine the subsequent fate of these Muslim émigrés, much less their contribution to the formation of some of the earliest Muslim communities in the Americas. These early Muslim immigrants to the Americas bear a striking resemblance to contemporary Muslim immigrants to Europe and the United States. The case of Ali Sarmiento for example is not unlike Muslim allies who worked with the US military in contemporary Iraq who were promised safe passage for themselves and their families to the West following their service as translators, native informants or allied militia fighters.

"For a quarter of a millennium at the end of the Middle Ages, Muslims of the Iberian Peninsula had a simple choice: either accept subject (*Mudéjar*) status within one of the Christian states (Aragon, Castile, Navarre) or live within the Islamic kingdom of Granada."[12] Some Muslims like Ali Sarmiento were granted safe passage out of Spain—primarily but not exclusively to North Africa—at Spanish government's expense. Lucrative deals were secured with Muslim "nobles," officials, and religious scholars.[13] Some Muslim elites were even financed on their own private estates.[14] However, because Spain's assimilated Spanish speaking *Mudéjares*, were romance language speakers, serious differences emerged between them and their Muslim brethren living in the Islamic state of Granada (Spain).[15] These differences are not unlike political differences between Muslims affiliated with the Nigerian state who remain politically and religiously oriented toward the West in contrast to Islamists in Nigeria's impoverished Northeast whose political and religious orientation remains decidedly toward Mecca and Islamist militancy.

Similar to debates among Muslims in the contemporary era, the Muslims of medieval Spain debated whether or not a true and practicing Muslim could or should reside in a Christian society. Muslims were exhorted by Islamic authorities (*al-fukaha*) in the strongest possible terms to leave Christian Spain, avoid Mudéjar or Christianized Muslim status, and embrace flight (*hijra*). For instance, one famous edict (*fatwa*) attributed to al Wansharishi warns Spain's Muslims, "not to live in the land of the disbeliever."[16]

The attractiveness of al Wansharishi's edicts were enhanced by the Spanish capitulations of 1491, which proclaimed that "anybody wishing to cross to North Africa might sell his estate and be transported with all his effects in a ship to any Muslim country he wished, without payment of passage money or other expenses, for three years."[17] A significant number of Spain's Muslim refugees elected to escape to North Africa while others remained behind in Muslim Granada to plot the re-conquest. Spanish policy and Muslim world policy encouraged emigration and separation, respectively, to be sure. But their effect on immigrant refugees have not always produced positive results. For instance, the push and pull of centrifugal and centripetal forces, driving thousands of Africans desperately to cross the Mediterranean into Europe leave many to die each year.

"As far back as the start of the thirteenth century, the arrival of Muslim refugees from Spain fleeing before the Aroganese and Casilian *reconquesta*," added new strength to Muslim corsairs of the Mediterranean even though "Spanish Moors were not always warmly received and frequently remained on the periphery of North African society."[18] Muslim corsairs of the Mediterranean including (a) Moors or *Moriscos* from Spain, and (b) Muslim *Janissaries* from Turkey and elsewhere clashed in bloody struggles for power and intrigue reflecting an intra-Muslim rivalry often overlooked by modern western historians. These intra-Muslim clashes plus Spanish Muslims' peripheral status in North Africa must have made flight to the Americas more appealing to Spanish Muslim refugees than flight to North Africa after 1492.[19]

Despite prohibitions against the transport of Jews and New Christians (*Moriscos*), both groups appeared in growing numbers in the New World after 1492. Difficult-to-enforce laws were further diminished by the fact that "*converses*" or New Christians were the very class of people most likely to possess the aptitude and capital needed to develop colonial trade and industry."[20] Haring lends credence to this view by noting,

> There were always ways of reaching America, clandestinely or for a price to the crown. In spite of prohibitive laws, therefore, Jews, and New Christians, both Spanish and Portuguese, were found in the Indies in increasing numbers. And it was against them that the Inquisition was mainly directed.[21]

A footnote designed to clarify an official Spanish decree against Moors, Jews, and New Christian traveling to the New World, reads: "Evidently some [Moors, Jews, or recent converts] were already there, or later slipped through the net at Seville, for the proctors sent to represent the colonists in Spain in 1508 complained that the natives were being corrupted by their teachings!"[22] Reference here to "their teachings" may represent a tacit acknowledgment of the presence of Islam among early natives in the Americas.

A consensus among scholars holds that many Africans brought to the Americas during the sixteenth and seventeenth centuries, were male captives of war that included Muslim struggles underway in Senegambia. For instance, a revolt occurred in Hispañola in 1522 and another five years later in Puerto Rico.[23] An uprising in Panama was suppressed "with great difficulty"[24] creating "constant danger" in the minds of colonialists "that fugitive slaves would join hands with rebellious Indians," as happened in an uprising on Hispañiola in 1533 led by a tribal chief, named Henríquez, which took ten years to suppress.[25]

A Black conspiracy in New Spain (Mexico) in 1537 caused such alarm the viceroy Mandoza requested the suspension of new importations from Africa.[26] These conditions lend credence to the view that a weak and ineffective Spanish colonial policy governing illegal immigration to the Americas existed at the time that allowed Jews, Moors, and heretics "to live unmolested in the loosely organized communities of the American frontiers,"[27] where life for them though far from certain, was no more dangerous than it might have been had they remained behind to face the Inquisition. This characterization captures the plight of Muslim refugees living in the West. But in addition to this, anti-immigrant fervor acquires a more sinister flavor when Muslim victims of violence are further victimized by xenophobic, Islamophobic classifications which psychologically depict them as "other" as seen in recent ugly cases found in CAR, Europe and the United States.

Active discrimination against Moors in Spain may have led many "to seek refuge in the vast open stretches of America, where they hoped to find an escape from the long arm of the government or of the Church at home."[28] Religious non-conformists in England and Spain were persecuted. But while the English Crown permitted religious dissenters to live and worship as they pleased in the colonies, Spain, officially, sought to enforce the same rigid orthodoxy in its colonies that it demanded at home in Europe.[29]

This policy fueled open defiance, by Moors, (Muslims) and Native Americans during the early years of Spanish colonialism. But Spain's practice of requiring formal though nominal conversion toward the end of its colonial rule allowed some of its New World subjects to continue to practice traditional religious "customs." These "customs" were more openly displayed in remote parts of Spain's colonies. But how did ordinary people, like those who might be described as crypto-Muslims find their way to the New World? As we have seen, the path of Spain's Muslim aristocrats, collaborators, and elites, like Ali Sarmiento, may have been facilitated by royal decrees and safe passages. But how did more ordinary Muslim refugees escape Spain after 1492? The answer to this lies in Spain's active seaports and loosely controlled voyages.

THE ELUSIVE ATLANTIC

While the public typically thinks of pirates, as action-oriented, exciting, romantic figures motivated by courage, greed, and a desire to challenge the establishment, real pirates during the golden age of piracy bore little resemblance to these fictional images. Pirates of the 1650s to the 1720s differed from pirates of the 1820s and 1600s. Muslim corsairs for example, unlike pirates of earlier and later years, plundered for the Glory of God as well as for individual greed and profit.[30] This form of plunder became especially significant following the Elizabethan war against Spain. At first, British officials made little effort to suppress pirates and corsairs, whose actions against the Spaniards were seen as a profitable and effective way to expand English commerce. They also represented a cheap way to wage proxy wars against Spain.[31] Hence, nearly every maritime hero of the reign of Elizabeth—Drake, Hawkins, Grenville, Raleigh, Frosbisher, and many others—spent time either as a pirate or privateer who engaged in piracy on the side, or as a raider, abettor or employer of pirates.[32] Corsairs and privateers who plundered for the Glory of God in the employ of Muslim patrons bear a striking resemblance to contemporary Islamist militants. While both reflect an affiliation with Islam and Muslims, violence and plunder rather than religion and peace were the primary motivations of the corsair and privateer. And both, as seen in the case of pirates and ISIS, sailed under the Black flag of terror.

Although little is known of the day-to-day life, beliefs, and social customs of pirates, many Irishmen and Englishmen were declared outlaws for their decision to "turn Turk" a widely used euphemism for becoming Muslim. Others like "archpirate" Captain Jack Ward became valuable allies of the Turks who rose to high positions despite remaining Christian.[33] While French and Iberian shipping remained the principal targets of these activities, a broad network of political and commercial support soon developed.[34] English pirates and corsairs developed allies among Muslim officials in Morocco and insurgents in the Caribbean. The latter served as principal sources of food, drink, equipment, women, and in some instances, family life.[35] English allies of the Muslims of Morocco, some of whom would convert to Islam, would become the political equivalent of Albanian, Greek, and Italian allies of the

Turks (1480–1580) in the Mediterranean. Europeans captured as boys from Christian nations and raised as Muslim became known as *Janissaries*. Just as the descendants of the *Janissaries* were among the first European Muslims to emerge in Europe, the descendants of English pirates and corsairs, who converted to Islam and fought against Spain, may represent the first European Muslims to emerge in the Americas. For some it is difficult to resist characterizing these activities as examples of "state sponsored terrorism," aimed at recruiting "foreign fighters" to wage "jihad" against the disbelievers in the interest of empire as seen in the case of ISIS and its goal of promoting the caliphate or Boko Haram and its related goal of restoring the past glory of the once powerful Kanem-Bornu empire of central Africa.

Irish pirates who sailed South in August or September plundering the coasts of Spain and Portugal taking prizes to their winter base in Mamora [Mehdia or Mahadya] on the Atlantic coast of Morocco, were welcomed by the Emperor of Morocco who condoned the wealth they brought which sold widely in Morocco at attractive prices.[36] Although the word corsair (from the word *corso*), is widely treated as synonymous with pirates in the West, Barbary pirates, as they were formerly known, operating from bases in what is today Algeria, Tunisia, and Libya, were distinguished from pirates in the mix of motivations that drove them to plunder.[37] Sailing out of Algeria and Morocco, Muslim corsairs and their English/Irish allies harassed European shipping throughout the Atlantic and Caribbean and were most feared for kidnapping and enslaving their captives.

To their victims, they were probably seen as just another brand of pirate. But Muslim corsairs "saw themselves as legitimate warriors of Islam," who sailed vessels and conducted plunder under commissions provided by Muslim authorities in the Mediterranean. Ship crews were a heterogeneous collection of Turks, Moors, and renegade Europeans that included Morisco refugees from Spain. Captains, officers, and specialists were European renegades. But while their motives were complex and far from uniform, "jihad" in addition to plunder was an important motivation of these corsairs whose primary targets were the ships of Christian nations. Again, the Muslim corsairs of this period display much in common with contemporary Islamist militants. The core of this form of terror as Fichtner notes was a kind of light cavalry, largely comprised of minimally armed, mobile ethnic Turks who did not always wait for the sultan's orders before striking their targets. One especially vicious group, the *Martolosan*, were Christians under Muslim commanders, although Crimean Tartars were another such allied group. Of course, even when these Muslim allies were formally under Ottoman command, they still retained vandalizing and territorial agendas all their own.

The Islam examined in this study is primarily the Islam of the Qur'an, the Prophet Muhammad, the tradition (*sunnah*), and the five pillars discussed in chapter 2. Yet, this strict approach to Muslim identity of necessity must be relaxed to include atypical though important instances of Islamist militancy as seen in the case of the assassin, Carlos the Jackal, and in the case of seventeenth-century Muslim corsairs depicted below.

> These turbaned warriors in their flowing robes served under their own aga and played little or no part in the sailing of the ship, sitting patiently smoking opium or tobacco until that moment of glory when the khodja, or purser, "read out verses from the Koran in a loud voice," as they swarmed over the sides of a prize [with] great curving scimitars in their hands, [to] swept through the doomed ship.
>   [W]ild-looking men with turbans and long knives who burst forth out of the mist and drag innocent families away to a lifetime of slavery. Few people realize, however, that they had exact Christian counterparts who attacked ships with Muslim passengers or goods aboard and raided the coast of North Africa and the eastern Mediterranean in a search for Muslim captives to sell into captivity. For Christendom, too, had its holy war, which Pope Urban II had launched in November 1095 when he set in motion the First Crusade.[38]

European labor shortages in early America may have helped some Muslims to reach the Americas as early as 1617, with the introduction of Moorish laborers by Spaniards who eventually set them free in the colonies.[39] Yet, while skeptics may be correct in doubting that Turkish corsairs had actually reached the Caribbean, the same cannot be said for their English, Moorish, and occasional French allies and their many Black and brown allies who waged a protracted campaign against Spain in the Caribbean and the Atlantic. Indeed, after reaching their peak in the 1620s, the Barbary corsairs and their largely English allies, dwindled in significance, before briefly engaging in a nineteenth-century (1801–1805) naval encounter against the United States that ended in the release of some three hundred American captives.[40] Later with the decline of corsair activities in the Americas, a number of former predators on Christian shipping were granted pardons and settled quietly in the New World.[41] But others like the notorious, Blackbeard, whose crews contained many Blacks and mulattoes, fought to the death.[42]

These men eluded colonial authorities through alliances they formed with indigenous anti-colonial insurgents that included Mosquito Indians, along with Black and Native American fugitives known as maroons. The Mosquito Indians of Nicaragua, who fiercely resisted colonialism and often allied themselves to pirates, may upon close scrutiny reveal a one-time Muslim identity. As late as the nineteenth century Charles Napier Bell claimed to have learned the traditions of the Mosquito Indians of Nicaragua from an elderly woman who was both Mende (a prominent West African group) and Muslim.[43] Political groups committed to "making America great again" have expressed alarm and dismay at the number of "non-Americans" living in the United States, like illegal immigrants from Mexico and beyond, the way colonial officials must have feared the presence of Muslims in early Americas.

The Spanish pronunciation of the word, mosquito bears some resemblance to *masjid*, the Arabic word for mosque, which may have originated in Spain, as a derogatory Spanish expression denoting the way Muslims may appear in prostration during prayer. Other interesting linguistic patterns include the English word, admiral, which like its French counterpart appears related to the Arabic title, Amir al-Baha or lord/governor of the seas. One Arab oral tradition even suggests that Honduras may have derived its name from pre-Colombian Arab explorers who first dubbed it Hind Ras, meaning India head or point in Arabic reflecting the standard nomenclature used by voyagers at the first sight of land.

To the great dismay of their Muslim brethren in the Islamic state of Granada, relations between Spain's Muslim minority, the *Mudéjares*, and Catholics were often "cordial," as perhaps reflective of United States and their Muslim allies in Iraq and Afghanistan. Both shared a common ancestry, language, and culture. Mudéjares "were not automatically hostile towards a Catholic King ruling over them and if well treated, proved to be staunchly loyal."[44] For instance, "Muslim builders working for Catholic patrons gave birth to a style of architecture known as *Mudéjar*, containing elements of Romanesque, Gothic, and Hispano-Muslim influence."[45] Yet despite their efforts and skill at assimilation, the history of the *Mudéjares* came to an abrupt end around 1500 when a series of decrees directed at them in the kingdoms of Castile and Aragon would command them to convert to Catholicism or leave Spain.[46] Those who remained became nominal Christians. But for those who chose to preserve their identity, flight to the Americas must have been an attractive alternative.

Given these incentives perhaps far more than Mudéjares architecture may have been transplanted from Spain to the New World. Much like their demeanor as immigrants in the contemporary West, "the Muslims of the Christian Kingdoms [of Spain] sought to have no history, to live discretely and unperceived."[47] The liberty to practice their religion quietly "indoors" before the dawn of the Spanish Inquisition must have been an appealing option to some if not all Spain's endangered Muslims. Utilizing their skills in the trades including in construction, woodcarving, ceramics, metalwork and the sale of foodstuffs—where they served as carpenters, joiners, potters, builders, and architects—Spanish Muslims offered valuable skills to Spanish sea vessels traveling to and from the New World. Official decrees forcing them to leave Spain plus edicts (fatwās) from their own Islamic scholars (*al-fukaha*) advising them to emigrate (*hijra*), illustrate the strong incentives that Spain's Muslims had to abandon Iberia. And after the fall of Muslim

Granada in 1492, among the two most frequently considered destinations for Spain's Mudéjares/*moriscos* (i.e., colonial America and North Africa), colonial America must have seemed the most desirable of the two, if not the ideal choice.

IN THE SHADOW OF 1492

What explains Muslim flight (*hijra*), struggle (*jihād*), and community (*ummah*) to the New World? The simple answer is the events of 1492 and their aftermath. The defeat of the Moors of Spain in 1492, the "discovery" of the New World in 1492, European competition in the Mediterranean and Atlantic, and of course the slave trade are the leading factors responsible for the arrival of *jihad*, Islam, and Muslims in the New World. Europe faced the ever-present threat of "Barbary pirates," (North African Muslims), Moors, and Mediterranean Turks, in the aftermath of defeat of the Moors in 1492. Muslim nations often in concert with European allies would attack European vessels at sea as far North as Iceland. During the 1960s Malcolm X made wry references to this in references to what he called the "Black Irish" of Britain; while Princeton emeritus historian Professor Bernard Lewis in a similar vein made similar references to these frequently ignored contests in post-September 11, 2001, lectures throughout the United States.

During an April 17, 2005, C-Span Television interview, Stanford Economist, Thomas Sowell, asserted that more Europeans had been captured by North African Muslims than in the entire Atlantic slave trade. Princeton Historian, Linda Colley, similarly notes that while far less is currently known about it, the Ottoman and North African transatlantic trade in Black and white "slaves," nevertheless lasted longer than New World slavery and at times may have been comparable to it, in scale.[48] Colley's description of Ottomans and North African corsairs as "highly effective predators" is perhaps best illustrated by the fact that even relatively secure Denmark was forced to devote about 15 percent of its Mediterranean trade profits "to paying [Muslims] off."[49]

Echoing Colleys' assertions, Fichtner notes that for Suleyman the Magnificent, such raiding was more "a form of punishment" more possibly linked to the victims' status as disbelievers or infidels than to anything remotely related to commerce. Nonetheless, as many as 362,000 Africans may have been imported by Ottomans during the nineteenth century alone.[50] Boko Haram's campaign of kidnapping and enslavement of victimized young girls and ISIS's enslavement of victimized Christian women in Iraq bears some resemblance to these practices. Media reports during the G. W. Bush years of terrorists promising to capture and enslave women among US military fighters, bear a similar if not distant resemblance to these practices.

Notwithstanding Jackson's reminder that Ibn Khaldun's *Al-Mūqaddimah* (1381) contains starkly racist images of Blacks, Ibn Khaldun represents a valuable first-hand account. More recent accounts describe how Spanish Muslims sought refuge in the coastal regions of Spain and North Africa and on the islands of the western Mediterranean following their defeat in Granada in 1492.[51] But before this defeat, Ibn Khaldun describes how Muslim power so dominated the whole of the Mediterranean that "not a single Christian board floated on it."[52] *Al-Mūqaddimah* describes how some "non-Arab [European] nations became servants of the Arabs and were under their control."[53] North African and Ottoman navies of the sixteenth and seventeenth centuries "employed seagoing nations for their maritime needs" and "embarked the army and warriors" of non-Muslim European allies "to fight against the unbelievers across the sea" according to Khaldun.[54] Do not these Muslim and non-Muslim allies from across Europe, Australia, and the United States resemble contemporary "foreign fighters," members of ISIS or similar such groups?

Although it is easy to overlook the impact of the Muslim naval presence during the time of Columbus, a major motive behind Spanish colonization of the New World nonetheless was the Christian-Muslim rivalry. Columbus' efforts to capture the Indies occurred in the context of the larger "holy war" under way against the Muslims. Muslim scholars underscore the vastly overshadowed role of Martin Alonzo Pinzon who piloted one of Columbus' three ships that first landed in the Americas. Pinzon, was Morisco and quite possibly a crypto-Muslim. Yet, regardless of how one interprets Columbus' "discovery," "the age [of Columbus] was one in which skilled navigators abounded, and Columbus can but have been aware that, in practical knowledge of maritime matters, he had many equals and perhaps many superiors even among those who sailed with him."[55]

Commenting on what he describes as "the language of holy war" that flourished in New England where writers clamored for a war against the "Mahometans," Matar concludes that "such anti-Muslim zeal may have been inspired by anxiety over the possibility that 'Turks' had actually landed in America [and]—that the Atlantic had not completely protected the colonists from their Muslim nemesis."[56] In response to reports that the French and Turks had surprised the English in New England, a nagging question confronting Europeans would be did "the 'Turks' [i.e., the Muslims] actually reach North America, perhaps as pirates cooperating with French pirates?"[57] It is conceivable that some men and women from North Africa may have fallen into the hands of British transatlantic slavers causing some to end up laboring on plantations in the American South.[58] Indeed, some Muslim corsair captains, considered highly dangerous by colonial authorities, may have ended up working along-side slaves as oarsmen aboard European ships in the New World.[59] While the full-extent of co-mingling between Muslims and others in the Americas remains unclear, in the fluid world of the colonial Atlantic, Muslim contact with persons already living in the New World seems highly likely.

 For example, "thousands of Britons were captured and hauled to the slave markets of North Africa" during the seventeenth century while Muslims captured at sea by the British were "either put to death or hauled into the jails of England."[60] British convicts being hauled to American penal colonies were also the targets of Muslim slavers. As a possible act of retaliation for this, "Muslim seamen were continually taken prisoners, sometimes rightly as pirates and sometimes wrongly as merchant seamen who were accused of piracy, so they could be sold as slaves or exchanged with British captives in North Africa."[61] Numerous scholars posit the idea of a Muslim nemesis inimi-cal to the West. For instance, Bernard Lewis, describes how sixteenth- and seventeenth-century Western colonial expansionism (or, if you like, imperi-alism) can be viewed as a European counter-offensive against centuries of subjugation at the hands of Muslim Moors, Turks, and Mongols.[62] This theme parallels what Lewis describes as "the Ottoman obsession."[63]

In a similar vein, Ottoman and Barbary naval attacks of the sixteenth and seventeenth centuries can be seen as a Muslim response to the fifteenth-cen-tury Muslim expulsion of the Moors from Spain. After 1680, Morocco's Sul-tan Moulay Ismail "systematized corsairing as a weapon of state finance."[64] Similar to "jihad" in the contemporary Islamic world, the *jihad* that began in Spain and the Mediterranean spread with devastating effectiveness to Europe and the Americas. But unlike contemporary *jihads*, the Muslim *jihads* of the sixteenth and seventeenth centuries enjoyed a rich historical documentation in the captive narratives of Europeans innocently trapped in the epic events of imperialism, "jihad," enslavement, and corsair raids throughout the Atlan-tic. The term "renegade" whites (*'allaj*, sing. *allooj*, *a'alaj*, pl.) was first introduced by Turkish and Arabic Muslims to designate Englishmen in the service of Muslims.[65] "Corsairs were not all Moors and Turks they were also Britons and other Christians who had Mahumetized and donned the turban."[66] Some of these ("Mahumetin") whites joined forces with Blacks and Indians to establish some of the earliest known multiracial maroon communities in the New World. John Walker Lind, the so-called American Taliban, captured from the battlefields of Afghanistan by US troops, now serving time in prison, may be a contemporary illustration of this phenomenon.

One renegade prominently featured in British captivity narratives is Alexander Dempster. As one of the more flamboyant renegades, Dempster is described as clad in Mohammedan dress," with a large red turban, and coming from a very respectable and ancient family. Another "renegade" was white "adventurer," William Augustus Bowles, who opposed white encroachment on Indian lands in Florida and defected from the British army after being reprimanded for insubordination. He quit the army, threw away his uniform, and married a Native American. Bowles joined the military at the age of thirteen. He first came to Florida in 1788 but was later captured by Spanish authorities who exiled him to Moro Castle, Cuba where he died in 1805. Bowles is prominently photographed wearing a turban and what some might describe as Arabic Muslim dress. British captive Peter Williamson provides another example of a white renegade. Williamson claimed his Native American capturers actually reared him from childhood, and led him to adopt the life of an Indian warrior among the Delaware Indians. Williamson would author a book on his childhood experiences. Of course, Lawrence of Arabia represents perhaps the best-known case of a white renegade who voluntarily joined forces with one contingent of Muslims.[67]

JIHAD AND HIJRA BY OTHER MEANS

Like West Africans who escaped their enslavement to join the Indians at every opportunity, a significant number of Europeans of the sixteenth and seventeenth centuries chose to "go over" to their Native American or North African Muslim captors. Coming from lower-class (and most often, Irish) backgrounds, many of these Europeans had been abducted in their youth and raised by their captures.[68] Turks actively recruited foreign-born youths primarily from Albania, Greece, Italy, and the Balkans, to serve as professional soldiers known as *Janissaries*. Others joined the Muslims for purely financial reasons as the demand for skilled gunners on board Muslim naval vessels was highly prized.[69] In the words of Ibn Khaldun, "every craftsman [among the non-Arabs] offered them his best services."[70] This pattern may reflect the all-to-familiar practice of "foreign fighters" that now includes African and African Americans who journey to join the "jihad" of ISIS in Syria, Iraq, and elsewhere.

Some Europeans reared in North Africa fully embraced Islam. Many learned Arabic and dressed and behaved as Muslims.[71] Still others entered military alliances with Berber pirates. As an example of their well-known mutual respect for one another, the monarch Ahmed al Mansur of Morocco and the Queen of England in 1603 may have plotted to implement a joint English-Moorish invasion of the American West Indies aboard British ships as a direct challenge to Spanish hegemony in the region.[72] But because both monarchs died a year later their likely schemes never materialized. "If there was one aspect of African life that struck Europeans, it was African religion."[73] A six-volume 1722 publication by a Catholic priest named Father Labat who served in the West Indies from 1693 to 1705, reveals the frustration that missionaries felt over their failure to convert Africans.[74] In the words of Labat "only in the presence of Europeans who could serve as constant examples would Blacks remain Christians."[75]

Most of the "galley slaves" aboard French ships of the seventeenth-century Atlantic "were Moslems, taken in warfare with the Barbary states, in fighting with corsairs, by purchase in the slave markets on the southern and eastern Mediterranean coast, and even in occasional slave raids on the North African coast."[76] The Pope and Christian Europe justified these practices as punishment for infidels and believed that such punishment ensured Africans' Christian conversion.[77] It is clear from documented historical accounts that corsairing and privateering for a time may have been almost equally practiced by Christian and Muslim empires.

Yet unlike the Christian practice, "English, Welsh, and Irish pirates flourished under Muslim flags."[78] For instance, Britons like Peter Lyle, Joseph Pitts captured at age fifteen, and Thomas Pellow captured at age eleven "(whose account appeared in 1739) renounced England and Christianity during their captivity in North Africa."[79] A Scotsman named Peter Lyle (Murad Rais), who converted to Islam, rose to the rank of admiral in the service of Tripoli Muslim ruler, Yussef Karamanli (probably Karim Ali). Pitts, Pellow, and other Europeans wrote memoirs describing their conversion to Islam. Another British captive case involving eighty-seven survivors aboard the British shipwreck *Inspector,* in Morocco in 1746, included two captives, Thomas John and John Armatage, both of whom are described as Black men. John Armatage reportedly accepted Islam ("turned Turk"), and joined the black slave army (*Abid al-Bukhari*) of the Moroccan Sultan.[80] Although some of Armatage's fellow British captives converted to Islam and settled in North Africa, others worked as mercenaries until they earned enough money to buy a pardon and return home. This rich history of Christian-Muslim warfare which might very well inform our contemporary understanding of Christian-Muslim world confrontation is in need of more careful examination in the West.

The experiences of those captives who managed to return are recorded in documents they wrote and are often published. For instance, British captive Joseph Pitts who returned to England to publish a highly successful book on his experiences in North Africa describes three fellow English captives he knew who had also voluntarily embraced Islam.[81] Many adopted Islam over Christianity and appear to have remained Muslim due to opportunities they enjoyed which they were unlikely to have had as members of England's lower classes.[82] The contemporary African American Muslim experience in the United States includes numerous examples of influential persons, like Imam Jamil al-Amin, Imam Talib Abdur-Rashid, W. D. Muhammad, Malcolm X, and members of the popular group known as the Last Poets which included at least two Muslims, who after "converting" to Islam in their youth became prominent spokespersons for Islam in the United States. Similar to their English counterparts of the seventeenth and eighteenth centuries, their prominence in the Muslim community (*ummah*) derived as much from their "conversion" to Islam, as it did to their perseverance under conditions of captivity and persecution. Moreover, the stature of African American Muslims among contemporary Muslims in the United States is enhanced by their symbolic links to the legacy of Black enslavement as well as to the transformational power of religion as an instrument of survival and deliverance.

The Moroccan captive, Mustafa Zemmoui is a notable case in point. Also referred to as Esteban, Estebanico, or Estevanico of Azamor, Esteban was captured during King Manuel I of Portugal's invasion of Azemmour in modern-day Morocco in 1511. Following his capture he was probably sold to a Spaniard who eventually joined the Panfilo de Narváez expedition that reached what is today the City of Tampa Florida in 1528. He was one of four sole survivors of the ill-fated Navaro expedition (1528–1536) and became a highly respected healer, explorer, and master of Indian sign language. Although he is described as an extremely large and powerful Black man, Esteban and his party were massacred by Zuni Indians after attempting to enter the first of the seven legendary cities of Cibola. Although there is no evidence that Estaban created a lasting religious impact, he was the first non-Indian to cross North America and the first Muslim to reach the region.[83]

Corsair communities led by British pirates Sir Francis Drake, Henry Morgan, and Sir Walter Raleigh, continued to prey on Spanish and Muslim vessels, despite a British peace treaty with Spain and good relations with the Muslim rulers of Turkey and Morocco.[84] Buccaneers and pirates of seventeenth-century America "were joined by a mixed bunch of runaway slaves, deserters, escaped criminals, and religious refugees."[85] English pirates became so numerous among the Muslims they became known as the "new pirates of Barbary."[86] French support for the Turks and their Muslim allies in the Mediterranean and opposition to Spain from 1480 to 1580, may explain, at least in part, the French sacking of Havana in 1538 and active support of French hostility by local maroons, that may have included fugitive Africans and others of Muslim backgrounds.

"When the thirteen American colonies split off from mother England, they lost British protection," and the US soon "found itself lumped in the pile of potential Barbary victims, alongside the likes of Sardinia and Sicily. From 1785 to 1815 more than 600 American citizens were captured and enslaved."[87] Europeans were forced to pay tribute to North African Muslims to avoid capture and enslavement. For example, "[t]wenty-one freeborn Americans would spend eleven years in slavery in Algiers from 1785 to 1796, before their stories would receive public attention in the US."[88]

Tripoli's ruler, Yusef Karamanli declared war on the United States to spark the first US war with a foreign power. When Tripoli captured the USS *Philadelphia*, 307 Americans were forced into slavery along the coast of Barbary, where Thomas Prince, a seventeen-year-old from Rhode Island, and three other Americans reportedly "decided to go Turk," and convert to Islam.[89] Many Westerners captured in this way managed to return home like the twenty-one freeborn Americans described above. But it is unclear whether Thomas Prince, his fellow Muslim converts, or the crew's only Black sailor, were among them. The war with Tripoli (now Libya) became immortalized in the line, "to the shores of Tripoli"[90] in the now famous US Marine fight hymn. The conventional approach to explaining seventeenth-century piracy as well as the recent kidnapping of hostages by militant Islamists in Paris, Raqqa' Syria, and Mali in 2015 has been to view them as acts of random violence. But a more accurate and compelling approach is to view them as part of a prolonged "jihad" against Western interests by Muslims and their allies.

As Jamieson's compelling study *Lords of the Sea* describes how "they [the Barbary corsairs] claimed the 'eternal war between Christendom and the lands of Islam as justification for their predatory actions." Colley similarly argues that it is possible to view the bulk of these encounters (solely directed at Christian shipping) as revenge by Muslim states and their sponsors for Muslim expulsion from Moorish Spain in 1492.[91] This jihad eventually reached the Americas and involved alliances between enslaved and formerly enslaved Muslims possibly living as maroons, that is, escaped fugitives, in the Americas *and* European "renegades" typically operating as pirates in the Caribbean. White renegades and allies of the Muslims during this period may also be viewed as forerunners to contemporary white American Muslims like John Walker Lindh the so-called "American Taliban," former US military officer and attorney, Brandon Mayfield, and white Australian Muslim, David Hicks, unwittingly trapped in a web of international "jihad."

These events reveal that neither the US-led WOT nor the worldwide Muslim struggle (*jihad*) have been able to escape the grips of international conflict and at times may be virtually indistinguishable from it. As the universal model and symbol of pious Muslim behavior, the Prophet Muhammad fought a vigorous jihad against the Meccans who had earlier forced him and his companions (*mujahirun*) to flee from Mecca to Medina, Arabia in the seventh century AD, Lucrative caravans controlled by the Meccans eventually were considered fair game and attacked by the Muslims. With the fall of Muslim Spain in 1492 and the Muslim expulsion from the Iberian Peninsula, Spanish enslavers, colonizers, and champions of the Inquisition must have also seemed like fair game to Muslims and their European corsair allies in the New World.

Turkish corsairs active in the Mediterranean who eventually moved West along the coast of North Africa to become close allies of fellow Muslim

Barbary corsairs (whose name probably derived from the Berber of North Africa). Christian-Muslim warfare had been going on in various forms and at various intensities since the seventh century. And although Turkish history perhaps celebrates its memory more highly than other nations, with a number of Turkish ships named after famous Turkish corsairs, the Barbary corsairs were the first major foreign enemy of the young American Republic in the late eighteenth century and were the principal reason for the creation of a permanent US Navy.

The first Barbary war (1801–1805), against Tripoli in Libya, and the second Barbary war (1815) against Algiers, loom large in the study of early American foreign policy.[92] While pirates in the minds of Arabs historically were defined as "sea robbers," the Barbary corsairs like European Christian Privateers operated within a legal framework. Unlike pirates, Barbary corsairs and Christian Privateers were obligated to receive permission from their rulers to send out privately owned war ships, and when they returned with prizes those captured ships, cargoes, and crews were disposed of according to set rules.[93] Yet Barbary corsairs were different from most European corsairs in that they engaged in a war that was "eternal" and therefore Barbary corsairs could sail against Christians whenever they wished.[94] Their attacks on Christian shipping and coasts made them widely feared because they represented the advance of the Ottoman Empire and rise of militant Islam.[95]

Although difficult to know with certainty, between 1530 and 1780 it is estimated that the Barbary corsairs captured as many as 1.25 million captives from Christian Europe, and in the sixteenth century alone may have taken more Christians captives than the number of Black slaves Christian nations shipped across the Atlantic from Africa to the Americas.[96] The notion of eternal war also ascribed to Muslims by Georgetown scholar Michael Scheuer raises important implications for the WOT. Globalization and the dispersal of Muslims worldwide have made classical Islam's distinction between Dar al-Islam and Dar al-Harb, largely obsolete. Britain was accused of hypocrisy for devoting more energy to abolishing the Black slave trade than to abolishing the last vestiges of the white slave trade by Barbary states of North Africa though Britain changed its mind and launched a bombardment of Algiers in 1816 forcing the Barbary states to promise to end the enslavement of white Christians.[97] The Ottoman Turkish Sultan granted permission to Turkish corsairs at the Western end of the Mediterranean and in North Africa to launch attacks against Christian shipping and coasts. The most famous of these corsairs was Kemal Reis who took along with him his nephew, Piri Reis, a skilled sailor best known for the seas charts he prepared including a pre-Columbian chart of the Atlantic coast, a copy of which appears on the cover of Abdullah Hakim Quick's (1997) *Deeper Roots* study of the earliest known African Muslims to visit the New World (cited below).

Reis was a title given to Turkish corsairs.[98] Although unable to intervene in enough time to forestall the fall of the Spanish Muslim kingdom of Grenada and the triumph of the Spanish Reconquest of Spain from the Moors of North Africa, Turkish corsairs and Morisco Muslim refugees from Moorish Spain who settled in Morocco continued to conspire against Spanish authority in Christian Spain long after the fall of Granada in 1492. For example, the expulsion of Moriscos from Spain in 1609 to 1614 was in part the result of Barbary corsair interference in the early 1600s (except for Salé Morocco which remain a remained a hotbed of Barbary corsair intervention against Spanish Christians). Rather it was the influx of Dutch and English corsairs with their advanced maritime skills and technology using square sails that allowed Barbary corsairs to menace and attack Spanish and later English shipping and coasts as far away as Newfoundland, Iceland, Ireland, and the New World.[99]

Similar to events in contemporary Mali and Iraq where Muslim fighters as witnessed in the case of Iraq dispersed to nearby countries like Syria, Jordan, and surrounding areas after the fall of Saddam Hussein, the expulsion of the Muslim fighters from Muslim Spain after 1492 may have succeeded in merely dispersing Muslims from Europe to new military theaters in North Africa, the Atlantic, and the Americas. If this is true, then the arrival of Islam, Muslims, and jihad in the Americas may be seen as a direct consequence of the emergence of these converging historical events. The strongest evidence supporting the presence of early Islam in the Americas exists in Latin America and the Caribbean. But a similar unfolding of events may help explain the appearance of whites among Boko Haram and Shabab and the corresponding appearance of Black African fighters of Boko Haram among fighters in Iraq and Syria. This explanation may explain seemingly random acts of violence across Europe in 2016/2017 often involving the progeny of Africans. Many feared the defeat of ISIS and dispersal of its fighters from their stronghold in Syria and Iraq would simply disperse them to theaters like Africa.

ANALYSIS

A striking similarity exists between contemporary Islamist militants and the pirate-buccaneer-privateer (corsair) alliance of the seventeenth and eighteenth centuries. These similarities include reliance on terror as a primary tool for instilling fear, use of lethal violence as an instrument of retaliation and/or revenge, kidnapping for ransom as a principle means of financing, a rejection of mainstream values, contempt toward mainstream symbols, displays of cruelty as punishment for code infractions small and large, ambush as a preferred fighting tactic, continuous recruitment to replenish highly fluctuating memberships primarily due to high battlefield casualties, injuries, and outright desertions, appropriation of selected Islamic symbols especially "jihad," emphasis on egalitarianism among its members, consensus-based decision making, reliance on broad ranging military alliances, collaboration with sovereign authorities publicly and privately as seen in Boko Haram's alleged secret links to sympathetic voices within the Nigerian government and privateer Sir Francis Drake's public ties to top level officials in the government of England, links to state sponsors and/or their affiliated agencies as seen in Muslim fighter (*mujahedeen*) collaboration with the CIA in Afghanistan against the Russians during the 1980s and regular pirate collaboration with auxiliary-state organs in Morocco for example, responsible for the repatriation, "liquidation," or redistribution of proceeds acquired from privateer plunder on the high seas. Contemporary Islamist militants and seventeenth- and eighteenth-century pirate-buccaneer-privateers also display a rejection of mainstream practices related to the treatment of vulnerable persons as seen for example in the practice of sodomy by pirates against vulnerable young boys known as "cabin boys" forced to share quarters with desperate pirate men on long seafaring voyages, the capture of young Christian Yazidi women by ISIS fighters for marriage or enslavement and the capture of the Chibok school girls of Nigeria for marriage or enslavement by Boko Haram militants.

The lengths to which pirates, buccaneers, and corsairs went in search of plunder and revenge in the early eighteenth century are noteworthy. For example, pirates cruised the North American coasts form Newfoundland to Caribbean, crossed the Atlantic to the Guinea coast of Africa, and rounded the Cape of Good Hope to Madagascar to plunder ships in the Indian Ocean. It is difficult to imagine how the impact of seventeenth- and eighteenth-century piracy might be described as anything other than spectacular in its scope and cruelty. Corsair warfare in the elusive Atlantic allowed the Muslim nations of North Africa to continue to battle the Christian nations of Europe to avenge the Muslim defeat at Grenada in 1492, the persecution of Muslims and Jews during the Spanish Inquisition and Crusades first launched by Pope Urban II in A.D. 1095 against Islam and therefore against the entire Muslim community (*ummah*). Islamist militants have cited everything from disaster in Syria to the prolonged suffering of the Palestinian people as reasons for their contemporary outrage. While "draining the swamp" of terrorism associated with ISIS, piracy which peaked in Somalia during the 1990s and murders associated with the Honduran-US-based street gang, MS 13, resonates as a preferred strategy with President Donald Trump, a more effective way to eliminate contemporary violence would be to eliminate the social contractions that give rise its emergence in the first instance.

Although Islamist militancy and its world view based on militants' interpretations of Islam and the sunnah gave Muslims and their allies reasons to avenge oppression and persecution by Spaniards and the Atlantic slave trade of the past, they facilitated the development of a piracy, buccaneering and privateering regime that served as a formidable tool of resistance. This idea is excellently explored in James Scott's (1990) *Weapons of the Weak: The Hidden Transcript* though largely by scholars. Militant Islamists in the early Americas under the banner of maroons and "religious refugees" did indeed fight back. Therefore, rather than merely view piracy as a system of organized plunder, privateering may be seen as a tool of resistance that allowed "religious refugees," fugitive "slaves," and others in early America to undertake struggle (*jihad*) from domains beyond the reach of authorities that often served as safe havens for those whom society labeled "criminals"— areas that Scott describes as the domain of the hidden transcripts. It may be no coincidence to note that pirates mounted coordinated attacks on colonial interests in the Americas, collaborated with maroons and "runaways" insurgents and supported nineteenth-century independence movements throughout Latin America.

While the United States may be "a land of immigrants" and of evolving generations of new arrivals, a gaping void exists in this narrative when it comes to crypto Muslims and crypto Jews arrivals to the New World who struggled to preserve and occasionally succeed in transmitting their values and heritage to their progeny. Without including both Muslim and Jewish narratives, an important slice of American history and experience is overlooked. The failure to recognize and understand the role of "indigenous" Muslim communities who long-since arrived in the Americas to practice their religions privately and transmit their beliefs and values sometimes unwittingly to their progeny reflects poorly on the United States which may one day come to recognize the importance of understanding Islamism as a major world force and its implications. The failure of historians to include crypto-Muslims and crypto-Jewish narratives into a single national narrative is a major deficiency that must be corrected. It is also clear from the foregoing that the reality of pirate and buccaneer life differed substantially from the romantic image portrayed of them in American family classics like *Treasure Island* and *Robinson Crusoe* for piracy, buccaneering and privateering entailed unspeakable acts of cruelty and terror imposed on its victims. Yet distinguishing between these differently motivated practices reveals a pirate at the very least to be a predator who robs and plunders at sea. But it is a mistake as one writer observes to view pirates as a maritime version of Robin Hood, for piracy like rape, depends on force and/or the threatened use of force and intimidation accompanied by extreme violence, torture and death in order to work. The example of a man who was nail to the deck through his feet using large nails, illustrates this point.[100]

The French played a major role in piracy as many became the most fearsome buccaneers who prowled the Spanish Main from French seaports. The original buccaneers were hunters in the woods and valleys of the island of Hispaniola and in the mountainous regions of Haiti and the Dominican Republic. They lived off the herds of cattle and pigs first introduced to the New World by the Spaniards. The name *boucaner* means to smoke dry or cure and comes from the strips of meat cooked over stoves or barbecued pits they used—a practice buccaneers borrowed from Arawak Indians living nearby. They dressed in hides with their butchers' knives in plain view, wildly unruly, with a look and smell reminiscent of a slaughterhouse. Yet beyond their appearance the pirate-buccaneer-privateer alliance provided political cover for "runaway slaves," "religious refugees," and maroons occupying many of the same areas used by pirates in the Caribbean and early Americas. Indeed, the notorious pirate/corsair, Frances Drake according to one observer, made contact with escaped Black slaves known as Cimaroons who lived in the surrounding jungle who were always ready to revenge themselves on the hated Spaniards. As further evidence of the significant role of blacks among pirates one study describes how "the pirates who came to the West Indies were drawn from a number of seafaring nations and many were black slaves."[101] It is also significant to note that at their death-beds, both Sir Frances Drake in the Caribbean and legendary Indian leader, Oceola of Florida, were surrounded by Blacks in their respective camps.

A privateer in contrast to a pirate was an armed vessel, or the commander and crew of such a vessel, holding a license to attack and seize the vessels of an enemy nation. From the 1650s through 1725 Spanish vessels were the prime targets of English vessels. European vessels representing Christian nations became the principle targets of Turkish vessels. But this designation was also extended to their allies in the Mediterranean including the seafaring nations of North Africa who prowled as far afield as Newfoundland and Denmark across the Atlantic. Spaniard and Christian nations (except English and French vessels) were the principle targets of "runaway slaves," "religious refugees," and maroon fighters serving alongside pirates, buccaneers, and privateers especially in the Caribbean. Revenge and greed remained the primary motivations for this ruthless and diverse band of fighters. This system enabled maritime nations to conduct proxy wars in pursuit of identifiable national interests. By issuing a letter of marque to private ships (resembling an impressive certificate written in legal jargon, elaborately decorated to impress the holder) nations were spared the cost of building and maintaining large standing navy. Such a system would no doubt be difficult to manage much less maintain in the contemporary era without disintegrating into chaos. Nevertheless, this system endured for decades among the major world powers.

The pirate-buccaneer-privateer alliance allowed for periodically coordinated campaigns against Spanish colonial interests in the Caribbean although European nations were also known to use it as a tool against Muslim nations in hopes of capturing victims who might be used as bargaining chips for the negotiated return of thousands of captured European Christian victims. Captain Francois le Clerc, picturesquely known as Jambe de Bois because of his wooden leg set sail in 1553 with a squadron of three royal ships and a number of privateers. Cruising along the coast of Hispaniola and Puerto Rico he succeeded in capturing a number of Spanish ships. The following year, in 1554, he launched an attack on the principal Spanish stronghold at Santiago de Cuba. With a force of eight ships and three hundred men he spent thirty days looting and sacking the town causing of level of devastation requiring years from which to recover. Meanwhile, the Frenchman Jacques de Sores who sailed out from France with le Clerc captured the city of Havana on the northern coast of Cuba where he was joined by local "runaway slaves" and maroons in a coordinated campaign against the Spaniards. When Sores failed to obtain the ransom he demanded, his forces proceeded to burn the city to the ground and in a display of possible religious contempt if not humiliation against the church desecrated the church and confiscated the sacred vestments worn by priests, which the attackers mockingly wore as cloaks.[102]

The sacking of Panama was the last major action of the buccaneers led by the infamous English corsair, Henry Morgan, in 1671. Morgan who always carried a commission from the governor of Jamaica making him technically a privateer, was a Welshman whose exploits along the Spanish Main made him a legendary figure. Similar to earlier successful attacks by the British and French and their maroon allies on the Spaniards of Cuba where maroons from African maroon communities were especially strong and numerous, Morgan led successful campaigns against Spanish colonial interests around Jamaica. Though the Spanish considered him a corsair for his involvement in actions similar to those of others (like Francis Drake and his cousin Sir John Hawkins) he no doubt considered himself a soldier fighting the enemies of his country on behalf of the king of England. A similar rationale exists among contemporary Islamist militants including ISIS and al-Qaeda fighting against the enemies of Islam. Corsair attacks on Panama led by Morgan and others who flocked to join his campaigns so humiliated Spanish authorities that the Spanish Crown demanded Morgan's removal, who was arrested and sent home aboard a frigate in 1672.

Once home he spent two years in London waiting to learn his fate but was never imprisoned. He was free to spend time visiting his friends and relatives. He is described as spending considerable time drinking and gambling in addition to mobilizing militia fighters and fortifying defenses against the Spaniards around Jamaica. He quarreled with English officials to exude the air of a frolicking free spirit while continuing to engaging in gargantuan drinking bouts with his friends. He consulted a Black physician who advised him to cover his skin with clay, water and urine but died miserably after suffering the effects of dropsy in 1687 in Jamaica. Despite the decline of buccaneering after Morgan, piracy continued to be practiced by free-lance raiders of all nationalities who rarely carried commissions authorizing their activities.[103]

Because slaves among pirates, buccaneers and privateers carried no weapons and were looked upon as mere property, one observer concludes that Black "slave" status within the pirate alliance differed little from that of slaves in society at large. But the example of "slaves" among the Seminole Indians of Florida may challenge this perception for Black "slaves" among the Seminoles were often granted entry into Seminole society as leading fighters and/or military "allies." "Slaves" among the Seminoles (many of whom appear to have been from African Muslim backgrounds) typically lived in separate villages separate from those of their Seminole "masters." The primary obligation of the "slave" in this arrangement resembled that of a twentieth-century sharecropper in the US South in that the "slave" was required to supply an agreed upon minimum quantity of crops, annually, plus participate to battles against enemies of the Seminole nation under the command of their own militia commanders. Because "slaves" and "allies" held reputations for being skilled agriculturalist and capable fighters, slavery among the Seminoles, where Blacks were indeed allowed to carry guns, had a reputation for being comparatively less harsh than the slavery practiced in most other US states. Given this history, similar conditions among pirates of the Caribbean may upon closer examination reveal a form of Black enslavement more closely akin to that of the Seminoles rather than to forms commonly associated with plantation societies.

But in other ways the system of piracy produced decidedly harmful effects on Africans enslaved in the Americas. Pirates generated handsome profits from "slave" transport and sale that financially undercut the profits of the established planation system, as seen in the examples of Drake, Hawkins and their "slaving" voyages to the Guinea region of Africa. These voyages inflicted unspeakable harm and suffering on Africans draggedd to the Americas to toil on "slave" plantations. A higher than average number of African Muslims war captives may have been swept up in sea voyages to the Guinea coast for "slaves." Diouf (1998) Mamdani (2005) and others make reference to these victims of *jihad*, transported to the Americas from Senegambia and their broader historical significance. A frequently overlooked consequence of this were higher than average numbers of Africans from Muslim backgrounds, skilled in Muslim struggle (*jihad*) and knowledgeable of Islam who landed in Florida, Georgia and the Carolinas.

Piracy with its penchant for smuggling "slave" imports into the United States "illegally" after the 1820s when slave shipments were outlawed transported enslaved Africans through long and difficult to monitor borders like those found along the Florida coast. These circumstances may have unwittingly facilitated the importation of African born victims known as *bozales* with first-hand experience with *jihad*. This plus their widely known reputation for resistance made them especially dreaded additions from the planters' perspective. Regular and persistent arrivals of *bozales* to plantations through illegal shipped "slave" shipments replenished the number of "enslaved" Africans in the Americas with first-hand knowledge, awareness and experience with Islam much to the chagrin of the "slavetocracy" but also to the dread of interests in the contemporary United States seeking to promote competing "Islam in America" narratives rooted in the alleged yet unproven belief that "Americas'" first "wave" of Muslims to arrive in the New World failed to survive due to the rigors of slavery and forced mass conversion to Christianity before offering entirely self-interested claims in its place.

This chapter lays to rest three widely embraced though highly erroneous views. The first is associated with Daniel Pipes's (2002) study, *Militant Islam Reaches America* that erroneously implies that militant Islam first arrived in the New World with the tragic events of September 11, 2001. The second erroneous view associated with the supporters of President Trump and the Muslim ban believes that banning what Mamdani labels 'bad Muslims' from entering the United States, will make Americans more safe. The third erroneous view is what I elsewhere ascribe to Wave of Immigration (WOI) theorists, the dominant paradigm among scholars of "Islam in America" who believe that Americas' first Muslim "wave" from Africa was obliterated by the rigors of enslavement and forced to convert to Christianity only to be replaced by immigrants to the US in the 1960s who became de facto spokespersons for the Islamic community in the United States. But WOI theorists offer no evidence of either the disappearance of Americas' earliest Muslims nor evidence that the Islam they first introduced was not successfully passed on to their progeny in the US.

Preliminary evidence presented in this chapter disputes these views. Evidence of the survival of Americas' earliest Muslims is most evident in works by Quick (1976), Austin (1984), Turner (1997), Diouf (1998), Dannin (2002) Gomez (1989, 2005), Jackson (2005), Hawthorne (2010), and Rashid (2013). Collectively these and other studies help document the survival of Islam in one form or another in the Americas including the United States. Although the strongest evidence of this survival unsurprisingly is found in the Caribbean and Brazil, evidence of the survival of Islam among the progeny of African Muslims has emerged in remote regions of colonial Florida and other parts of the Antebellum South including Georgia and South Carolina. There is a need for studies that de-marginalize African Muslims and their progeny in the Americas to compliment similar efforts underway to marginalization the experience of Islam and Islamist militancy in Africa. The history and experience of African Muslims in light of the worldwide Islamist challenge are simply too important to continue to ignore.

This chapter has explored: (1) "Muslim flight"; (2) "The Elusive Atlantic"; (3) "In the Shadow of 1492"; (4) "*Jihad* and *Hijra* by Other Means"; and (5) "Analysis." The following chapter continues to offer a deeper look at the Islamic Challenge among Africans and their progeny in the Americas by challenging the widely held assumption among American historians of the failure of early Islam and Islamism among Africans and their progeny to survive in the United States. Chapter 7 also offers preliminary evidence of the surviving presence of the Islamic institutions of *jihad*, *hijra*, and *ummah* among the progeny of Africans in the Americas.

NOTES

1. Rashid, *Black Muslims in the US: History, Politics and the Struggle of a Community*, 38. Also see Bryan Burrough, *Days of Rage America's Radical Underground, the FBI, and the First Age of Terror* (New York: Penguin Books, 2015).

2. Michael A. Gomez, *Black Crescent: The Experience and Legacy of African Muslims in the Americas* (New York: Cambridge University Press, 2005), ix.

3. Ibid. Also see L. P. Harvey, *Muslims in Spain 1500–1614* (Chicago, IL: University of Chicago Press, 2005).

4. Harvey, *Muslims in Spain 1500–1614*, 5.

5. Ibid.

6. Ibid. Also see Gomez, *Black Crescent*, 13–14. According to Bethell, during the period, 1850–1750, "those with 'New Christian'—that is, Jewish ancestors or relatives were considered religiously and culturally suspect and suffered legal and financial disabilities, [however] both cypto-Jews and those who had not the slightest attachment to Judaism were lumped together by the society as a suspect group." See Leslie Bethell, ed., *Colonial Brazil* (New York: Cambridge University Press, 1987), 139.

7. See Herbert S. Klein, *The Atlantic Slave Trade* (New York: Cambridge University Press, 2005), 13, and Sylviane Diouf, *Servants of Allah: African Muslims Enslaved in the Americas* (New York: New York University Press, 1998), 17–20.

8. Ibid., 7–9.

9. Nick Hazelwood, *The Queen's Slave Trader* (New York: Morrow, 2004), 28–29. Also see Les Roundtree et al., *Diversity Amid Globalization* (Upper Saddle River, NJ: Prentice Hall, 2003), 157.

10. Diouf, *Servants of Allah*, 17–20.

11. See L. P. Harvey, *Islamic Spain 1250–1500* (Chicago, IL: University of Chicago Press, 1990), 336–37.

12. Ibid., 41.

13. Ibid., 337.

14. Ibid.

15. Ibid., 15.

16. Ibid., 56 and 90.

17. Ibid., 314.

18. Jacques Hers, *The Barbary Corsairs: Warfare in the Mediterranean, 1480–1580*, translated by Jonathan North (Mechanicburg, PA: StackpoleBooks, 2001), 216 and 220.

19. Hers, *The Barbary Corsairs*, 123, 160.

20. Peter Smith, *The Spanish Empire in America* (Gloucester: Harcourt Brace Jovanovich Inc., 1973; originally published by C. H. Haring), 189.

21. Ibid.

22. Ibid., 10.

23. Smith, *The Spanish Empire in America,* 206.

24. Ibid.

25. Ibid.

26. Ibid., 10 and 206.

27. Ibid., 35.

28. Ibid., 34.

29. Ibid., 35.

30. Peter Earle, *The Pirate Wars* (New York: Thomas Dunne Books, 2003), 9–10.

31. Ibid., 23.

32. Ibid., 23.

33. Ibid., 28.

34. Ibid., 31.

35. Ibid., 32.

36. Ibid., 32–33.

37. Ibid., 39–40.

38. Ibid., 43–46.

39. Nabil Matar, *Turks, Moors, and Englishmen* (New York: Columbia University Press, 1999), 28.

40. Ibid. Also see Perez-Mallaina, *Spain's Men of the Sea,* 38.

41. Ibid., 38.

42. Ibid., 11.

43. Ibid., 193–94, 216.

44. Michael McClain, "The Mudejares of Muslim Spain," *Dialogue*, September 1999, 6.

45. Ibid.

46. Ibid.

47. Harvey, *Islamic Spain: 1250–1500,* 68.

48. Linda Colley, *Captives* (New York: Pantheon Books, 2002), 56.

49. Ibid., 63. Also see Fichtner, *Terror and Toleration: The Habsburg Empire Confronts Islam, 1526–1850,* 42.

50. Michael A. Gomez, *Reversing Sail: A History of the African Diaspora* (New York: Cambridge University Press, 2005), 51–52.

51. Ibn Khaldûn, *Al Muqaddimah*, ed. N. J. Dawood, trans. Franz Rosenthal (Princeton, NJ: Princeton University Press, 1989), 212. Also see Sherman Jackson,

Islam and the Black American: Looking for the Third Resurrection (New York; Oxford University Press, 2005), Richard Zacks, *The Pirate Coast* (New York: Hyperion, 2006), and a "Riveting Look at America's 1st War in North Africa," *Chicago Tribune*, July 24, 2005.

52. Khaldûn, *Al Muqaddimah*, 210.

53. Ibid., 209.

54. Ibid.

55. Cecil Jane, ed., *The Four Voyages of Columbus*, translated and edited with "Introduction" and "Notes" by Cecil Jane (New York: Dover Publication, Inc. 1998, first published in 1930), "Introduction," xl.

56. Ibid., 165.

57. Ibid.

58. Colley, *Captives*, 146.

59. Gomez, *Black Crescent*.

60. Matar, *Turks, Moors, and Englishmen*, 24.

61. Ibid., 91.

62. Post 9–11 guest lectures by Bernard Lewis, Indiana University, Bloomington, IN, 2002.

63. Bernard Lewis, *Islam and the West* (New York: Oxford University Press, 1993), 72–84.

64. Colley, *Captives*, 52.

65. Matar, *Turks, Moors, and Englishmen*, 59.

66. Ibid.

67. See Edwin Reynolds, *The Seminoles* (Norman: University of Oklahoma Press, 1957), and Colley *Captives*, 321.

68. Matar, *Turks, Moors, and Englishmen*, 49, 51, 53, and 63.

69. Ibid., 49–54.

70. Ibn Khaldûn, *The Muqaddimah*, trans. Franz Rosenthal (Princeton: Princeton University Press, 1967), 210.

71. Matar, *Turks, Moors, and Englishmen*, 71, and Colley, *Captives*, 95, 107, and 118.

72. Matar, *Turks, Moors, and Englishmen*, 9–10.

73. William B. Cohen, *The French Encounter with Africans: White Response to Blacks, 1530–1880* (Bloomington, IN: Indiana University Press, 2003), 15.

74. Ibid., 18.

75. Ibid., 19.

76. Ibid., 43–44.

77. Ibid., 44.

78. Matar, *Turks, Moors, and Englishmen*, 63.

79. Ibid., 71 and Colley, *Captives*, 96, 107, 118, and 119.

80. Colley, *Captives*, 39, 95, 107, 119, 190, and 192, Zacks, *The Pirate Coast*, and "A Riveting Look at America's 1st War in North Africa," *Chicago Tribute*, 24 July 2005.

81. Matar, *Turks, Moors, and Englishmen*, 63. Also see Colley, *Captives*, 118.

82. Ibid., 56.

83. Ibid., 56–57.

84. Ibid., 56.

85. David Cordingly, *Under the Black Flag: The Romance and the Reality of Life among the Pirates* (New York: Random House, 2006), 39.

86. Matar, *Turks, Moors, and Englishmen*, 60.

87. Zacks, *The Pirate Coast*, 12.

88. Ibid., 4 and 12.

89. Ibid., 46 and 54. Zacks describes how "the only Black sailor among the captured USS Philadelphia's crew ended up days later as a royal cook. The sailor was singled-out by a "holy man" among the Barbary pirates. The rest of the captured American crew wound-up enslaved under wretched conditions.

90. Ibid.

91. Alan G. Jamieson, *Lords of the Sea: A History of the Barbary Corsairs* (Chicago: University of Chicago Press, 2012), 11 and Colley, *Captives,* 45–46.

92. Jamieson, *Lords of the Sea: A History of the Barbary Corsairs*, 12.

93. Ibid., 13.

94. Ibid.

95. Ibid., 14.

96. Ibid., 17.

97. Ibid., 20. This may have been a possible motive behind the British abolition of slavery, years ahead of the Emancipation Proclamation viewed as abolishing slavery in the US in 1860.

98. Ibid., 29.

99. Ibid., 85–86.

100. David Cordingly, *Under the Black Flag: The Romance and Reality of Life Among the Pirates* (New York: Random House, 2006), "Introduction," xiv.

101. Ibid., "Introduction," xviii, 27 and 12.

102. Ibid., 37.

103. Ibid., 53–55.

Chapter 7

Islamism, Africans, and the West

This chapter advances the idea that the Islamic institution of flight (*hijra*) facilitated the arrival of many African Muslims first from Spain and later from West Africa to the Americas to form what Afroz calls the nucleus of the Muslim community (*ummah*) in the United States.[1] A theory known as the "black rice thesis," articulated by Wood (1974), Littlefield (1981), and Carney (2001) posits that skilled rice farmers from the Upper Guinea region of West Africa introduced technology that led to the establishment and expansion of an eighteenth-century rice seed plantation system in lowland South Carolina and Georgia that survived with great success in the Antebellum South.[2] But rice technology was not the only innovation that Africans from Upper Guinea introduced to the Americas, for the Muslim institutions of struggle (*jihad*), flight (*hijra*), and community (*ummah*) as key cultural features of Upper Guinea may have been unwittingly transferred in the process.[3] This chapter explores manifestations of Islamism among African Muslims and their progeny in the United States via discussions devoted to (1) "An Evolving African Muslim Identity"; (2) "Islam, Islamism, and the Islamist Challenge, Revisited"; and (3) "Reimagining Africa."

AN EVOLVING AFRICAN MUSLIM IDENTITY

Since their arrival in the Americas during the age of Columbus, African Muslim identity remains little-known outside of African communities and those who study them. Nonetheless, the African Muslim community worldwide continues to evolve and grow. And although Islamist ideology consciously rejects the legitimacy of modern secular authority, the impact of the latter on the former is difficult to deny. For instance, proponents of Islamism continue to celebrate the importance and centrality of group identity, as seen in the Qur'anic verse: "Oh mankind! We created you from a single [pair] of a male and female, and made you into nations and tribes, that ye may know each other, [not that ye may despise each other.] Verily the most honored of you in the sight of God is [he who is] the most righteous of you. And God has full knowledge and is well acquainted (with all things)."[4] Commonplace among many political conservatives in the United States and Europe is opposition to the idea of diversity, which is often promoted by right wing elements of the conservative movement opposed to the ascendancy of Muslims, minorities, and others who are increasingly seen as the antithesis of America's "greatness." To these groups, there is *no* need to celebrate Muslim values, black history, or Jewish history as doing so advances at the expense of mainstream American values and the erstwhile goal of "making America great again." In France, for instance, public displays of religious symbols have been banned and Russia's long-standing practice of Russification among other things transforms Muslim names like Karim and Malik described as among the "beautiful names" in the Qur'an to Russian names like Karimov and Malikov. These practices stand in stark contrast to the Qur'anic observation "And among His signs is the creation of the heavens and the earth and the variations in your languages and your colors; verily in that are signs for those who know."[5] The survival of Islamic religion in the United States, due in part to constitutional protections, is a phenomenon that many supporters of President Trump may be reluctant to embrace, much less acknowledge. President Trump was a prominent member of the "birther" movement that rejected the first African American president based on the erroneous belief that Mr. Obama was not born in the United States.

Yet, despite all this, Gomez's *Black Crescent* (2005) documents a surviving African "legacy" of Islam among the progeny of Muslims in the Americas among "near indigenous" people living in South and Central America.[6] Turner's *Islam in the African American Experience* (2003) and Rashid's *Black Muslims in the US* (2013) add further support for the idea of a surviving Islamic legacy in the United States.[7] Other works documenting the survival of Islamism and influential Islamic institutions, beliefs and practices among the progeny of African Muslims in the Americas, include Lincoln (1961), Austin (1984), Muhammad (2000), Diouf (1998, 2003, 2014), Dannin (2002), Gomez (1998, 2005), Kline (2005), Jackson (2005), Quick (1976), and Abdullah (2010). Perhaps the earliest and most dramatic cases of Islamism in the New World have been found in Haiti, Brazil, Jamaica, Trinidad, and Guyana. These cases join preliminary evidence of Islamism among of blacks in Georgia, Florida, Louisiana, and Virginia and the cities of New York, Los Angeles, Detroit, Chicago Minneapolis, Philadelphia, and Atlanta. Each offers evidence of a surviving belief in Islam among "the faithful" in the

Americas who of necessity may have clung more closely to their religion in some instances than fellow coreligionists "back home" in Africa.

The late Moroccan writer and Islamist feminist, Fertima Mernissi's personal observation of black Muslims during the 1960s in the United States who took their religion more seriously than did Muslims back home in her native Morocco, is a case in point.[8] Some five decades later, it is not uncommon to find other Arab visitors to the United States as seen in the Friday sermon (*al-Khutbah*), mostly delivered by foreign-born Imams across the United States acknowledging the contributions of black Muslims to the development and spread of Islam in the Americas. Younger Muslims in the United States are often exhorted to treat older indigenous black Muslims in the United States with respect. These practices offer concrete evidence of an African Muslim presence in the Americas that predates debates sparked by President Trump and others over the feared arrival of militant Islamists into the United States. Even colonial officials in early America expressed fears over the possibility that Muslims (i.e., Turks, Moriscos, and others) had reached the New World during the age of Columbus.[9] Indeed, Columbus's decision to sail West instead of East for India may have been influenced in part by the need to avoid hostile areas in Africa and the Middle East controlled by Muslims. With the possible exception of China and Russia, the West continues to view the Muslim world as its primary political nemesis. As early as November 27, 1095, Pope Urban II called for the first Christian Crusade to "liberate" Jerusalem (Palestine) from the Seljuk Turks (Muslims). "Turks and Muslims were inimical intruders into the culture of Christendom where they had no place."[10] Indeed, "notions about the Islamic conquest of the Iberian peninsula in the early eighth century and the medieval crusades in the Levant and Holy Lands . . . were a major factor in turning the Muslim into the 'normative enemy' of Christendom."[11] Because similar fears had been expressed toward Muslims during the 2016 presidential campaign, it was no accident that newly elected president Trump imposed a "Muslim ban" on Muslims traveling from select Muslim countries like Somalia to the United States. Despite its widely unpopular rejection by educated urban residents of the United States who collectively constitute the majority of persons living in the United States, the Muslim ban nonetheless has been upheld as settled law by the US Supreme Court.

Enslaved Africans built many communities in the South[12] including the City of St. Augustine, Florida established by the Spaniards in 1565 as the oldest continuously occupied European city in North America.[13] Field research conducted there in 2000, revealed that St. Augustine's black section, known as Lincolnville and before that as Africville, may be the oldest such "Black" community in the United States. Several of the city's oldest structures, including its major defense installation at Fort Marion (or San Marcos), were built in whole or part by African labor under the direction of Spanish colonial authorities.[14] According to documents stored in the St. Augustine Historical Society, African labor was transported by the Spaniards from Cuba to St. Augustine to complete the city's landmark infrastructure.[15] One St. Augustine structure built by enslaved Africans in the sixteenth century may represent the oldest housing structure still standing in the contemporary United States. These structures and the story of their builders, predate by over a century, the history of better-known structures built by African labor that include the US White House in Washington, DC, and US Capitol grounds widely believed to have been designed by free black architect, Benjamin Banneker (1731–1806), a mathematician and astronomer who assumed lead responsibility for its design after George Washington had a falling out with city planner, Pierre Charles L'Enfant, who left the project taking all its designs with him, leaving matters in disarray before Banneker came to the rescue.[16] Nevertheless, it seems ironic to note that Washington, DC's, National Mall may at one time have been "the best place in town to sell slaves."[17]

The first Africans brought to the New World by European slavers may have arrived in April 1502, aboard a ship that brought the first governor of Hispaniola, Nicolas de Ovando. Africans escaped in the woods to join Native Americans fugitives. "Later that year Governor Ovando sent a request to King Ferdinand that no more Africans be sent to the Americas," because "they fled among the Indians and taught them bad customs and never could be captured."[18] Africans' greater labor productivity compared to Native Americans and near immunity to tropical diseases like malaria and small pox led the Spaniards to abandon all thoughts of excluding them from shipment to the Americas. As early as 1510 King Ferdinand, visions of gold dancing before his eyes, quickly ruled out all restrictions on sending Africans to the Americans.[19] After acknowledging the fact that one black "slave" could do the work of four Native American Indians, even Governor Ovando forgot his earlier opposition as importing African labor convinced him that the value of African labor well outstripped its price.[20] But while importing more (Muslim) Africans may have been good for profits it only intensified the phenomenon of "runaway" Africans and Native Americans known as maroons. Could the "bad customs" referred to by the governor have been a reference to Islamism? Preliminary evidence of Muslim maroon resistance in Brazil, Haiti, Jamaica, and Surname suggests it may have been.

Restall's examination of what he calls "the myth of the white Conquistadores," debunks the marginalization of Africans, Native Americans, and "mixed blood" participants in the conquest of the New World.[21] Many of those recruited by Spain, according to Restall, to participate in these campaigns were African Muslims brought from Spain to serve alongside Native Americans, Amerindians, and other blacks already living in the New World.[22]

Many were without military standing or rank. Recruits from Spain and elsewhere throughout the Americas were lured by the promise of plunder and riches.[23] Wolof (Muslims) were especially prized by Spain, with some justification, as "good fighters."[24] Spain had been at war with Muslims since their arrival in Iberia after crossing Gibraltar in 711 AD and experienced firsthand, the fighting skills of the Moors (Muslims) who finally capitulated at Grenada in 1492. African Muslims and their progeny remained a prominent feature of Spanish colonial defenses in the Americas. Indeed, with New World conquest and defense "under their belt," inter-colonial rivalries between the Spanish, Britain, France, and Dutch colonial powers provided regular opportunities for African (and Indian) fighting recruits throughout the Americas. And to a degree greater than most American historians seem to realize, African allies during these colonial campaigns appear to have quietly retained much of their distinctive culture and religious identity. Perhaps as a consequence of this, Islamic institutions that include flight (*hijra*), struggle (*jihad*), community (*ummah*) and dissimilation (*taqiya*) may have unwittingly survived intact throughout colonial America for longer than most observers seem to realize.

The belated realization that blacks may have served in US military campaigns dating from the American Revolution to the present may be eclipsed by African Muslim participation in the Conquistadores conquest of the Americas as documented by Restall. Long before the rise of Islam and African Muslims, blacks gained recognition for their martial arts skills in the armies of ancient Kush (or Nubia) in present-day Sudan along the Nile. Kush rose to conquer Egypt and rule the twenty-fifth dynasty of the Pharaohs beginning with Pianky (or Piya) which reined for a brief period (700–656 BC). Kush traded with Egypt primarily in gold produced in Nubia for over a thousand years. But Kush's hatred of Egypt's domination with its routine references to "vile Kush" and depictions of the Kushites in derogatory roles in Egyptian art led Kush to exploit Egypt's vulnerability and eventually conquer Egypt. While they were later checked by the Assyrians and reconquered by the Egyptians, the Kushites under the leadership of a one-eyed African woman queen successfully resisted the Romans to maintain their independence.[25]

By 1522, "Europeans in the America first learned that slavery did not easily or painlessly lead to enormous wealth," when on Christmas Day in 1522 African and Indians enslaved on a plantation owned by Diego Columbus on the Island of Hispaniola rose and killed their masters in perhaps the first major conspiracy of its kind in the New World.[26] Similar, though smaller, conflicts had spread across the island in the weeks before Christmas. Over the next ten years, violent resistance spread to Colombia, Panama, Cuba, Puerto Rico, and Mexico, leading terrified Mexican officials temporarily to halt any further importations of Africans. Before whites succeeded in destroying their alliance, blacks and Native American Indians presented stiff opposition against white settler intrusion in Florida before 1819 when the territory became sold by Spain to the United States for $5 million. Native Americans came to depend on the valuable assets of Africans including their agricultural, building, herding, languages, military, and diplomatic skills especially when dealing with whites.[27]

Colonial military campaigns in early America involving a significant number of Native Americans such as the Seminoles, the Natchez, the Chocktow, and the Chickasaw and their African allies in what is now the American Deep South, are instructive.[28] Joining these Native American groups were a significant number of blacks who based on their African links to Senegambia may well have included blacks from African Muslim "tribes" like the Fulani, Wolof, and Mandingo that predominate (to this day) in areas from whence they were captured. These groups are described in the literature as blacks and brown people who wore turbans, displayed great military skills, fasted, covered their women, concealed their women and children and built their graves so that the faces of the deceased faced East. Once in the Americas many from these groups continued to live in communities with Islamic sounding names like Islamorada, the Turks and Cocos Islands, Musa Creek, Fort Musa and Tallahassee, Florida, despite American historians' collective ignorance of them. The largely ignored African (and Indian) presence in Florida appears to have rendered ample opportunities for Islam and Islamism to survive (1500–1819) in a period when religions in early Florida are routinely described as being of "unknown" origin.[29] The State of Florida became a US territory only in 1819 and a state in 1821. But the territory itself was not fully explored nor mapped until 1900 and for most of its international history from roughly 1500 to 1819 was beset by simultaneous and competing claims by one or another US or European powers. In light of this fluid situation and lack of clear-cut control by American or European powers, early Florida (1500–1819) was often described as "lawless," even though conditions among Florida's refugees and maroons though far from idyllic in contrast to those faced by whites, were anything but "lawless."

Other Africans lived with Native Americans in secluded autonomous enclaves known as maroon villages throughout the region with names like Musa, Angola, and Pelikihaha along the St. John's River in northern and central Florida and along the Gulf coast of Florida before the massive intrusion of white settlers into the region following the end of Seminole Indian Wars of Florida from 1816 to 1838. Africans from African Muslim backgrounds resisted white intrusion into the area before passage of the Indian Removal Act of 1830 which ultimately succeeded in forcing the remaining Indian warriors and the black allies to leave the region in what historians have labeled as the infamous "Trail of Tears" or Indian removal campaign. Again, Africans from Muslim backgrounds played major roles in these historical events even though their presence is often overlooked perhaps unsurprisingly, by most white southern historians. The Seminole Indian Wars fought in Florida gained a reputation for being the most costly "Indian wars" in US history up to that point in time. Primary source accounts suggest that a large part of these battle outcomes were shaped by the fighting skills of Florida's African "allies." These campaigns came to an abrupt halt when the US government simply agreed to terminate the fight (though a number of Seminoles are known to have retreated farther into the Florida Everglades.) One writer describes the Seminole and their African allies (and "slaves") as the "unconquered people" of Florida.[30]

Distinguished military campaigns were not the only accomplishments associated with African and more specifically, African Muslims, in the New World. For instance, the sixteenth-century African explorer Estephan (also Estephanicho, Estephanico, and Little Steven), born in Morocco, became the first non-Native American to cross the continental United States. A mural in his honor hangs in the New Mexico state house.[31] Some credit Africans in the New World employed by the Spaniards with being the first "cowboys" given the experience of African Muslims, like the Fulani, who then and now serve as skilled, semi-nomadic cattle herders.[32] The Fulani, as noted earlier, were among the earliest victims of Boko Harm and form one of two dominant ethnic groups represented among Boko Haram fighters. Africans are widely credited with being the first to introduce rice-growing technology and techniques to the Americas which had a profound impact on US agriculture in the antebellum period. Before there was cotton or tobacco, there was rice, and popular brands in the United States, for example, Uncle Ben's rice still display the likeness of an African.[33] Because the earliest "slaves" and indentured servants in the United States were drawn from Muslim areas of West Africa as noted by Diouf, Muslim language and speech may for a time have been the dominant lingua franca among enslaved populations in the early United States.[34]

This evidence suggests that African Muslim influence, including the influence of Islam and Islamism may have continued to spread beyond African shores to the New World, including the United States. At roughly 10 percent of the enslaved population in the United States, African Muslims were widely credited with being the first to introduce the religion of Islam (and Islamism) to the New World. Although black or African American Muslims remain approximately 20 percent of the Muslim population in the United States, their total numbers among the Muslims of the United States remain among the largest.[35] This statistic is underscored by the fact that no one Muslim group in the United States holds an absolute majority. Second only to the Muslim community in Saudi Arabia, the Muslim community in the United States remains perhaps the most ethnically, racially and religiously diverse population of Muslims in the world. The survival of Islamism among the progeny of contemporary society raises the need to explore what I elsewhere describe as the "hidden transcripts" of African Muslim presence in the Americas. Chinese and Jewish immigrants like Africans have been widely dispersed throughout the world. Yet it would be absurd to conclude that Jews living outside Israel are any less Jewish because of where they happen to reside. Likewise, the dispersal of African Muslims throughout the New World primarily as a result of enslavement and forced flight (*hijra*) after the Spanish Inquisition make Africans in the New World no less African than the Moors of Spain or the Senegambians of West Africa. This observation is reinforced by the simple fact that Islamists among blacks in the United States as elsewhere, continue to identify themselves first and foremost as simply Muslim.

While historians generally acknowledge an African Muslim presence in the Caribbean and Latin America, preliminary evidence suggest the presence of African Muslims and their progeny among the enslaved brought to the United States tended to be found in relatively few areas that include the Carolinas, Georgia, Louisiana, Florida, and Virginia. Beyond this geographic nucleus, contemporary migrations of black Americans from the American South to the North during the great migration (1917–1970) and more recent migrations of African immigrants to communities in New York, Minneapolis, Washington, San Diego, Chicago, and elsewhere have further refreshed the African American Muslim community in the United States. These migrations are expected to contribute to a predominantly nonwhite majority in the United States by 2050. These demographic trends have also contributed to a growth in the number of Islamist militants in the United States which includes a significant number of Islamists from African Muslim backgrounds. It is perhaps no coincidence that the longest-serving Muslim members of the US Congress are the progeny of African Muslims, a fact that has not gone unnoticed by those fearful of them.

The terrorist Michael Adebolajo and Michael Adebowale of London who attacked and nearly decapitated British soldier Lee Rigby in 2015 illustrate the worldwide reach of militant Islamists and their menacing and sinister impact on the West. The brutal attack on the British Parliament at Westminster in London by Khalid Masood, an Afro-British assailant, in March 2017 killing five and wounding many others is another case of Islamist militancy against the West. British citizenship in both instances did little to deter militant Islamist rage. Likewise, the enslavement of Pacifico Lucitan (*Bilal*) of Brazil during the 1835 Muslim-led "slave revolt," as we have seen, did little to deter Islamist militants' pursuit of Muslim struggle (*jihad*). If immigrants from Iraq or Afghanistan are no less Iraqi or Afghan, respectively, from living in the United States, then it seems possible to imagine how African Muslims living in the West might conceivably feel no less African Muslim given the history of enslavement, discrimination, and pressures to abandon their identity, values, and religion. Evidence of the survival of Muslim identity, values, and religion may explain the survival and spread of flight (*hijra*), Muslim struggle (*jihad*), and community (*ummah*) among the progeny of African Muslims in the United States. Similar, if not more frightening, instances of militant Islamism often perpetrated by the progeny of North and West Africans in Europe were witnessed from 2015 through 2017 in London, Brussels, Paris, Normandy, Nice, Berlin, Manchester, and Barcelona. While authorities have worked tirelessly to dampen public anxiety over these violent events, their seriousness cannot be denied.

According to a Pew Research Center study directed by Mark Hugo Lopez and released in April of 2015, the number of black immigrants living in the United States has more than quadrupled since 1980.[36] The primary source of this population increase was a 137 percent increase in African immigrants totaling 1.4 million.[37] Black immigrants have been described as strongly identifying with their home countries. Instead of assimilating quickly as earlier immigrants had done, these new black immigrants have been reluctant to assimilate even into "indigenous" black America and are most likely to be equally reluctant to assimilate into mainstream America like their white immigrant counterparts had done in the past. Instead, they preferred to hold fast to their ethnic-religious identities—in ways that differ from their white immigrant counterparts of the past. Moreover, black immigrants are described as being twenty-five times more likely than their American-born counterparts to possess a bachelor's degree and all black immigrants were less likely to live in poverty from the Arab Middle East.[38] This pattern among self-identified black immigrants in a 2015 Pew study contributes to the widely reported trend of a growing nonwhite majority in the United States. The likelihood of a similarly significant number of immigrants from African Muslim backgrounds seems modestly likely, given the relatively large number of English-speaking Africans from Nigerian, Senegal, Ghana, Eritrea, and Ethiopia already living in the United States and continued fear of Arab Muslim immigrants.

This pattern seems similar to patterns witnessed in the past when Africans brought to parts of the United States and especially Florida were often smuggled in illegally long past the time when slavery was outlawed in the United States (1808), in the United Kingdom (1808), and in France (1794). Africans arriving in Florida primarily from Muslim areas in Guinea and Senegambia were called bozales or "slaves" who were born in Africa who played vital roles in replenishing New World African populations with firsthand knowledge of the teachings and practice of Islam. A total of 1.8 million black immigrants lived in the United States in 2013.[39] Perhaps most significantly, black immigrants' share of the total black population according to Pew is projected to rise from 9 percent (in 2013) to 16 percent by the year 2060.[40]

ISLAM, ISLAMISM, AND THE ISLAMIST CHALLENGE, REVISITED

What is the Islamist challenge? What is it not? What shall we call it? Is it a threat? What does it seek? What is its ultimate goal? What is its significance? What is its scope? The Islamist challenge as distinct from Islam and Islamism is an ideological rejection of the existing world order punctuated by militant Islamism and the desire to establish Islamic law (*shari'ah*) as an alternative to the failed Western projects of Westernization, imperialism, chattel slavery, colonialism, and secularism. The Islamist challenge rejects Western modernity in the political realm, the Western state system first introduced by the Treaty of Westphalia in 1648 and its associated institutions. But Islamist militant ideology rejects the prevailing Western system of nation-states as fraudulent and artificial and condemns international borders as man-made and therefore forbidden (*haram*). To the strict salafist, man-made innovations (*bid'a*) are forbidden (*haram*) for true Muslims. Profiting from interest, otherwise known as usury, is also forbidden (*haram*) by Islam. Even the idea of Africa itself is rejected by militant Islamists as seen in rants by Boko Haram leader Abubakar Shekau against the secular Nigerian state and its national symbols, including the Nigerian national flag and its overwhelmingly Western identity. Yet, the horror and victimization experienced by Nigeria's moderate Muslims cannot be ignored by feelings of outrage and rejection toward the secular state displayed by Islamist militants.[41]

The Islamic Brotherhood of the 1980 called for a return to the fundamentals of Islam while the Izala movement of northern Nigeria actively promoted the slogan: "There is no government but Islam."[42] The first identifiable signs of the group, Boko Haram, appeared in 1995 when a group of Islamic scholars met under the name *Ahlulsunna wai jama' ah hijra*, led by Islamic scholar, Abubakar Lawan. The group was composed of moderate, middle-class middle-aged men interested in the study of orthodox Sunni Islam. But when Lawan left the country to study in Saudi Arabia, the younger more radical Muslim scholar Muhammad Yusuf filled the void.[43] Although Yusuf's revolutionary zeal was acquired in the nearby impoverished region of Chad and Niger, it is also significant to note that Yusuf, like many of his followers, had little formal Western education.[44]

The organization known as Boko Haram ascribes to the formal name, the People of the Sunna for preaching Sunna and jihad (*Jama 'ahl as-Sunna lid-Da'wah wa'l-Jihad*). Under Yusuf the group's moderate elements drifted away. Nevertheless, the group attracted a wide variety of Muslims from impoverished inner city youth to university students. By 2008/2009 the group attracted wider attention and experienced greater clashes with security authorities, culminating in major riots in 2009 following a police raid that triggered days of social unrest.[45] During this time many Boko Haram members were killed and the group's leader was caught hiding in his father-in-law's barn, interrogated (on tape), and killed in broad daylight outside a Nigerian police station. He became the group's first martyr and was replaced by his lieutenant, Abubakar Shekau, who is widely regarded as mentally unstable.[46] While Yusuf is typically described as a reluctant militant, Shekau is described as "part gangster part theologian." Despite undeniable intelligence and fluency in several languages Shekau is only nominally educated, at best. Although authorities claim to be unsure of the organization's structure and leadership, Shekau's lieutenants include Khalid al-Barnawi and Abubakar Adam Kambar. A handful of prominent members of Boko Haram have been tracked to training camps in Algeria and Somalia. According to the United Nations Security Council, another handful may have received training in a Tuareg Islamist training camp in Mali (Azawad).[47] Banks, cash convoys, and extortion have become legitimate spoils of war for Boko Haram. Boko Haram's lethality has become more deadly with more attacks occurring in early 2015 than in all of 2014.

Although Boko Haram victims numbered over 6,600 in 2014 as noted in the introduction of this study, the largest and most deadly series of Boko Haram attacks may have occurred between January 2 and 7, 2015 against the town of Baga on Nigeria's northeast border with Cameroon.[48] According to one observer "the Boko Haram insurgency is a direct result of chronic poor governance by Nigeria's federal and state governments, the political marginalization of northeastern Nigeria, and the region's accelerating impoverishment."[49] Similar attacks against neighboring Chad and Niger have led some to believe that Boko Haram has been active alongside other Islamist groups in the region including AQIM of Mali. But the failure of the Nigerian state remains a primary enabler of Boko Haram activity. For instance, the popular local meaning for the Economic Community of West African States Monitoring Group or ECOMOG, which is controlled by Nigeria is "every car or moving object gone" (from theft).[50] It is perhaps no coincidence that more than a few African states have been described by scholars as "kleptocracies." Some of the atrocities committed by the Nigerian military have been captured on video and although they are difficult to deny, the government has done so, repeatedly. The Kanuri "tribal" group constitutes the majority of Boko Haram

fighters. Experts fear that the group's influence is spreading, given its influence on groups like Ansaru with links to al-Qaeda in the Islamic Maghreb
(AQIM), al-Qaeda the Arabian Peninsula (AQAP), and the Islamic Movement of Uzbekistan (IMU) from efforts by Cameroonian militant, Umman
Nur.[51]

REIMAGINING AFRICA

African Muslims have contributed significantly to the development and
spread of Islam and to the survival of small though identifiable communities
in Africa, Europe, the Middle East, and the Americas. Therefore, scholars
must avoid limiting their analyses of African Muslims to Africa, as doing so
ignores the mosaic character of the Islamic community (*ummah*) and black
Muslims' role in the development and spread of Islam outward from the
Arab peninsula. Throughout this study, we have seen how African Muslim
survival in distinct communities in Nigeria, Somalia, CAR, Kenya, Mali,
Britain, Libya, Iraq, and the United States—has contributed to the history and
fabric of these societies despite the fact that the societies themselves have not
always been willing to recognize and celebrate this survival. Moreover, while
Africa may be the primary focus of the Africanist's or orientalist's focus,
efforts to differentiate Africans from other Muslims and/or Islamists, may
unwittingly create a distorted image of African Islamists identity.

Though Africa may be the land of their forefathers, African Islamists
appear to prefer to call themselves simply Muslim. As Africa or Arabia may
be centuries removed from their current place of residence, black Islamist
militants prefer to identify themselves as merely Muslims, resisting the narrow names, labels, and identities thrust upon them by others. Close examination of African Muslim identity reveals an intersectionality that blends
multiple, otherwise distinct, identities such as Sunni and Kanuri. Therefore,
there is a need to reimagine Africa or "African" as a distinct lived experience
rather than merely as a geographic space—in our efforts to understand African Islamists. When attempting to understand Islamist militants in particular,
one must be prepared to reimagine (if only for the sake of analysis) an alternative conceptualization of identity and geography that function as alternatives
to secular forms of self-identity considered man-made and therefore without
merit in the Islamist worldview.[52]

Media accounts devoting an inordinate amount of attention to Donald
Trump sometimes obscure the fact that there are many Donald Trumps in
the United States and Europe. But there are also many like Muhammad Ali,
the late cultural icon, who quietly embrace the religion of Islam despite rising Islamophobia in the United States and Europe.[53] It is a paradox that for

decades, black Muslims in the United States have actively exploited the public's general ignorance of their existence to enhance their own anonymity and obscurity and fortify themselves against racial, ethnic, and religious bigotry. Indeed, widespread public debate sparked during the US presidential campaign in 2016 over the adoption of a Muslim ban in the United States treated Muslims in the United States as though Muslims in the United States were all Arab immigrants from the Middle East. Virtually no attention is devoted to the fact that like Muhammad Ali not all Muslims in the United States are immigrants. While African American is what they are called by others, African America is not necessarily what they call themselves or prefer to be called by others. When it comes to black Muslims, escaping (for a time at least) the dual challenge of being black and Muslim in hostile environments by avoiding public scrutiny may have been welcomed as an asset. Yet, escapism (*hijra*) or separatism if you like, is ultimately a tragedy for scholarship for it conceals the long-standing survival of the progeny of African Muslims in the United States. Perhaps, Dannin says it best when he describes how ignorance of the Muslim past in the United States conceals an important chapter of American history.[54] Nevertheless, black Muslim skill at conducting Muslim struggle (*jihad*), often in concert with non-Muslim allies (e.g., Indians, non-Muslim blacks and corsairs) less skilled in the use of flight (*hijra*), has enabled them to acquire an influence that far surpasses their numbers in the United States.

Recent immigrant arrivals from the Middle East have not always been able to recognize African American Muslims, much less duplicate their success at surviving bigotry in the United States. What I elsewhere describe as Waves of Immigration (WOI) theorists and the "Islam in America" literature they produce assumes the disappearance of the Islam first brought to the Americas by Africans. This decidedly self-serving view has been promoted without the slightest hint of scientific validation since the mid-1980s when WOI theorists concluded that the Islam first brought to the Americas by African Muslims was abandoned with the wholesale conversion of blacks in the United States to Christianity where they remain to this day. But Wood's study of slave resistance in eighteenth-century South Carolina challenges this assumption by noting "that many of the most effective means," of resisting domination and control, "fall at the low (or invisible) end of the spectrum." And "to the benefit of the slave and the frustration of the historian, such subversion was always difficult to assess."[55] Scott (1990) explores this phenomenon which Muslims call *taqiyya* ("dissimulation") or what he calls the "hidden transcripts." Scott's hidden transcripts theory offers a detailed theoretical perspective for recognizing difficult-to-monitor resistance and survival which captures and explains the survival of Islamist militancy among African Muslims in difficult to monitor settings. The following and final chapter of this study offers conclusions and advice for policy makers.

NOTES

1. See Sultana Afroz, *Invisible Yet Invincible: The Islamic Heritage of the Maroons and the Enslaved Africans of Jamaica* (London: Austin-Macauley Publishers Ltd., 2012). Also see "The Jihad of 1831–1832: The Misunderstood Baptist Rebellion in Jamaica," *Journal of Muslim Minority Affairs*, vol. 21, no. 2, 2001, 227–243.

2. Walter Hawthorne, *From Africa to Brazil: Culture, Identity, and an Atlantic Slave Trade 1600–1830* (New York: Cambridge University Press, 2010), 138–139.

3. This idea, though not thoroughly explored here, is an integral part of arguments put forth in Rashid, *Black Muslims in the US: History, Politics and the Struggle of a Community*, 50–53.

4. *The Holy Qur'an*, Abdullah Yusuf Ali translation, chapter 49, verse 13, 1407.

5. Ibid., chapter 30, verse 22, 1056.

6. Gomez, *Black Crescent: The Experience and Legacy of African Muslims in the Americas.*

7. Rashid, *Black Muslims,* 2013.

8. See Fatimah Mernissi, *Islam and Democracy: Fear of the Modern World* (New York: Addison-Wesley Publishing Co., 1992), 111. Also see Sherman Jackson, "Preliminary Reflections on Islam and Black Religion," in Zahid Bukhari et al., eds., *Muslims in the American Public Square* (New York: Altamira Press, 2004).

9. See Matar, *Turks, Moors and Englishmen*, 28.

10. Fichtner, *Terror and Toleration: The Habsburg Empire Confronts Islam, 1526–1850*, 47.

11. Ibid., 21.

12. William Loren Katz, *Black Indians: A Hidden Heritage* (New York: Anthem Books for Young Readers, 1986), 114.

13. See Jane Landers, *Black Society in Spanish Florida* (Gainesville, FL: University Press of Florida, 1999), and Kathleen Deagan and Darcie MacMahon, *Fort Mose: Colonial America's Black Fortress of Freedom* (Gainesville, FL: University Press of Florida, 1995).

14. Ibid.

15. Ibid.

16. See https://blogs.weta.org/boundarystones/2016/02/08/benjamin-bannekers-capital-Contributions Also see Jesse J. Holland, *Black Men Built the Capitol* (Guilford, CT: Lyons Press, 2007), 26–32.

17. For a fascinating firsthand account of an African enslaved in Yellow House, a notorious "slave" holding pen located on what is today's Washington, DC's National Mall, see Jesse J. Holland, *Black Men Built the Capitol* (Guilford, Connecticut, 2007), 26–32.

18. Katz, *Black Indians: A Hidden Heritage*, 29.

19. Ibid., 31.

20. Ibid., 33.

21. Matthew Restall, *Seven Myths of the Spanish Conquest* (New York: Oxford University Press, 2003), 35.

22. Ibid., 49–63.

23. Ibid., 61.

24. Ibid.

25. See Henry Louis Gates's televised PBS series "The Black Pharaohs of Egypt," January 2017,

26. Katz, *Black Indians: A Hidden Heritage*, 34–35.

27. Ibid., 30.

28. Joel W. Martin, *Sacred Revolt: The Muskogee's Struggle for a New World* (Boston: Beacon Press 1992).

29. See Robert Hall, "African Religious Retentions in Florida," in David Colburn and Jane L. Landers, eds., *The African American Heritage of Florida* (Gainesville: University Press of Florida, 1995), 45–48.

30. Brent Richard Weisman, *Unconquered People: Florida's Seminole and Miccosukee Indians* (Gainesville: University Press of Florida, 1999).

31. Abdelhamid Lotfi, *Muslims on the Block: Five Centuries of Islam in America* (Ifrane, Morocco: Al Akhawayn University Press, 2002), 26–27.

32. See Rashid, *Black Muslims in the US: History, Politics and the Struggle of a Community.*

33. See Daniel H. Usner Jr., *Indians, Settlers and Slaves in a Frontier Exchange Economy: The Lower Mississippi Valley Before 1783* (Chapel Hill: University of North Carolina Press, 1992), 286, and Daniel C. Littlefield, *Rice and Slaves: Ethnicity and the Slave Trade in Colonial South Carolina* (Urbana: University of Illinois Press, 1991), 52.

34. Joseph E. Holloway, "The Origins of African American Culture," in Joseph E. Holloway, ed., *Africanisms in American Culture*, second edition (Bloomington: Indiana University Press, 2005), 40–42.

35. Estimates of the total number of Muslims in the United States are consistently understated as they often fail to include indigenous Muslims described as black Muslims in official estimates, to the delight of many black Muslims. Regarding the number of black Muslims in the United States, Muslim spokesperson Malcolm X once famously stated that "those who know do not say and those that say do not know."

36. "Black Immigrants Have Quadrupled Since 1980, Study Says," *New York Times*, April 10, 2015.

37. Ibid.

38. Ibid.

39. Ibid.

40. Ibid.

41. "Boko Haram: The History of Africa's Most Notorious Terrorist Group," Charles River Editors, Kentucky, 2017, 2.

42. Ibid., 7.

43. Ibid.

44. Ibid., 9.

45. Ibid., 10.

46. Ibid., 11.

47. Ibid., 15.

48. Ibid., 17 and 18.

49. Ibid., 20.

50. Ibid., 22.

51. Ibid., 29 and 30. Also see John Campbell, "US Policy to Counter Nigeria's Boko Haram," *Council on Foreign Relations*, Special Report no. 70. November 2014.

52. Wayne argues that the election of Barack Obama and other recent developments raise questions for black Americans over the defining characteristics of their community. Yet, similar questions can be raised concerning what it means to be an African Muslim living in the United States and abroad, more generally. See Michael Wayne, *Imagining Black America* (New Haven: Yale University Press, 2014).

53. In an interesting case of Muslim practice in the United States, beyond the reach or awareness of many people a prison Imam, Jon Young, recently claimed that "80 percent of the Muslim inmates in Sing Sing [prison] had converted to Islam after entering prison . . . . The [New York] prison houses 250 registered Muslims," "Navigating A Holy Month for Muslims, Behind Bars," *New York Times*, July 7, 2016.

54. Robert Dannin, *Black Pilgrimage to Islam* (New York: Oxford University Press, 2002).

55. See Peter H. Wood, *Black Majority: Negroes in Colonial South Carolina From 1620 Through the Stono Rebellion* (New York: W. W. Norton & Company, 1975), 287.

Conclusion

The Western world's encounter with the Islamic world entails a long and well-documented history of encounters to which "Africans" have contributed significantly yet about which westerners have not always been keenly familiar with thanks to myths and stereotypes of Africa and Africans. To minimize this error and its consequences in the future, policy makers must acquaint themselves with this historical record and resist the temptation to view the Islamist challenge as exclusively driven by one group, one leader, or one region of the world. Policy makers must acknowledge publically that the ongoing war on terror (WOT) is a world rather than a regional war. For too long, US foreign policy has been preoccupied with Saudi Arabia, Iraq, and Syria and by extension with Afghanistan and Pakistan to the exclusion of other important players and theaters in the Islamic world. As a result, the United States has ignored the equally important region of Africa that includes lesser-known but increasingly important states of Nigeria, Mali, Sudan, Kenya, and Somalia. Africa is now a major sanctuary for militant Islamist shelter, arms, and training with epicenters in North Africa that increasing spread their influence southward to region of the Sudan via the vast and seemingly limitless expanse of the Sahara desert. Africa could very well replace Afghanistan as the principal haven for international Islamist terrorist groups in the coming years.

Policy makers in the Trump administration must abandon the practice of overreacting to the Islamist challenge by seeking cooperation with Russia in the fight against ISIS. Although it is true that the West and militant Islamists have been longstanding foes, it is also true that beyond the West and Islamic world rivalry mutually, productive outcomes have been reached in part because of this rivalry. For instance, this rivalry can be linked to the advent of modern printing introduced to Europe from the Middle East following its initial introduction in China, the introduction of the scientific method used for centuries in Moorish Spain and the introduction of Arabic numerals and numerous household commodities such as sugar, coffee, chess, and pepper from the Muslim world. Despite President Trump's frequent references to earlier (failed) attempts by President G. W. Bush, Secretary of State Clinton and President Obama to ally with Russia, US-Islamic world cooperation has historically produced longer-lasting and more fruitful benefits than potential benefits witnessed thus far from a United States–Russian alliance.

The primary motivation behind 2017 efforts to derive a "deal" with Russia appear to have more to do with ethno-nationalism and presumed common Christian heritage with Russia than with overlapping national self-interest between Russia and the United States. The first country to recognize the fledgling United States of America following its Declaration of Independence from England was not Russia but the African Muslim nation of Morocco with whom the United States has held the longest diplomatic relations of any nation in the world. Abandoning the Islamic world (to say nothing of what this would mean for US European allies) in addition to the logistical nightmare associated with Mr. Trump's initial roll-out of its Muslim ban undermines US efforts in the WOT by in effect abandoning, Muslim allies who once supported the United States in the WOT. The ramifications of this are enormous. Long term, the United States must also resist making the same mistakes it made during the Cold War of being quick to label African nationalist insurgents communist for the flimsiest of reasons. Labelling certain African insurgents "terrorists" may be similarly misleading as terrorism is a technique not an ideology linked to Muslim *and* Christian nations, historically.

When it comes to the Islamist challenge and Africans, US policy makers must be prepared to reimagine African identities as most Islamists regard western nation-states and the identities they create such as Nigerian as artificial, alien, and secular identities imposed by Europeans on black Muslims. Boko Haram's rejection of the Nigerian state and of secular identities such as Nigerian or African for that matter is challenged by a preference for being called simply a Muslim. One of the consequences of the reimagining of Africa means that policy makers must be prepared to engage militant Islamist among black Muslims for whom religious identity holds more currency than western conceived racial or national identities, as the latter are seen as "artificial" identities imposed on Muslims by outsiders. Policy makers must therefore resist the temptation to see the world exclusively through European eyes. Policy makers must also do more to educate the public to the important significance of Africa and Africans in the WOT and its place in European, US, and world history. Finally, policy makers must do more to acknowledge the counterproductive practices of some of its overseas allies that include

Nigeria, that create additional burdens for policy makers seeking the common goal of eliminating terrorist violence among Africans.

From former Secretary of State Hillary Clinton to Defense Secretary James Mattis, policy makers candidly admit, "we are not winning" the WOT. If the West is to ever defeat the terrorists and preserve the alliance it created and desperately depends on, it must abandon its careless and insensitive use of words like "radical Islamic extremists," "jihadist," "jihadism," and "jihadi" to denote Muslim terrorists in the US-led WOT. Words matter to Muslims as seen in the Charlie Hebdo attacks in Paris of November 2015. Consequently, policy makers must adopt greater restraint when using words in this way because they suggest Muslims are terrorists because most embrace struggle (*jihad*) as an essential obligation. If most Muslims behaved as "jihadists" or terrorist, there could be no consistently reliable Muslim support for the US-led WOT. If continued support for the West in its WOT is to be assured, then more careful use of language by US policy makers at all levels is required. The word "Khawar'ij," is the Arabic word used by Muslims to denote extremists and not "jihad," "jihadist," or "jihadism."

Opponents of the West point to this careless use of language argue that the WOT is indeed a war on Muslim struggle (*jihad*) and therefore a war on Islam since nearly all of the world's 1.8 billion Muslims embrace Muslim struggle (*jihad*) as a sacred religious obligation. No other practice is more threatening to the US-Muslim world relations than this, for in the words of former CIA official and leading US foreign policy critic, Michael Scheuer of Georgetown University, the Muslim world hates Americans not for what they believe but rather for what they do. For instance, President Obama took great pains to avoid using the term "radical Islamic terrorism," while President Trump seems to relish in the use of this and other toxic words that fuel conflict, division, and pain. Republican supporters of Mr. Trump typically dismiss "liberal" warnings like these as useless attempts at "political correctness." Yet, the even more conservative 1.8 billion Muslim world rejects deliberate use of words they believe should never be uttered as adjectives of the religion of Islam.

Mindful of the adage, "with friends like these who needs enemies," US policy makers must do more to sanction Muslim allies especially in Nigeria and Kenya who do more to produce Islamist militants than they do to discourage their emergence in the first instance. Policing practices in Nigeria, Kenya, Cameroon, and Somalia produce the very violent outcomes their governments have been sworn to oppose. US government policies must do more to rein-in these states and their security forces while resisting the temptation to adopt heavy-handed counterproductive measures including public chastisement or the withholding of vital arms shipments as seen in the case of Nigeria. Furthermore, counterproductive measures such as these undermine the morale needed to bolster the confidence of US-trained allies in the Muslim world where instances of retreat, surrender, and capture have occurred similar to military setbacks witnessed in Iraq and Afghanistan in 2014/2015.

US policy makers must do more to support allies with clear-cut records of success, like the seasoned fighters of Chad for whom Boko Haram apparently fears. Yet, rather than support effective military allies like Chad, the Trump administration included Chad on one of its newly revised list of terrorist states for 2017 whose citizens were blocked from entering to the United States. If Muslim authorities in charge of Nigeria's security forces are to secure the moral high ground in their war with Boko Haram, they must embrace practices that are morally superior to those of the terrorists. Thus far at least, the achievement of this goal remains largely unmet and if the Nigerian state continues to fail at its current rate, the militants rather than the Nigeria state, will capture the moral high ground. The United States must remain mindful of President G. W. Bush's observation that the WOT is a battle to win "the hearts and minds" of the broader Muslim world.

Policy makers must resist the urge to micro-manage the legitimate Muslim struggle (*jihad*) waged by Nigeria, Mali, Somali, and other Muslim allies in the WOT. Although this may be difficult to do, policy makers must remember that Muslim allies in Africa similar to Muslim allies in the Islamic Middle East have longstanding experience with Muslim struggle (*jihad*) and are therefore fully capable of waging war effectively as seen in the case of the African fighters of Chad. But to retain their continued respect and support, US policy makers must do more to promote greater transparency regarding the broad goals of US foreign policy in Africa. The crash of Air Algérie Flight 5017 near the town of Gossi, Mali, in 2014 and "ambush" of US Special Forces and Nigerien forces in Niger in October 2017 were rife with conflicting official accounts. A need exists for more timely and detailed accounts of terrorist violence among Africans beyond reports produced by the British Broadcasting Service (BBC) self-described as the leader in breaking international news.

But just as US allies produce more Islamist militants than they deter African multilateral peace keepers—perhaps the largest in the world—must be better managed if they wish to regain credibility in Africa. As a display of widespread public outrage against them, Islamist militants bombed UN headquarters in Abuja, Nigeria, in 2011. With recorded instances of theft by ECOMOG "peacekeepers" to ethnic favoritism in CAR, peacekeeping actions in Africa have a horrendous track record. Lombard's study of UN peacekeeping in CAR documents UN involvement in the pregnancy of local women, theft of mineral gems, and corrupt business practices involving Cameroonian and possibly French peacekeepers. These occurrences led Lombard to conclude in her 2016 study that UN personnel stationed in CAR were the primary beneficiaries of the peacekeeping operations in the state. Peace-keepers according to Lombard drove bigger vehicles, earned higher salaries, and reaped greater economic gains than most citizens of CAR. In addition to this, victimized Muslims communities targeted by anti-Muslim militias in CAR have been attacked and killed with impunity, sometimes under the watchful eyes of UN peacekeepers stationed nearby reminiscent of practices observed in Haiti and other peacekeeping theaters of conflict. The United States must do more not just to shoulder a greater share of its financial burden but to embrace more credible rules of engagement governing when and how its forces intervene to halt the killing of innocent civilians. These measures require greater behind-the-scene diplomacy than the currently understaffed US State Department under President Trump seems capable of providing. However, these tasks will remain required if the UN wishes to regain badly needed credibility in Africa.

US officials must be careful to insure that interventions to halt group violence in Africa are rooted in sound and just principles and not just western favoritism toward one side or another in local conflicts as possibly seen in US-EU intervention in Libya culminating in the death of Muammar Gadhafy and unraveling of Libya in 2011. Indeed, US intervention in Somalia may have had more to do with revenge for the infamous black Hawk Down incident and hatred of the Islamic Courts and Shabab than with any real military importance and significance to the United States. Somalia had been without an organized central government since the collapse of the Somali state following the flight of strong man Mohammed Siad Barre from Mogadishu in an armored vehicle in 1991. Similar to its record in Africa during the Cold War when it routinely labelled Africans with East European bloc weapons and training "communists," the United States must resist labelling Islamists "terrorists" for the flimsiest of reasons.

This questionable practice facilitated the invasion and occupation of Somalia from 2006 to 2011 by a US-trained forces largely comprised of Somalia's regional enemy, Ethiopia, who drove the Somalis from their indigenous land without clear evidence of a threat to the United States or its interest in the area. This action triggered a bloody insurgency that might have been avoided. Conflict with Shabab, the bloodiest Islamist challenge among Africans after Boko Haram, has steadily escalated since then. Twin bombings in Mogadishu, the capital and largest such attack in Somalia, claimed the lives of more than 350 victims in October 2017. Illustrating both the tragedy of terrorist violence in Africa and marginal attention it continues to receive a *Wall Street Journal* report published in February 2018 estimates that "more than 31,000 people have died in the decade long war [in Nigeria]," with 2 million people forced from their homes. And the tragedy does not end there. The same report describes an attack in the town of Dapchi where more young schoolgirls are feared to have been captured by Boko Haram. Contradicting earlier reports cited in chapter one, the report acknowledges that between October 2016 and May 2017, the 103 Nigerian schools released for five imprisoned Boko Haram fighters also came with a ransom price of $3.7 million.[1] In the words of one militant, the West is paying for Muslim struggle (*jihad*).

Contrary to images of Africa as the "dark continent" far removed from the mainstream currents of world events, Africans as these events reveal are playing major roles in the US-led WOT. No other challenge threatens to undermine Africa's positive contribution to world affairs more than the emergence of terrorist violence. While the United States has made great strides in its rediscovery of Africa, its increased troop presence in Djibouti, built new drone installations in Niger and elevated the status of US Africa Command (AFRICOM), much more remains to be done as seen in the tragic crash of Air Algérie Flight 5017 over Gossi, Mali, in 2014, and the "ambush" of US special forces in the nearby Mali/Niger border region in October 2017. These and other events raise nagging questions including why the body of US Sgt. La David Johnson was separated from three other American Special Forces and left on the battlefield unburied for days before being recovered by Nigeriens? Was he tortured? Was he kidnapped? And if so why? What were Americans doing in Niger? And if they were there as "trainers" then what does "training" actually mean? Is the United States engaged in combat in Africa? Were US troops on a mission to capture a reputed terrorist leader? These questions raised by US congressional US Representative Fredricka Wilson, a democratic congressperson from Florida and personal friend of the Johnson family, became the latest in a series of nasty confrontations involving President Trump. Questions raised by this episode seem entirely reasonable given the hardships already endured by US families and the dearth of information that is known about US troops in Africa.[2]

Peacekeeping operations in Somalia notwithstanding, a greater US involvement in Africa is long overdue. While it is true that US Special Forces have operated across the continent for years, the US goal of continuing to operate across Africa without leaving a visible military footprint may no longer be possible to achieve. For a region of fifty-four different nation-states, in an area three times the geographic size of the continental United States, sub-Saharan Africa cries out for a larger and more transparent US presence. If the existence of terrorist violence anywhere raises the threat of terrorist violence everywhere, then greater US commitment to Africa seems worth the investment. Africa may be the only area of critical self-interest to the United States whose operational headquarters are located a continent away in Stuttgart, Germany.

If Africa is to become a real priority, efforts to raise US military presence similar to the US troop buildup in Afghanistan in 2017 may also be needed.

Such a development at the very least requires moving AFRICOM from Stuttgart to sub-Saharan Africa to possible locations in Addis Ababa, Accra, or Nairobi. Such a move would signal a more serious willingness to halt terrorist violence among Africans. US policy makers must also eliminate overly bureaucratic protocols governing troop interventions to Africa in the interest of faster and more effective military responses to the continent's growing crises. US intervention protocols against Boko Haram, which occurred at least four years after the insurgency had already begun in 2009, must be avoided and retooled. We may never know how many lives could have been saved had the United States intervened far sooner than it did.

Policy makers must take the moral high ground and avoid tainting the public discourse with anti-terrorist propaganda, which to date has delivered few lasting results. Scheuer's 2005 YouTube video speech "How and how not to fight terrorism," frequently cited in this study, reminds us that terrorists hate the US not what it believes or for its way of life. Terrorists hate the US for what it does and the greatest gift to the terrorists is an American foreign policy that promotes counterproductive practices like military intervention and torture that invite retaliation from Islamist militants.

If this is true, then policy makers must avoid such practices and make adjustments in US foreign policy, where needed. On a related matter, policy makers must reject the practice of torturing terrorist suspects. The leadership of Arizona senator John McCain, the only member of Congress to have been tortured as a prisoner of war (POW), remains a beacon of light on this question that remains an issue in Washington as seen in debates during confirmation hearing for a new CIA head in 2018. Scheuer and others join McCain on this point to remind us that terrorist suspects held at Guantánamo Bay and elsewhere have in many cases gained release from prison only to reappear on the battlefield in the WOT. The best propaganda in times of war must be honesty and truth for truth is always the first casualty of war.

Contrary to the way that Boko Haram is translated in the western media, MacEachern, who is an expert on Boko Haram, reminds us that the term "Boko Haram" "is probably better understood as 'deceitful education' or 'useless education,' as opposed to traditional Koranic education" is forbidden.[3] This observation if true provides one more reason to avoid deceit in western foreign policies toward African Islamists. Scheuer, a former CIA official, offers related advice that draws attention to the simple, transparent, and laudable image of Osama bin Laden whom Scheuer implies may be worthy of the description "honorable adversary" or "worthy opponent" as bin Laden in Scheuer's view "says what he means and means what he says."

To ignore this is to play into the hands of the terrorists or in the words of Scheuer, "being too clever by half."[4]

Boko Haram would not be the only indigenous Muslim community that perceives secular authority as devilish and deceitful. For instance, the so-called Black Muslim community in the United States prior to its revival in 1975 and turn to mainstream Sunni Islam under the leadership of W. D. Muhammad, son of Nation of Islam (NOI) founder, included many similar ideas widely familiar at least to black Americans exposed to NOI "teachings." The national spokesman for the pre-1975 NOI as it was once called was Malcolm X, who along with Muhammad Ali were among the best known "indigenous" Muslims in the United States. NOI notions such as "masters of deceit" and secular world "tricknology" were familiar elements of the NOI's anti-secular, anti-racist, and antiwhite ideology. Most observers who are unfamiliar with Wahhabi-Salafi principles would reject these notions as entirely "home grown" which itself is a form of marginalization of Africa/ black Muslims. But the theme of rejecting that which is deemed deceitful, inauthentic, and made-up as opposed to that which is created by God (Allah) lies at the heart of the Wahhabi-Salafi critique of secularism.

For example, the Wahhabi-Salafi notion of innovation (*bid'da*) referring to that which is manmade, fabricated, or "fake" might be applied to the idea of the WOT itself. This may be an additional reason for President Obama's gradual refusal to use the term "WOT" (although for those who believed he was a Muslim who was born in Kenya, this idea and quite possibly any idea presented by Mr. Obama would be difficult to accept). Yet, Islamists militants, with some justification, reject the idea of WOT because terrorism is essentially a tactic. Because by implication, the idea of making war on a tactic makes no sense, those who argue that the WOT in reality is a war on Islam and Muslims may have a point. As I have argued elsewhere, "people, not tactics, are the targets of war." As it turns out, this is not a novel idea as former September 11, 2001, commissioner, Nebraska senator Bob Kerry, expressed a similar idea on April 7, 2004, while testifying during a televised public hearing when he said, "Terrorism is a tactic. The administration is not waging a war on a tactic, but a war on 'Muslim extremists,' therefore 'we have to figure out how to engage in a dialogue' with Muslims."[5]

Finally, this study encourages US policy makers to examine the historical record and authoritative sources of Islam to clarify more accurately the meaning, significance, and motives behind the Islamist challenge and distinguish once and for all "jihad," that is, terrorist violence, from legitimate Muslim struggle (*jihad*), flight (*hijra*), and community (*ummah*). Developing these capabilities may help to diminish many seemingly endless debates. Because Islam when properly understood is respectful of others, it seems fitting to end with the hope that if statements included in this study have disparaged anyone in anyway, my sincerest apologies are offered in advance. But if this study has helped to improve in any small way our understanding of the challenges and opportunities that lie ahead, then all praise is due to Allah for only the mistakes are mine.

NOTES

1. "Boko Haram Militants Seized More Nigerian Schoolgirls," *Wall Street Journal*, February 22, 2018.

2. "New Niger Details Revealed," *The Wall Street Journal*, October 24, 2017.

3. MacEachern, *Searching for Boko Haram: The History of Violence in Central Africa*, 11.

4. This quote is derived from a public speech delivered by Scheuer at Indiana University in Bloomington. For an excellent presentation of Michael Scheuer's approach to foreign policy, see his national best-selling Michael Scheuer, *Imperial Hubris: Why the West Is losing the War on Terror* (Washington, DC: Potomac Books, 2005).

5. Rashid, *Black Muslims in the US: History, Politics and the Struggle of a Community*, 133–34.

Selected Bibliography

Afroz, Sultana, "From Moors to Marronage: The Islamic Heritage of the Maroons in Jamaica," *Journal of Muslim Minority Affairs*, vol. 19, no. 2, 1999, 161–79.

Afroz, Sultana, *Invisible Yet Invincible: The Islamic Heritage of the Maroons and the Enslaved Africans of Jamaica* (London: Austin-Macauley Pub. Ltd., 2012).

Afroz, Sultana, "The Jihad of 1831–1832: The Misunderstood Baptist Rebellion in Jamaica," *Journal of Muslim Minority Affairs*, vol. 21, no. 22, 2001, 227–43.

Ajayi, A. F. Ade, "Africa on the Eve of European Conquest," in *General History of Africa, Africa in the Nineteenth Century Until the 1880s*, J. Ade Ajayi, ed. Abridged edition (Berkeley: University of California Press, 1998), 239–46.

Al-Yassini, Ayman, "Wahhabiyah," in *The Oxford Encyclopedia of the Modern Islamic World*, John L. Esposito, ed. (New York: Oxford University Press, 1995), 419–20.

Austin, Ralph, "Africa and Globalization: Colonialism, Decolonization and the Post-Colonial Malaise," *Journal of Global History*, vol. 1, no. 3, 2008, 403–409.

Bates, Robert H., *When Things Fell Apart: State-Failure in Late Twentieth Century Africa* (Cambridge: Cambridge University Press, 2007).

Bauer, Wolfgang, *Stolen Girls: Survivors of Boko Haram Tell Their Story*, translated by Eric Trump (New York: The New Press, 2017).

Bethell, Leslie, (ed.), *Colonial Brazil* (New York: Cambridge University Press, 1987).

Bolster, Jeffrey, *Black Jacks: African American Seamen in the Age of Sail* (Cambridge, MA: Harvard University Press, 1998).

Bratton, Michael, and Nicolas van de Walle, *Democratic Experiments in Africa* (Cambridge, UK: Cambridge University Press, 1997).

Bright, Jake, and Aubrey Hruby, *The Next Africa: An Emerging Continent Becomes A Global Powerhouse* (New York: St. Martin's Press, 2015).

Brenner, Louis, (ed.), *Muslim Identity and Social Change in Sub-Saharan Africa* (Bloomington: Indiana University Press, 1993).

Brown, Carl L., *Religion and State: The Muslim Approach to Politics* (New York: Columbia University Press, 2000).

Burrough, Bryan, *Days of Rage: America's Radical Underground, the FBI, and the First Age of Terror* (New York: Penguin Books, 2015).

Campbell, John, *US Policy to Counter Nigeria's Boko Haram*, Council Special Report no.70. (New York: Council on Foreign Relations, 2014).

Cavanagh, William T., *The Myth of Religious Violence* (New York: Oxford University Press, 2009).

Charles River Editors, *Boko Haram: The History of Africa's Most Notorious Terrorist Group* (Lexington, KT: Charles River Editors, 2017).

Chazon, Naomi, Peter Lewis, Robert Mortimer, Donald Rothchild, and Stephen J. Stedman, *Politics and Society in Contemporary Africa*, third edition (Boulder, CO: Lynne Rienner, 1999).

Clapham, Christopher, *Africa and the International System* (New York: Cambridge University Press, 1996).

Chivvis, Christopher S., *The French War on Al Qa'da in Africa* (New York: Cambridge University Press, 2016).

Cobrin, Jane, *Al-Qaeda: The Terror Network that Threatens the World* (New York: Nations Books, 2002).

Cohen, William B., *The French Encounters with Africans: White Response to Blacks, 1530–1880* (Blooming: Indiana University Press, 2003).

Colley, Linda, *Captives* (New York: Pantheon Books, 2002).

Cordingly, David, *Under the Black Flag: The Romance and Reality of Life among the Pirates* (New York: Random House, 2006).

Cyert, Richard, and James March, *Behavioral Theory of the Firm* (New York: Blackwell Business, 1992).

Dannin, Robert, *Black Pilgrimage to Islam* (New York: Oxford University Press, 2002).

Davidson, Basil, *The African Genius* (New York: Little, Brown, and Co., 1969).

Davidson, Basil, *The African Slave Trade* (New York: Little, Brown, and Co. 1980).

Davis, John et al., (eds.), *Terrorism in Africa the Evolving Front* (Lanham, MD: Lexington Books, 2010).

Davis, John, "The African Response to Terrorism: An Assessment," in *Terrorism in Africa: The Evolving Front*, John Davis et al., eds. (Lanham, MD: Lexington Books, 2010), 240–27.

Diouf, Sylviane, *Servants of Allah: African Muslims Enslaved in the Americas* (New York: New York University Press, 1998).

Edgerton, Robert B., *Hidden Heroism: Black Soldiers in America's Wars* (Boulder, CO: Westview Press, 2002).

Edgerton, Robert E., *Africa's Armies: From Honor to Infamy: A History from 1791 to the Present* (Boulder, CO: Westview Press, 2007).

Elster, Jon, *Reason and Rationality* (Princeton, NJ: Princeton University Press, 2009).

Esposito, John L., (ed.), "The Prophet Muhammad," in *The Oxford Encyclopedia of the Modern Islamic World* (New York: Oxford University Press, 1995), 153–66.

Fichtner, Paula Sutter, *Terror and Toleration: The Habsburg Empire Confronts Islam, 1526–1850* (London: Reaktion Books, 2008).

Franklin, John Hope, and Loren Schweninger, *Runaway Slaves: Rebels on the Plantation* (New York: Oxford University Press, 1999).

Geertz, Clifford, *Islam Observed: Religious Development in Morocco and Indonesia* (Chicago: The University of Chicago Press, 1968).

Gomez, Michael A., *African Domain: A New History of Empire in Early and Medieval West Africa* (Princeton: Princeton University Press, 2018).

Gomez, Michael A., *Black Crescent: The Experience and Legacy of African Muslims in the Americas* (New York: Cambridge University Press, 2005).

Gomez, Michael A., *Exchanging Our Country Marks: The Transformation of African Identities in the Colonial and Antebellum South* (Chapel Hill: The University of North Carolina Press, 1998).

Gomez, Michael A., *Reversing Sail* (New York: Cambridge University Press, 2005).

Haley, Alex, *The Autobiography of Malcolm X* (New York: Dial Press, 1973).

Hall, Robert, "African Religious Retentions in Florida," in *The African American Heritage of Florida*, David Colburn and Jane L. Landers, eds., (Gainesville, Florida: University Press of Florida, 1995).

Hamdun, Said, and Noel King, *Ibn Battuta in Black Africa* (Princeton: Marcus Wiener Pub., 1975).

Hamm, Mark S., "Prison Islam in the Age of Sacred Terror," *The British Journal of Criminology*, vol. 49, no. 5, 2009, 667–85.

Hamm, Mark S., *The Spectacular Few: Prisoner Radicalization and the Evolving Terrorist Threat* (New York: New York University Press, 2013).

Harvey, L. P., *Islamic Spain 1250–1500* (Chicago: The University of Chicago Press, 1990).

Harvey, L. P., *Muslims in Spain 1500–1614* (Chicago: The University of Chicago Press, 2006).

Hawthorne, Walter, *From Africa to Brazil: Culture, Identity, and an Atlantic Slave Trade 1600–1830* (New York: Cambridge University Press, 2010).

Hazelwood, Nick, *The Queen's Slave Trader* (New York: Morrow, 2004).

Hegel, G.W. F., *Phenomenology of Spirit* (New York: Oxford University Press, 1997).

Hers, Jacques, *The Barbary Corsairs: Warfare in the Mediterranean, 1480–1580*, translated by Jonathan North (Mechanicsburg, PA: StackpoleBooks, 2001).

Holland, Jesse J., *Black Men Built the Capitol* (Gilford, CT: Lyons Press, 2007).

Holloway, Joseph E., (ed.), *Africanisms in American Culture*, second edition (Bloomington: Indiana University Press, 2005).

Human Rights Watch/Africa, *Mauritania's Campaign of Terror: State-Sponsored Repression of Black Africans* (New York: Human Rights Watch, 1994).

Hussain, Shahrul, *A Treasury of Sacred Maxims: A Commentary on Islamic Leal Principles* (Leicestershire, UK: Kube Publishing, Ltd., 2016).

Jackson, Sherman, *Islam and the BlackAmerican: Looking for the Third Resurrection* (New York: Oxford University Press, 2005).

Jackson, Sherman, "Preliminary Reflections on Islam and Black Religion," in *Muslims in the American Public Square*, Zahid Bukhari et al., eds. (New York: Altamira Press, 2004).

Jamieson, Alan G., *Lords of the Sea: A History of the Barbary Corsairs* (Chicago, IL: The University of Chicago Press, 2012).

Jane, Cecil, (ed.), *The Four Voyages of Columbus*, translated and edited with introduction and notes by Cecil Jane (New York: Dover Pub., Inc., 1998; first published in 1930).

Jervis, Robert, *Perceptions and Misperceptions in International Relations* (Princeton, NJ: Princeton University Press, 1976).

Katz, William Loren, *Black Indians: A Hidden Heritage* (New York: Anthem Books for Young Readers, 1986).

Kaufman, Joyce P., *Introduction to International Relation: Theory and Practice* (Lanham, MD: Rowman & Littlefield, 2013).

Keagan, Kathleen, and Darcie MacMahon, *Fort Mose: Colonial America's Black Fortress of Freedom* (Gainesville: University Press of Florida, 1995).

Keenen, Jeremy, *The Dark Sahara: America's War on Terror in Africa* (New York: Pluto Press, 2009).

Keenan, Jeremy, *US Imperialism and Terror in Africa* (London: Pluto Press, 2013).

Khaldun, Ibn, *The Muqaddimah: An Introduction to History*, translated from Arabic by N. J. Dawood, and edited by Franz Rosenthal (Princeton, NJ: Princeton University Press, 1989).

Klein, Herbert S., *The Atlantic Slave Trade* (New York: Cambridge University Press, 2005).

Landers, Jane, *Black Society in Spanish Florida* (Gainesville: University Press of Florida, 1999).

Lauziére, Henri, *The Making of Salafism: Islamic Reform in the Twentieth Century* (New York: Columbia University Press, 2016), ebook.

Levtzion, Nehemia, and Randall L. Pouwels (eds.) *The History of Islam in Africa* (Athens: Ohio University Press, 2000).

Lewis, Bernard, *Islam and the West* (New York: Oxford University Press, 1993).

Lewis, Bernard, *Race and Slavery in the Middle East* (New York: Oxford University Press, 1990).

Lewis, Bernard, *The Multiple Identities of the Middle East* (New York: Schocken Books, 1998).

Littlefield, Daniel C., *Rice and Slaves: Ethnicity and the Slave Trade in Colonial South Carolina* (Urbana: University of Illinois Press, 1991).

Lo, Mboye, *Muslims in America: Race, Politics and Community Building* (Beltsville, MD: Amana Pub., 2004).

Lombard, Louisa, *State of Rebellion: Violence and Intervention in the Central African Republic* (Chicago, IL: The University of Chicago Press, 2017; originally a Zed publication).

Lotfi, Abdelhamid, *Muslims on the Block: Five Centuries of Islam in America* (Ifrane, Morocco: Al Akhawayn University Press, 2002).

MacEachern, Scott, *Searching For Boko Haram: A History of Violence in Central Africa* (New York: Oxford University Press, 2018).

Mamdani, Mahmoud, *Good Muslim, Bad Muslim* (New York: DoubleDay, 2005).

Mangala, Jack, (ed.), *New Security Threats and Crises in Africa: Regional and International Perspectives* (New York: Palgrave Macmillan, 2010).

Martin, Joel W., *Sacred Revolt: The Muskogee's Struggle for a New World* (Boston, MA: Beacon Press, 1992).

Matar, Nabil, *Turks, Moors, and Englishmen* (New York: Columbia University Press, 1999).

Mayer, Ann Elizabeth, *Islam and Human Rights: Tradition and Politics* (Boulder, CO: Westview Press, 1995).

Mazrui, Ali, "Islam and the Black Diaspora: The Impact of Islamigration," in *The Black Diaspora: African Origins of New World Identities*, Isodore Okpweho, Carol Boyce Davies, and Ali Mazrui, eds. (Bloomington: Indiana University Press, 1999).

Mernissi, Fatimah, *Islam and Democracy: Fear of the Modern World* (New York: Addison-Wesley Pub. Co., 1992).

Muhammad, Amir Nashid Ali, *Muslims in America: Seven Centuries of History, 1312–1998* (Beltsville, MD: Amana Pub., 1998).

Mulroy, Kevin, *Freedom at the Border: The Seminole Maroons in Florida, and Indiana Territory* (Lubock: Texas Tech University, 1993).

Perry, Glenn E., *The Middle East Fourteen Islamic Centuries*, third edition (Upper Saddle River, NJ: Prentice Hall, 1996).

Pipes, Daniel, *Militant Islam Reaches America* (New York: W. W. Norton & Co., 2002).

Porter, Kenneth W., *The Black Seminoles: History of a Freedom Seeking People*, revised and edited by Alcoine M. Amos and Tomas P. Senter (Gainesville, FL: The University Press of Florida, 1996).

Pouwels, Randall L., and Nehemia Levtzion, (eds.), *The History of Islam in Africa* (Athens: Ohio University Press, 2000).

Quick, Abdullah Hakim, *Deeper Roots* (London: Ta Ha Pub., 1976).

Rahman, Fazlur, *Islam* (Chicago, IL: The University of Chicago Press, 1979).

Rahnema, Ali, (ed.), *Pioneers of Islamic Revival* (New York: Zed Books, 1994).

Rashad, Adib, *A History of Islam and Black Nationalism in America* (Beltsville, MD: Amana, 1995).

Rashid, Samory, *Black Muslims in the US: History, Politics and the Struggle of a Community* (New York: Palgrave Macmillan, 2013).

Rashid, Samory, *Black Muslims*, Oxford Bibliographies online, African American Studies, 2016.

Reis, João José, *Slave Rebellion in Brazil: The Muslim Uprising of 1835 in Bahia*, translated by Arthur Brakel (Baltimore: Johns Hopkins University Press, 1993).

Reno, William, "The International Factor in African Warfare," in *Africa in World Politics: Engaging a Changing Global Order*, John W. Harbeson and Donald Rothchild, eds. (Boulder, CO: Westview Press, 2017).

Restall, Matthew, *Seven Myths of the Spanish Conquest* (New York: Oxford University Press, 2003).

Reynolds, Edwin, *The Seminoles* (Norman: University of Oklahoma Press, 1957).

Robinson, David, *Muslim Societies in African History* (New York: Cambridge University Press, 2007).

Robinson, Marsha, *Matriarchy, Patriarchy, and Imperial Security in Africa: Explaining Riots in Europe and Violence in Africa* (Lanham, MD: Lexington Books, 2012), e-book.

Rodison, Maxime, *The Arabs*, Translated by Arthur Goldhammer (Chicago, IL: The University of Chicago Press, 1981).

Rogers, J. A., *World's Great Men of Color* (New York: Collier Books, a division of MacMillan Pub., 1972).

Rotberg, Robert, and Robert Burrows, (eds.), *Terrorism in the Horn of Africa* (Washington, DC: Brookings Institution, 2005).

Roundtree, Les, *Diversity amid Globalization* (Upper Saddle River, NJ: Prentice Hall Pub., 2003).

Rubin, Barry M., *Guide to Islamists Movements* (New York: M. E. Sharpe, 2010), e-book.

Said, Edward, *Orientalism* (New York: Vintage Books, 1978).

Schaffer, Matt, and Christine Cooper, *Mandiko: The Ethnography of a West African Holy Land* (New York: Alfred A. Knopt, Inc. 1980).

Scheuer, Michael, "How and how Not to Fight Terrorism," YouTube video speech, Independent Institute, 2005.

Scheuer, Michael, *Imperial Hubris* (Washington, DC: Potomac, 2005).

Scheuer, Michael, *Through Our Enemies Eyes: Osama Bin Laden, Radical Islam, And the Future of America* (Washington, DC: Brassey, Inc., 2003).

Schmidt, Elizabeth, *Foreign Intervention in Africa: From the Cold War to the War on Terror* (New York: Cambridge University Press, 2013).

Scott, James C., *Domination and the Art of Resistance: Hidden Transcripts* (New Haven, CT: Yale University Press, 1990).

Shillington, Kevin, *History of Africa* (New York: St. Martin's Press, 1995).

Smith, Mike, *Boko Haram: Inside Nigeria's Unholy War* (New York: I. S. Tauris, 2016), 76–79.

Smith, Peter, *The Spanish Empire in America* (Gloucester: Harcourt, Brace, Jovanovich Inc., 1973; originally published by C. H. Haring).

Subcommittee on Counterterrorism and Intelligence, *Terrorism in Africa: The Imminent Threat to the United States* (Washington, DC: US Government Printing Office, 2015).

Sylviane, Diouf, *Fighting the Slave Trade in West Africa* (Athens: Ohio University Press, 2003).

Terrill, Robert, *Malcolm X: Inventing Radical Judgement* (East Lansing: Michigan State University Press, 2004).

"The Danger in the Desert, Jihad in Africa," *The Economist,* vol. 26, no. 8820, 2013, 21.

Thornton, John, *Africa and Africans in the Making of the Atlantic World 1400–1800*, second edition (New York: Cambridge University Press, 1998).

Turner, Richard Brent Turner, *Islam in the African American Experience* (Bloomington: Indiana University Press, 2003).

Thom, William, *African Wars: A Defense Intelligence Perspective* (Calgary, AB: University of Calgary Press, 2010).

Usner, Daniel H., *Indians, Settlers and Slaves in a Frontier Exchange Economy: The Lower Mississippi Valley before 1783* (Chapel Hill: The University of North Carolina Press, 1992).

Voll, John O., "Religion and Politics in Islamic Africa," in *Religious Challenge to the State*, Mathew C. Moen and Lowell C. Gustafson, eds. (Philadelphia, PA: Temple University Press, 1992).

Waines, David, *The Odyssey of Ibn Battuta: Uncommon Tales of a Medieval Adventurer* (Chicago, IL: The University of Chicago Press, 2010).

Wayne, Michael, *Imagining Black America* (New Haven, CT: Yale University Press, 2014).

Weisman, Brent Richard, *Unconquered People: Florida's Seminole and Miccosukee Indians* (Gainesville: University Press of Florida, 1999).

Welch, Alford T., "Muhammad: Life of the Prophet," in John L. Esposito (ed.) *The Oxford Encyclopedia of the Modern Islamic World* (New York: Oxford University Press, 1995), 153–161.

Westerlund, David, (ed.), *Questioning the Secular State: the Worldwide Resurgence of Religion in Politics* (New York: St. Martin's Press, 1996).

William, Paul D., *War & Conflict in Africa*, second edition (Cambridge, UK: Polity Press, 2017).

Williams, John Alden, "Khawar'ij," in *The Oxford Encyclopedia of the Modern Islamic World*, John L. Esposito, ed. (New York: Oxford University Press, 1995).

Wood, Peter H., *Black Majority: Negroes in Colonial South Carolina from 1620 Through the Stono Rebellion* (New York: W. W. Norton & Co., 1975).

Young, Tom, *Readings in African Politics* (Bloomington: Indiana University Press, 2003).

Zacks, Richard, *The Pirate Coast* (New York: Hyperion, 2006).

Zartman, I. W., "The Diplomacy of African Conflicts," in *Africa in World Politics: Constructing Political and Economic Order*, John W. Harbeson and Donald Rothchild, eds. (Boulder, CO: Westview Press, 2017).

Index

About the Author

Samory Rashid is a professor of political science at Indiana State University. He holds an MA and a PhD from the University of Chicago, where he was a student of Fazlur Rahman. He was born in Chicago and served as a visiting associate professor of political science at the University of California, Los Angeles (UCLA). He has traveled extensively and is the author of *Black Muslims: History, Politics and the Struggle of a Community* (2013).